NEGOTIATION EVOLVED

First published in Australia in 2013 by Filip Hron.
www.negotiationevolved.com

National Library of Australia Cataloguing-in-Publication Data
Hron, Filip, author.
    Negotiation evolved : increase rapport, trust, value, understanding, agreement,
    commitment and satisfaction / Filip Hron with Steve York and Ladislav Blažek.
    9780992341206 (pbk)
    9780992341213 (mobi)
    9780992341220 (ePub)
    Includes index.
    Negotiation.
    Influence (Psychology)
    Other Authors/Contributors: York, Steve, author. Blažek, Ladislav, author.
302.3

Cover design, typesetting and eBook production by Captain Honey.
www.captainhoney.com.au

5 4 3 2 1   13 14 15 16 17

NEGOTIATION EVOLVED

Increase rapport, trust, value, understanding, agreement, commitment and **satisfaction**

FILIP HRON

WITH STEVE YORK AND Ladislav Blažek

CONTENTS

I wish to acknowledge the extraordinary generosity of Felicity Thomson in sponsoring the editing and publishing of this book. As a result of her kindness and the resources she made available this book will now reach more people, appeal to more people, and ultimately help more people.

ACKNOWLEDGEMENTS

Let me begin by saying that I believe some version of every single insight in negotiation, and every single insight in this book, can in some way, shape or form be traced back hundreds or thousands of years. There are even entire cultures that live according to values and processes mentioned in this book.

Also, when discussing something as general and pervasive as human interaction, I believe it possible to independently come up with exactly the same insight that someone else has thought of ten, a hundred, or one thousand years ago, without necessarily having access to that original source.

With that introduction, I wish to acknowledge many of the sources that have inspired me and helped me progress as a negotiator:

- *3-d Negotiation* by David A. Lax, James K. Sebenius

- *Beyond Yes* by Peter Fritz, Allan Parker, Sherry Stumm

- *Body Language* by Allan Pease

- *Building Agreement* by Roger Fisher, Daniel Shapiro

- *Communication in Crisis and Hostage Negotiations* by Arthur A. Slatkin

- *Crisis Negotiations* by Michael J. McMains, Wayman C. Mullins

- *Difficult Conversations* by Douglas B. Stone, Bruce Patton, Sheila Heen, Roger Fisher

- *Dynamic processes of crisis negotiation* by Mitchell R. Hammer, Randall Rogan, Clinton R. Van Zandt

- *Experiments with people* by Robert P. Abelson, Aiden Gregg, Kurt P. Frey

- *Getting past* no by William Ury

- *Getting to yes* by Roger Fisher, William L. Ury, Bruce Patton

- *Getting together* by Roger Fisher, Scott Brown

- *How to get the truth out of anyone* by David Lieberman

- *Kennedy on negotiation* by Gavin Kennedy

- *Influence* by Robert Cialdini

- *Mind-lines* by Michael Hall, Bobby G. Bodenhamer

- *No contest* by Alfie Kohn

- *Negotiate and win* by Dominick Misino

- *Negotiating rationally* by Max H. Bazerman

- *Negotiating with giants* by Peter D. Johnston

- *Negotiation analysis* by Howard Raiffa, John Richardson, David Metcalfe

- *Persuasion* by Daniel J. O'Keefe

- *Precision* by Michael McMaster, John Grinder

- *Psychological aspects of crisis negotiation* by Thomas Strentz

- *Secrets of power persuasion* by Roger Dawson

- *Social motivation* by David Dunning

- *Stalling for time* by Gary Noesner

- *The 7 habits of highly effective people* by Stephen R. Covey

- *The negotiator's toolkit* by Allan Parker

- *The power of a positive no* by William Ury

- *The spirit of NLP* by Michael Hall

- *Thinking strategically* by Avinash K. Dixit, Barry J. Nalebuff

- *Value negotiation* by Horacio Falcao

- *You can negotiate anything* by Herb Cohen

I would like to give particular mention to three excellent negotiation experts, Horacio Falcao, Allan Parker and Steve York, for having been strong positive influences as colleagues and mentors at various points in my development as a negotiator. I am standing on the shoulders of giants who have extraordinary wisdom and experience. Specifically, I will in many places throughout this book aim to stay consistent with their terminology and organisation of insights, while I attempt to provide one unified perspective.

I wish to thank Steve York and Ladislav Blažek for their contributions to my practice and to this book. While it is my voice you hear throughout, that is a result of me drawing the shortest straw and being tasked with putting our collective thoughts on paper. They are listed as co-authors because their work has helped make mine possible. And I also wish to acknowledge and thank Michael Cradock, Steve Lancken, Rodrigo Londono, Kate O'Donnell, Rachelle Terry and Felicity Thomson for making invaluable contributions towards making this book reality.

INTRODUCTION

——— — ———

I will break a major negotiation rule and make a huge assumption without knowing anything about you: I believe that you are likely to have an interest in improving your negotiation skills. If I'm right, then the good news for you is that there are a lot of great insights out there that you can learn from.

The bad news is that these insights are scattered across a large number of sources. More bad news is these great insights are mixed with an abundance of bad advice. Unfortunately, unless you are already a negotiation expert, the distinction between the two may not always be apparent to you.

More bad news is that much good negotiation advice is presented in a manner that makes it appear incompatible or inconsistent with other good negotiation advice. As a result negotiators typically subscribe to a small portion of good insights, and reject large volumes of other good insights. Instead of engaging in a debate about which approach is "right", I would suggest that we accept that all insights have the potential to be the most valuable insight depending on the circumstances.

So this book will aim to cast a wide net, summarise what I feel are the most valuable insights in negotiation and organise these insights in a scalable framework that you can continue adding to after reading this book.

I don't believe that one person can do justice to a topic so huge and complex, so I asked Steve York, former head of hostage negotiation for the New South Wales Police Force in Australia, and Ladislav Blažek, former head of hostage negotiation in the Czech Republic, to incorporate their perspectives, insights and experiences into this book. Hostage negotiation is a great source for insights about any kind of negotiation. Hostage negotiators have to deal with the most difficult people, in the most difficult situations, and with the highest stakes — and if hostage negotiators don't do their jobs well then everyone will hear about it in the news. They are therefore under much more pressure to understand human behaviour and respond to it in ways that actually work, and work in the most difficult circumstances.

I don't claim that this book captures all the best negotiation insights. My hope is that *Negotiation Evolved* will be a good option for those who just want to read one book, and want maximum improvement in negotiation skills per page read.

I also hope I pique your interest in negotiation, and that you will continue to read more widely and build on the solid foundation I want *Negotiation Evolved* to provide.

In the early chapters I hope to clearly define negotiation and the various elements that comprise and influence it. Later chapters will expand on these elements and how they might help you in your every human interaction. Throughout are practical exercises that will illuminate how our minds work in relation to ourselves, our peers, our colleagues, superiors, friends and family members. In understanding this, I hope you will find negotiation easier and more fruitful.

A CASE IN POINT

During the period when I was writing the final chapter of this book, I one day found myself in a meeting with a business acquaintance. Let's call him Tom. Tom is one step from the top of a large and very reputable organisation. He has a very impressive CV with solid commercial and academic experience. He is now a few years from retirement, and he is very much concerned with making a difference and leaving a legacy.

Halfway through the meeting another person, let's call him Ivan, walks through the door. Without checking whether the timing is good, Ivan immediately starts explaining a technical fix for Tom's replacement laptop.

Tom loses his temper in an instant, and starts yelling at Ivan. Key sentences spoken include:

"...I asked to have this fixed and was told it would take one day, but it has taken three weeks..."

"...I'm not just anybody: if I want it fixed it should get fixed..."

"...I have pressures from above; I can't give them excuses; they expect me to deliver..."

"...I need to run a video conference with three screens twice per week with people in other parts of the world..."

Ivan repeatedly interrupts Tom with responses to each individual point:

"...the delay is not my fault — Dell hasn't shipped us the parts we need..."

"...I'm waiting to hear if the laptop will be fixed under warranty, because I can't approve spending money on anything..."

"...I am also under pressure to close a number of open support issues..."

"...you won't be able to use three screens ever again because we've upgraded to Windows7 and the driver for the screens don't work..."

This conversation was going nowhere fast. Both parties are at this point standing up, with voices raised, their faces fixed and red and about forty centimetres apart.

Who is at fault? What is the problem? What is the solution? What is important to each party? How could either party bring this conversation back on track? I encourage you to take a couple of minutes and write down what you think is taking place, and what you think could have been done differently.

I was sitting quietly in a guest chair and started taking notes for this book. The scenario I just shared with you is very typical of how interactions easily degenerate when we lack awareness about what goes on behind the scenes in human interaction, influence and negotiation. In fact, even if we *do* have this awareness, we may still find ourselves in situations where we temporarily forget to apply what we know and simply react instead. At the end of this book we will revisit this scenario. By then I expect that you will have perfect clarity about what took place behind the scenes, and what could have been done about it.

On that topic, was this a negotiation? Absolutely! All the insights that apply to negotiating a $10 billion mining deal apply to our everyday interactions as well.

1

WHAT IS NEGOTIATION?

——— ——

I'll start by sharing that there is no single definition of negotiation. Different dictionaries will define it differently. Different languages will define it differently. Some languages even have multiple words depending on the context.

Nevertheless, it turns out that it is extremely beneficial for us to adopt a very broad definition of negotiation, examples of which follow.

- Negotiation is a way to improve outcomes where people are involved.

- We are negotiating every time we try to satisfy parties' needs, whether those of one other party or more.

- Negotiation is the skill set for successful and valuable interactions.

- Negotiation is when we influence thoughts, emotions, perception, beliefs or behaviours.

Which means, of course, that we are negotiating all the time! And we have the opportunity to apply all the insights in this book in every one of our interactions. And we therefore have the opportunity to improve our outcomes in every interaction.

I think that is what's called *bang for your buck!* Tell me again, how much did you pay for this book…?

Hopefully you are already starting to see what makes me and other professional negotiators so excited about this topic. We firmly believe that negotiation is the number-one skill for achieving better outcomes in business and in life. We even suggest that all the lingering challenges we face globally could be improved, and many could be resolved, if stakeholders adopted a different approach to negotiation. Specifically, throughout this book we will advocate an approach that maximises rapport, trust, understanding, value, agreement, commitment, satisfaction and that allows us to build lasting relationships.

Also note that the flipside of this coin is that having poor negotiation skills is one of the main predictors of bad business outcomes, destroyed value, poor communication, and damaged relationships. Throughout this book we will refer to anything that detracts from parties reaching desirable outcomes through negotiation as *pollution* of the negotiation process.

What are some situations where we negotiate?

Here are a very few examples of such situations. I'm sure you can think of a hundred more without even trying!

- ◆ two businesses seeking to do a deal together

- ◆ two people seeking to build or repair a romantic relationship

- ◆ a team seeking to deal with differences and work effectively

- ◆ countries seeking to resolve conflict, whether caused by different values, limited resources, economic or environmental circumstances, miscommunication, perception of blame, etc

- ◆ a presidential candidate influencing public opinion

- ◆ a marketing division of a company influencing potential buyers

What are some reasons we negotiate?

Again, this is not a complete list.

- to get what we want

- to get the other party to change their behaviour

- to win

- to not lose

- to make the other party lose

- it's a ritual

- to solve a problem

- to create a problem

- to stall for time

- to test boundaries

In fact, there may be multiple reasons why we have one specific negotiation, and those reasons may change during the negotiation. The good news is that we don't have to keep all of these in mind. Invariably, we negotiate for the purpose of satisfying our needs!

What are "needs"? These represent what parties truly want, which is often different from what they ask for. We will unpack them in quite some detail as we go.

Note that the stated reason for a negotiation may completely differ from the real reason. We may be guilty of intentionally deceiving the other person, but more often than not we simply are not aware of why we negotiate. For instance, we may believe that we are negotiating to get a fair salary, but in reality we are trying to "win" the negotiation, or we are seeking some recognition that can help us psychologically justify having stayed in the job for so long. So before asking the other party why they negotiate, we may wish to check why *we* are negotiating.

THE THREE ELEMENTS OF NEGOTIATION — ALL NEGOTIATION — ARE:

- content;

- process; and

- relationship.

Obviously we'll go into this in much more detail later on, but briefly: content is whatever the negotiation concerns — the What; process is the set of activities and behaviours through which we achieve our outcomes — the How; and relationship is the bonds and tensions between the people involved — the Who.

It is important for us early on to highlight one of the most common patterns in dysfunctional negotiations. This is where parties focus on their respective content demands, while ignoring or neglecting the process and the relationship.

When we struggle to reach content outcomes, it is often because the process we follow is not set up to produce those outcomes. As a result we need to renegotiate the process. Whether or not we can get the other party's agreement to change the process is in part dependent on the strength of the relationship.

Our ability to negotiate with and influence others is primarily a result of how well we manage the last two elements. This point is worth reading twice, because it means that negotiation and influencing skills are independent from content, and thus transferrable to any area of business and life.

THE FOUR GAMES OF NEGOTIATION

When speaking to a large number of people about negotiation, we find that there are clusters of opinions: for example, some people view negotiation as a war or competition, and some people see it as an exercise in collaboration in pursuit of jointly preferred outcomes. Rather than arguing for which view is right or wrong (which you will come to understand is a dead end in negotiation), we acknowledge all viewpoints and recognise that there are several negotiation games — or processes of negotiation — that can be played.

We refer to the first game as *division*. Here parties have inflexible and ostensibly incompatible starting positions. These positions may be different price points, or different views on who is right and wrong. Like a traditional approach to war, parties spend their efforts trying to get the other party to retreat from their position. Value — the benefits available for division between the parties — is believed to be fixed. Views are believed to be incompatible, and therefore the perceived task at hand is to disqualify the views of others. While it is possible to cooperate when playing the division game, in practice this game typically becomes competitive very quickly, and each party tries to claim as much of that value as possible at the expense of the other party. If framed in terms of agreement instead of value, then this game is focused on making the other party agree with us, or to make the other party do what we want.

We refer to the second game as *integration*. Here parties try to find ways to increase value for both (or all) parties involved in the negotiation. This approach was made popular by the book *Getting to Yes!* (Fisher, Ury and Patton) in 1981. If framed in terms of agreement instead of value, then this game is focused on collaborating to find an outcome that both (or all) parties involved find desirable and can agree to.

We — the negotiators of today — believe we can do better than integration, and therefore introduce a third game: *maximisation*[1]. In this game we seek to maximise value for all stakeholders, whether represented at the table or not. The approach is based on systems theory and sustainability, where we acknowledge that the flow-on effects from a negotiation between two parties may have positive and/or negative effects on other parties in the system. If framed in terms of agreement instead of value, then this game is focused on changing the system so that parties already get what they want, often without having to negotiate with each other.

If we wish to represent all negotiations then we need a fourth game as well: *crisis negotiation*. In a crisis, whether we are negotiating a hostage situation or an uncontrollable oil leak in the Gulf of Mexico, the focus changes from dividing or creating value to resolving the immediate crisis only, and preventing enormous value destruction. If framed in terms of agreement instead of value, then this game is focused on identifying and satisfying the emotional needs that will make most material demands void and disappear.

To frame the relationship between the different games, it may help to have an analogy in mind. Let's pick something we can all relate to — traffic!

- The division game is what we would play where two lanes suddenly turn into one. Here we may see drivers either cooperate or compete. In the end one car will have to give way so that the other can pass. Sometimes this game deteriorates into congestion, and no car moves forwards. While this game has negligible potential for creating value it certainly has potential for destroying value.

- The integration game is what we play when we try to figure out exactly what two drivers next to each other want, and then figure out a way to make that happen. It may for example turn out that two drivers are going to the same destination every day and can therefore share a car rather than compete for the space on the road. The drivers may continue to create value: one of them might sell his or her car and share the saved travel costs. They might split the fuel bill and costs for road tolls. They might also value the company, and/or take turns using the travel time in the passenger seat to do work or fit in another hour of sleep.

- The maximisation game is where we look at traffic in the area, city or region as a whole. We try to figure out how to change the system so that everyone derives maximum benefit. This might include considering alternative modes of transport, coordinating traffic, expanding the number of lanes, building a new business district outside the city, providing incentives for car pooling etc.

- The crisis game is what we would play if the central business district were suddenly shut down during rush hour due to an accident involving a truck transporting toxic chemical waste. Our goal would be to resolve an extraordinary situation that may involve higher than usual stakes, emotions and time pressures. Part of the difficulty with a crisis is balancing efforts to resolve the crisis with managing the real risk that the crisis deteriorates into a disaster.

It is critical to stay aware of which game we are presently engaged in. Each game tends to affect other characteristics of the negotiation. For instance, open communication is one of the main tools for creating value in the integration game. However, freely sharing information in a competitive division game may dramatically increase the likelihood of getting exploited by the other party.

Those four games are not static recipes or step-by-step-guides. Rather they capture four broad groups of negotiation dynamics that we think collectively capture all negotiations. Which game we play may change at any point in the negotiation, and many of the tools and insights will be the same for different games.

MARTIAL ARTS:
A CROSS-DISCIPLINARY EVOLUTION

What we are proposing is a situational and agile approach to negotiation. One where the focus is on developing *your* skills so that they can be adapted to any situation or context. Here is another way to look at it:

Martial arts have been around for many centuries, yet in the last twenty years both the level of insights about what works and the skill level of fighters have increased dramatically. How come?

Martial arts were traditionally divided into a number of distinct styles.

Each discipline included a set number of techniques that had changed little over the course of centuries. Proponents of each style would have a philosophy, and a somewhat religious adherence to that style as "the right one".

A wide range of disciplines were available, and each came with advantages and disadvantages. One focused on punches and kicks, another on kicks only, another on wrestling, another on joint locks, another on joint locks with the assumption fighters would wear certain clothing, and so on. Competitions did not cater equally to fighters from different styles, so there was no way of figuring out which style was most realistic or provided the most effective form of combat or self-defence. Of course, this didn't stop representatives from the different styles claiming that their style was the best.

A trend was for individual martial artists to follow a pattern of training until they reached a senior black-belt level, and then start their own school. At that school the martial artist would, per definition, always be the most senior fighter: the master. Since the master was no longer surrounded by people who could test his or her skills, his or her development as a fighter would stagnate. Masters from different schools of the same style would rarely risk their reputation by fighting each other. The result, just as between the styles, was that many masters within a style would claim to be the best. (The belt system was one mechanism for circumventing this conversation: a higher belt meant a better fighter. However there were no set criteria for what was actually required in order to qualify for a specific belt, so again there was no objective measure of superiority.)

In the 1990s, though, a mixed martial-arts tournament was created, and fighters from all different styles showed up. Today virtually no fighter from those traditional styles wins such a tournament, of which there are now many. The fighters who do keep winning the mixed competitions share a profile that is different from the traditional martial artist's. Rather than religiously sticking to a set of techniques (or insights) that haven't changed in centuries, these new fighters "cherry-pick" the most effective techniques (or insights, or knowledge) from *all* martial arts styles. Because each fighter has different ideas (mindsets) about fighting, and different physical abilities, each fighter tends to end up with a unique repertoire. Styles are, in more ways than one, history.

The analogy between the evolution of martial arts and the evolution of negotiation is striking (pardon the pun). Traditionally there have been a couple of philosophies (or styles) of negotiation, and negotiators tended to stick religiously to one of those. And, just as the martial-arts masters ceased to evolve in their own schools, people who reached the point of believing they were great negotiators rarely continued their development.

More encouraging is that we now see negotiators who apply the mixed (or cross-disciplinary) approach to negotiation, and relentlessly try to become the best they can be. This involves seeking out and understanding *all* approaches to influence, training with multiple experts, and building a unique repertoire of skills that suits that particular negotiator. The paradigm has shifted from "Which style is best?" to "Which insights will help make me the best negotiator I can be?"

A negotiator's most helpful tools today might come from cognitive psychology, social psychology, communication, motivation, systems theory, sustainability, economics and game theory, interrogation techniques, neuro-linguistic programming (NLP), or any other field. The goal is not to qualify for an artificial "black belt" to get status within our own school, but rather to become the most skilled negotiators we can be.

This obviously makes our task of writing one book that caters to all readers a difficult one. Each reader will discover that they already master some of the skills we cover. But he or she will have different strengths and weaknesses, and will therefore want to focus on different things. So we are not saying that everything in this book is new to *you*. What we are saying is that if you want to master negotiation then you want to master everything in this book and beyond. If you are already halfway there, then that can only be a good thing.

SOLVING AND PREVENTING PROBLEMS

One powerful way to look at negotiation is as a problem-solving process enabled by effective communication. The negotiation often, but not always, exists because there is a problem that needs to be resolved. Negotiators use skilful communication to uncover what parties want, how that can be achieved, what possible obstacles are present, how to work around them, and so on. With our problem-solving hats on, negotiators become constructive investigators who identify and clarify problems before coming up with practical solutions for those problems.

But there is an even more powerful view of negotiation, and that is to look at it as a process of prevention. Problems are consistently cheaper, easier and less painful to prevent than they are to resolve. As we increase our awareness of how negotiation and influence work, we will be able to predict and prevent problems before they occur, or at the very least capture and resolve the problem at its inception.

To illustrate the power of this thinking, let us again use a traffic analogy. Motorcyclists have very poor odds of survival in any accident at speed. Therefore defensive motorcyclists maximise space between themselves and other vehicles to allow for mistakes and corrective action. For a motorcyclist, prevention is the only option.

In contrast, drivers of cars are much more likely to survive a crash, and therefore tend to be less obsessed with maximising empty space around them. However, fixing *any* damage to your car as a result of an accident is still significantly more complex, expensive and painful than preventing the accident altogether.

Good negotiators are problem solvers. Great negotiators are problem preventers.

MAKING PEOPLE PREDICTABLE

I am proud to admit that once upon a time I was actually a terrible negotiator. I was a brilliant problem solver, though! I could take problems of extraordinary complexity and produce very simple, clean and effective solutions. I would focus on what I deemed objectively good outcomes. My expectation was that people could see the logic, the rationale, and that it was obvious they would agree with me.

But then I would go to my boss and say: "Hey, you know that solution you came up with ten years ago? Well it is rubbish! People have complained about your solution for years. The great news is that I, your subordinate, have come up with a solution that is dramatically better. How about we tell everyone in the company? I reckon it would be great for my career aspirations if my colleagues could learn that I took initiative and insisted on building a solution for everyone's benefit even though you specifically told me not to."

I might be guilty of exaggerating a bit for comic effect here... Nevertheless, what do you think happened? That's right, no deal! But that makes no sense! My solution was *great*! Everybody had been hoping for something like this for years! Why wouldn't my boss jump on the idea? I could not understand it and wrote him (and all people) off as being unpredictable.

Do you find people unpredictable? When I ask this question in my seminars the majority of participants tend to nod. Well, as your skills as a negotiator improve, you will start to find people (and their thoughts, emotions, perceptions, beliefs and behaviours) much more predictable. And as you start understanding the insights in this book, the process of negotiation will become a lot more predictable too. (Similarly, my grandmother finds computers unpredictable, while a computer science graduate would say computers are absolutely predictable.) This predictability will allow you to better control the negotiation process, and ultimately improve your ability to get the outcomes you want.

EVERYTHING WE DO INFLUENCES

Negotiation and influence go hand in hand, but what *is* influence? One useful definition is that we influence every time we change the way someone thinks, feels, perceives, believes or behaves (which incidentally is also one of our suggested definitions of negotiation!). Of course, we may also wish to inoculate someone against change by influencing him or her to *not* change how he/she thinks, feels, perceives, believes or behaves!

In every interaction, everything we do has an impact on us, on the other party, and on the outcome — it influences! This impact may be tiny or it may be major. It may be positive or negative. It may be reversible or not. It may create one flow-on effect, or one hundred flow-on effects. It may impact the interaction and relationship immediately or a year from now. Some of this influence we exert will be conscious, and much of it will be unconscious. Some of it will be intentional, and much of it will be unintentional.

Clients often ask me to teach them how to influence people. I would suggest that we instead consider the possibility that we are clearly already able to influence, and what we seek is:

- greater understanding of how influence works; and

- greater control over how we influence, and thereby greater control over outcomes.

There are also differences between negotiation and influence. Often we can clearly map the process steps we take (e.g. take a brief, define issues, select a team, discover needs, etc) as part of the negotiation process. In contrast, the points in the negotiation where most influence takes place may be seemingly random (e.g. an informal conversation by the water cooler, an increased perception or feeling of rapport and trust, or the point where we stop talking because the other party non-verbally signalled that they are in agreement).

Many concepts and frameworks used in the negotiation world require an assumption that parties thoroughly and completely evaluate the choices available to them, and make a rational decision to arrive at the objectively *best* outcome. However, this does not reflect how we are influenced. The world we live in is far too complex for us to be able to process everything that is going on. As a means of coping we instead take short cuts. For example, few of us properly evaluate what an item is truly worth to us. Rather we look at one or two attributes, and apply a rule of thumb. For example, we assume that the average price of a product is a fair price, and a higher price signals higher quality. Similarly, we hear confidence in someone's voice and we assume they know what they are talking about. Or we see someone in a uniform and we assume we are supposed to follow his or her instructions.

Thus the comprehensive approach to negotiation we propose in this book is one where we integrate influencing into our every interaction.

2

WE ARE NOT BORN NEGOTIATORS

————— — —————

There are plenty of natural obstacles to effective negotiation. You will be relieved to know, though, that merely recognising them gets you a long way towards avoiding or overcoming them!

STOP POLLUTING

If we apply the insights in this book two very wonderful things will happen. The first is that we will be equipped with the tools to deal with hundreds of behaviours, patterns and traps that cause human interaction to be more difficult and ineffective than it needs to be. This will essentially allow us to remove pollution and keep our negotiations on track.

Have a think about these questions.

- ◆ Do you ever interrupt other people?

- ◆ Or do you ever assume that you are right?

- Or do you ever use the time when the other party is talking to think up your next counter argument?

- Or do you ever make hasty assumptions or judgements about people based on what they look like, how they speak or how they act?

- Or do you ever fail to acknowledge merit in the other person's argument before disagreeing, or fail to acknowledge the other person's contribution before changing the topic?

- Or do you ever label the other party as being "the problem"?

- Or do you ever find yourself in a situation where another person feels insulted and offended by you even though this was not your intention?

- Or do you ever find yourself ranting about other people's behaviour when they are not present?

- Or do you ever try to have a conversation with someone without checking that this is a good time for that conversation?

- Or do you ever leave a conversation, negotiation or disagreement without being able to explain the other party's view accurately enough for them to feel that you understand them?

- Or do you ever tell people what they are feeling or what they are thinking? Do you like when other people do that to you, particularly if they get it wrong?

- Or do you ever tell someone "I would've expected you to do that differently" even though you know it is too late to change what happened, and that this statement only serves to place blame?

We are *all* guilty of unconstructive (and even destructive) behaviours that, despite our best intentions, only serve to pollute our interactions with others.

Let's also think about what we want in the end. We probably want agreement. We probably want both parties to be committed to that agreement. We probably want understanding. We probably want to feel a sense of satisfaction about the process and the outcomes. And we probably want both parties to exhibit a set of behaviours that will ensure that we in the end achieve what we agreed to do. We probably want a strong relationship with trust and rapport. And we probably want to avoid a range of things, such as misunderstandings, negative behaviour, value destruction, and so on.

Managing human behaviour (in ourselves and in others) is critical to successful negotiation. Expert negotiators have a thorough understanding of how we think, what we feel, what we want, what we perceive, what we believe and how we behave. Expert negotiators also understand the mechanics for how to influence each of these.

LEARN HOW TO CREATE VALUE

The second benefit is that the insights in this book will help us create more value. A *lot* more value! In the end we ultimately negotiate to get what we want. Perhaps counter-intuitively, each of us is more likely to get what we want if we enter the negotiation with the mindset of trying to ensure that we *all* get what we want.

Value in negotiation is not necessarily measured in monetary terms. Rather the term "value" includes all the things that are valuable to us. As we will see, we have a wide range of needs — those things we value — many of which are far more important to us than money.

STAY AWARE AND ATTENTIVE

This book will increase our awareness of what goes on in negotiation. This awareness will help us know what to look for, i.e. where to focus our attention.

Imagine you and I stand by the road for one full day looking at passing cars. At the end of the day I ask you:

How many yellow cars did you see?

How many buses did you see?

Chances are that you will find these questions difficult to answer. However, if you were told at the beginning of the day what to look for, this would become a trivial task.

Similarly, if you and I today had a conversation about one of your past negotiations, you would likely find it challenging to answer the following questions:

- What were the psychological needs of the other party?

- How many times did you interrupt the other party?

- What percentage of time did each party spend talking?

- Which of your comments caused visible non-verbal reactions in the other party?

- Which psychological biases interfered with understanding or caused *pollution*?

Just as with the "yellow cars and buses" exercise, once we know what to look for it becomes much easier to keep track of this throughout the negotiation, and adjust our behaviour in response. After reading this book you will be able to create a list of hundreds of such parameters, each of which can help us influence others.

We can also influence the awareness and attention of the other party. We may, for instance, seek to guide a depressed person's attention away from options such as suicide, or guide a hostage taker's attention away from harming the hostages or police.

Aware of assumptions and beliefs

I propose that one of the main obstacles to creating exceptional outcomes in negotiation is the belief that we can't. If I ask my seminar participants to go and negotiate "the best deal they can" on anything, e.g. a course or a membership, then I expect the results to be fairly mediocre. Part of the reason is that we are exceptionally good at rationalising why we can or can't do something.

In negotiation the general predisposition of parties seems to be towards why we *can't* get everything we want. Now, all I have to do is to share with my participants that I negotiated to get that course for free, or that I managed to negotiate a lifetime free membership, or that I paid $0 for a new car, and I can guarantee you that my participants will collectively achieve better outcomes than before. In their minds the statement "It is not possible. I can't do it." has instantly been replaced with "Oh my god, it is possible. How can I do it too?" The latter is a *much* more constructive internal dialogue for negotiators.

In my experience I have found that skilled negotiators tend to subscribe to empowering assumptions along the lines of the first list below, and reject the counterproductive assumptions similar to those in the second list.

- Our desired outcome is *possible.*

- Negotiation is everywhere and we negotiate all the time.

- Anyone can become a great negotiator. It is a learnable skill.

- There is an abundance of value out there. We just have to find it. In fact, it is our job as negotiators to find it (or create it).

- We are more likely to get what we want if we frame the negotiation around trying to get *everyone* what he or she wants too.

- Perception is our reality. We all see the world differently, we all believe our view is *right*, and we take the action that makes the most sense given how we perceive the situation.

- Assume good intent.

- Truthful, precise and explicit communication reduces complexity and pollution in the process.

Counterproductive assumptions and beliefs.

- The pie is fixed, meaning that what one party gets, the other party misses out on.

- If the game is competition, we will win.

- We will never deal with this party again.

- Asking questions makes us look dumb.

- We influence by telling.

- We negotiate to win, as opposed to getting what we want.

- The other party is irrational, crazy or difficult.

- The particular option or solution isn't viable *in the real world*.

- We can't negotiate.

- We are the world's best negotiator.

- We have no choice.

- Finders keepers — losers weepers.

- We can't achieve better results than we've achieved in the past.

- We *will* achieve better or different results by not changing our approach and instead just doing what we've always done.

- That [insert any person here] will say "*no*".

- That we can't [insert limiting belief of your choosing here!]

Aware of self

Gaining self-awareness is often a difficult task, because it requires us to accept not just that we do some things well, but also that we do some things poorly.

The realisation I was a terrible negotiator helped me adjust hundreds of my behaviours because that was required if I wanted better negotiation results.

- I used to hog the airtime by telling the other party what I wanted. Now I spend most of the time listening to what the other party wants.

- I would immediately correct the other party when I thought he or she was wrong. Now I first demonstrate that I understand their view.

- I used to get upset when people insulted or attacked me. Now I try to understand why they are upset, and I allow for the possibility that I was incorrect in perceiving the insult or attack.

- I used to argue with people who argued with me. Now I let them vent, feel heard, and often that is all that is required.

- I used to start the conversation with the problem that needed to be resolved. Now I start with areas of agreement.

- I used to think *you vs. me*. Now I think *we*.

- I assumed that people were one hundred per cent logical so I focused on creating compellingly rational arguments. Now I spend much more effort on ensuring that people's emotional and psychological needs are met.

- I used to use all my supporting arguments and justifications, which may have come across as overbearing (or desperate). Now I can non-verbally identify the point where no further arguments are needed.

- I felt getting fair credit and recognition from the other party was important. Now I understand how leaving my own ego out of the equation can dramatically improve the likelihood that I get what I want.

Unfortunately self-awareness is difficult for many reasons. Just one is that we are limited to using our current knowledge when trying to explain our behaviour. For instance, let's say that you have a stomach-ache. Let's say that you are unaware that this is caused by a newly developed allergic reaction to your toothpaste. A doctor is more likely than you to know enough about how your body works to eventually figure this out. But if you are not a doctor, and you don't go to one, then you will still try to find an explanation. That might be to blame stress, or the takeaway meal you ordered, or hormonal fluctuations.

The same applies to negotiation and human behaviour. If we are not today experts in human behaviour, then our explanations for why an interaction turned out the way it did are unlikely to be correct. Luckily, our explanations will become a lot more accurate as we progress through the book.

For now, I would suggest that a healthy mindset is for us to assume that we are not yet qualified to explain what takes place behind the scenes in interactions of which we are a part.

Aware of the other party

At the time when I started collaborating with one seasoned negotiator Allan Parker, I had already attended countless negotiation courses, worked with several negotiation companies, read a large number of texts on negotiation, and advised on a range of large-scale negotiations. Still, most of that experience was centred on rational strategy: given what the parties *say* they want, how can we find outcomes that will work for all?

In my first meeting with this negotiator he interrupted me, grabbed my forearms and said: "Notice how you gesture in this direction every time you talk about options?" Unconvinced, I continued explaining my concept. I believe I said something along the lines of: "I have the picture in my head, it's just difficult putting words to it." He looked at me and said: "Yes, I can see that you see a picture, and your gestures are actually drawing the picture in the space in front of you."

He was right. How could I have spent so much effort on mastering negotiation and influence, while missing this flood of information that parties send each other every single moment of every interaction?

Paying attention to what the other party does helps us understand how he or she thinks. Knowing how the other party thinks allows us even greater control in influencing him or her. The first challenge is how to know what to observe, i.e. where to focus our attention. The second challenge is avoiding polluting what we observe with our own opinions and judgements. Undertaking training in neuro-linguistic programming (NLP) is a good start for dealing with the first challenge. Reading the section on perception in this book is a good start for dealing with the second.

TURN OFF YOUR AUTOPILOT

Have you ever thought about how you negotiate? At the outset of my negotiation courses I usually ask participants to reflect on the common pattern in their last five negotiations. Then I ask them to take five minutes to draw or otherwise document their approach to negotiation. I strongly suggest you try the same exercise now!

Generally, only a small proportion of people have ever truly assessed their own negotiation methods. This is an important realisation. This means the majority of us have not developed an intentional, informed and comprehensive approach to negotiation. What do we do instead? We operate on what we refer to as "autopilot".

When on autopilot we run a range of different patterns of behaviour. We have typically run these patterns thousands of times, and are often completely oblivious that we are running them. For example, one common pattern in relationships would be where one person tries to engage in a conversation to resolve a problem, and the other person tries to withdraw to avoid conflict. The more the first person tries to engage, the more the other person tries to withdraw, and the harder the first person will try to engage. We can probably speculate where this pattern of interaction will eventually take us.

Some of the patterns we run do not satisfy *any* of our needs. We may simply be guilty of mimicking or copying someone else's behaviour. I have over and over observed managers treat their subordinates badly, and once the subordinates become managers they exhibit exactly the same behaviour. In some cases the patterns we run actually de-satisfy needs that are important to us.

Other patterns serve to satisfy *some* of our needs, but fail to satisfy more important needs. A predictable response when being accused of something is to either become defensive or aggressive. Both of these responses could serve to satisfy one's short-term need to have a healthy self-image. But the pattern that we run may not necessarily help us achieve more important long-term needs, such as learning from our mistakes, or understanding how the other person sees the world.

Yet other patterns may be very effective in getting us what we want… only in *some* situations and contexts. For instance, negotiating ruthlessly based on power may work when the other party is competitive yet dependent on us, but may result in disaster in situations where we enjoy a great relationship or where the dependency doesn't exist.

A key to dealing with patterns is to first recognise what they are and what triggers them. Perhaps we are great at focusing on the other person's needs in our negotiations, but when we speak to our parents we fall into the old pattern of expecting that they have responsibility for our wellbeing. Some destructive patterns may be very strongly anchored to situations, people and behaviours, and we may need to break that connection. Other patterns are effectively part of our DNA, e.g. the need we feel to reciprocate if someone does something nice for us.

We also wish to analyse what needs are being met, and what important needs are left unmet by following the pattern. This in itself should be reason to re-evaluate whether these patterns are helpful or unconstructive.

Finally, we need to interrupt the undesirable patterns when they do happen. We may even ask the other person to help us with this, e.g. asking our romantic partner to pull a comical facial expression whenever we raise our voice or stop listening. In a more formal business setting we might educate the other party on a selected pattern and involve them in interrupting it, e.g.: "For our negotiation I think it may be relevant for you to know that in my current role I'm responsible for minimising risk, so I have a tendency to look for risks and problems. If you at any point in our negotiation feel that I'm being too negative, just remind me that I've fallen back into my day-to-day role."

Our patterns are influenced by our personality, our emotional state and by our experiences. What is our experience with the person we are dealing with? Or with other people? Do we imitate traits of any other person? Have we previously attempted to consciously create a new pattern? This mixed bag of random patterns is not necessarily a good thing to bring to our negotiations!

The key message so far is that our default autopilot is not a good driver for how to negotiate. But there is a second major insight here. When we are on autopilot we run the same patterns over and over. This makes us predictable. Once someone can predict our patterns, they can use that insight to influence or manipulate us.

LEAVE OUR EGO OUT OF THE NEGOTIATION

Diplomacy is the art of letting
someone else have your way
— DANIELE VARE

A key attribute of a skilled negotiator is to *not* bring our ego into the negotiation. As we go through this book together, you will see how difficult it would be to execute several of the strategies if we deem it too important to protect our ego at the same time. In fact, having a sensitive

36

ego is incompatible with being a skilled negotiator.

Here are some of the powerful elements of effective influence and good negotiation (addressed in greater detail throughout in the book) that are incompatible with having a sensitive ego.

- Letting the other party win.

- Not getting caught up in trying to get even.

- Letting the other party believe they deserve the credit, or that they are in control.

- Letting someone else negotiate on our behalf if they are more likely to succeed.

- Remaining constructive at all times, regardless of how we are treated.

- Prevention (which means the problem never occurs and we therefore won't get credit for fixing it).

- Demonstrating willingness to be proven wrong and to be influenced.

- Maximum flexibility, agility and adaptability.

Remember, our goal is not to make the other party accept that we are an amazing negotiator. Our goal is to have our needs met. Don't mix those two goals up! (I say this, but will predict that the vast majority of readers will still mix them up in the heat of battle…no, *negotiation*. I meant in the heat of negotiation!)

We have emphasised leaving our ego out of the equation. Along the same line, let's make a point of avoiding any actions, words, expressions or behaviours that may trigger the other party bringing his or her ego into the negotiation. Unless we have planned an intentional strategy that relies on stroking the other party's ego, we are well advised to keep all of them out of the room.

3

THINGS ARE NOT ALWAYS
WHAT THEY SEEM

——— —

As I mentioned in Chapter 1, *content | process | relationship* is a powerful top-level framework to which we can attach almost all other insights in this book. However, there is one complicating factor, and that is human *perception*. As we will discover, we can't trust our senses, we can't trust the way we think, and we don't have the facts.

Have you ever listened to a friend complain to you about problems and grievances about other people? Did you find your friend's recount of the situation a bit self-serving? Was your friend the undisputable victim? Was the other party the undisputable perpetrator?

People will often perceive the same thing or event very differently. They focus on different aspects. They interpret them differently. They rationalise them differently. And they distort the information to protect their sensitive egos. All of this is *so* obvious to us as impartial observers.

Now let me ask you one more thing: have *you* ever had an argument with someone else where you were confident that *you* had the facts, where the other party was misinformed, one hundred per cent to blame, and should crawl back you with an apology?

Whereas some professions reward us for coming across as being confident and possessing all the facts, as negotiators it serves us well to adopt childlike curiosity and consistently assume that we don't have all the facts. By realising (and accepting) that everything we see, hear or observe is unlikely to be "fact", we will be more likely to seek out the facts, and less likely to engage in unconstructive battles to place blame.

I do hope that after reading this section you will be shocked at how inaccurately we think and how inaccurately we communicate. I also hope that you will use this increased awareness to anticipate the million ways miscommunication can and does occur. And when miscommunication does occur, I hope you will accurately attribute this to the limitations of communication, and not to limitations in the other person.

OMISSION | DISTORTION | GENERALISATION

As negotiators we want to be aware of how an idea, thought, concept, feeling or event might be perceived differently by different people. This difference comes down to one or a combination of three functions.

- The understanding that a person has may have parts missing. We refer to this as deletion or *omission*.

- Some of the understanding a person has may have been altered, changed, or *distorted* in one way or another.

- Some of the understanding a person has may be added to, extrapolated or *generalised* from what was perceived.

Note that this occurs whether we are aware of it or not. Everything we perceive is likely to have parts that are generalised, distorted and omitted.

VISUAL | AUDITORY | KINAESTHETIC

Reality is merely an illusion, albeit a very persistent one!
ALBERT EINSTEIN

We don't see the world the way it is. None of us do. Rather we are limited to using our senses to *make sense* of the world. Our eyes will capture a small range of the colour spectrum and our ears will capture a small range of the noise spectrum. We will also feel the world, either with touch or with sensations within our body. And we will smell and taste the world as well.

Each of these senses is imperfect, doesn't capture as much information as we would like, and is not as accurate as we would like. Numerous (fairly entertaining) experiments in psychology demonstrate how easy it is to trick all of our senses. For instance, hearing a sound made by one person while seeing the lip movements of another person changes the way we hear the sound!

Thankfully, our senses at least capture *some* information of the real world. The real danger is that we assume we accurately captured reality when we didn't. Instead our brains use the captured information to create our own internal representation — or *map* — of reality.

No two people will have identical maps of reality, and no person has a complete map of reality. But people will make the best decision that is available to them, given their map of reality. This insight goes a long way to explain that much behaviour we may deem irrational in other people is actually very rational given their perceptions and view of the world.

In negotiation, understanding whether a person has a bias towards visual, auditory or kinaesthetic intake can help us gain a better understanding of how he or she thinks and processes information. By focusing on the other party's preferred channel(s) we improve our ability to build rapport, ensure mutual understanding, and ultimately to influence him or her.

FRAME OF REFERENCE OR PERCEPTION FILTER

Common sense is a collection of prejudices
acquired by age eighteen
ALBERT EINSTEIN

Let me share a short story: I grabbed my bag and I hurried to class. That's it.

Do you already have one or multiple ideas for what this story is about? What kind of bag do you think I'm talking about? A gym bag? A briefcase? How did I get to the class? What type of class was it? Was I a participant or an instructor?

Obviously you have no way of knowing. The point of this example is that we will fill in the blanks with assumed information (i.e. we generalise), and the information we create will be highly individual. Some of the assumed information will be positive (often causing unrealistic expectations), and some will be negative (often causing unfounded resistance to ideas and options). As we get more information we will start to replace assumed information and our mental representation will (hopefully) become more and more accurate.

Particularly if we are visual thinkers and we create pictures in our minds, then our pictures will *always* contain assumed information.

Picture a house.

That's a pretty simple exercise. A visual thinker, however, will already have created an image of a house that may have a colour, a number of windows, placement of the door, a certain shape of the roof, even though I specified none of that.

While in this simple scenario we can quickly become aware that we have made assumptions, in more complex interactions it becomes increasingly difficult. At some point we may even lose track of what we have assumed and what is actual information that we were given. As we will see later, even individual words with a clear dictionary meaning can still create different meaning in different people's minds!

We each see the world differently because we observe it through a filter that we can call our *perspective, frame of reference* or *perception filter*. This filter distorts information we receive in a number of ways.

- We will interpret what we see now based on our conclusions of all other experiences we have had prior. A person on the street wearing dirty and torn clothes and holding out his hand is, we presume, homeless.

- We will pay more attention to what we are interested in. Once we have decided to buy a particular model of car then we will notice that model considerably more often than before.

- We will interpret what we see to be consistent with our belief system. A non-religious person and a Christian person may have very different explanations for any particular story or segment in the Bible.

- We see the world the way we are. If we tell a lot of lies, then we are more likely to suspect that other people lie in similar situations.

- We are subject to the way our brains process and store information. A primarily auditory person may remember all the words that were spoken, whereas a primarily visual person might not remember a single word, but might instead construct a diagram, picture or movie that captures the information.

- And as we saw in the example above about the house, we will add information that is not there, but that we need in order to make a representation in our minds.

One way to describe our perception filter is to say that it is the sum of all our experiences to date. This has a number of implications. One is that our perception filter is constantly changing as we get older and have more experiences. Another is that no two people on the planet have had exactly the same experiences; therefore no two people on the planet will view the world in exactly the same way!

Note that information will flow through our perception filter in two directions — it not only distorts information we receive, it also distorts information that we send!

MULTIPLE FRAMES OF REFERENCE

Since our frame of reference is the sum of all our experiences, it is probably not surprising that we don't apply that entire frame all the time. Rather we (quite conveniently and self-servingly) pick specific sub-frames. There are probably an unlimited number of sub-frames, and here are some examples.

- Comparison frame: "Is what I'm considering better or worse than your proposal?"

- Esteem frame: "How will I feel if I go ahead?"

- Identity frame: "Who am I as a person if I do that?"

- Historical frame: "What do I usually do?"

- Audience frame: "What will Mum think about what I'm about to do?"

- Ethical frame: "What is the right thing to do?"

- Role frame: "What is the appropriate way to act given that I'm a parent/husband/nurse?"

The frame we use will strongly influence the meaning, opinion and judgement we associate with events, behaviours and outcomes. So if we wish to change someone's opinion, we may wish to consider changing which frame they use to evaluate what they observe. For example: "You say that helping John finish his project by the deadline is not your responsibility (role frame). I am just curious: would it be the right thing to do, understanding that we work for a charity and many people in need will be disadvantaged further if John misses the deadline (ethical frame)?"

THE THREE PERCEPTUAL POSITIONS

By default we see things from our perspective. But because everyone has a unique perspective, we need make an effort to ensure that we understand the other party's perspective too. Additionally, both our perspectives will have degrees of pollution, so we may also wish to consider a neutral perspective. To help us in this process, negotiators continually revisit the following three perspectives throughout our negotiations. But before we do, please take a minute to complete the next exercise.

> Take a minute to think back over a positive experience you had in the last month. Something that made you feel good. Replay the event in your mind. How do you recall the experience? Do you find yourself experiencing the event as if it was happening all over again, with all the emotions, feelings, maybe even sounds and smells as well? Or do you simply observe what happened, as if the experience was separate from you, like a film on a screen?

The first of these is called an *associated* state, and the second a *disassociated* state. We'll refer back to these when discussing the three perceptual positions.

First Position: "My world"

Have you while reading a book or studying for an exam suddenly realised that you hadn't paid attention to what you were reading? Or perhaps you watched a DVD, and found yourself having to rewind because your mind wandered and you missed something critical in the story? Or perhaps someone was talking to you and you heard your internal dialogue instead.

These are strong signals that you are in first position.

This is our associated state. More specifically, we are associated with ourselves. When I am in the first position my attention is squarely on me. I am fully aware of how I feel. I am conscious of the external factors that are affecting me. I will interpret what is said based on how it affects me, or how I react to it. In first position I am likely to want to share my view of the world, and will therefore have a high ratio of statements to questions in my communication. My sentences will include many mentions of "I", "me", and "mine". Because I am focused on what I want to say I am more likely to interrupt you mid-sentence. My voice will include more inflection to reflect my mood. I risk neglecting you and others.

First position is the most likely position to be polluted by a range of cognitive biases and mental traps (introduced later in this chapter). This is where we form our judgements and opinions. And it is also where we add meaning to what we hear, see or feel — meaning that may not be accurate.

This is the default position for the vast majority of us. Unfortunately, we typically revert to first position when interactions become difficult, and therefore struggle to consider other perspectives. If we want to excel in negotiation then we need to consider all perspectives of the parties involved.

My girlfriend shared a great example of someone temporarily being in first position. A colleague of hers from her days as a flight attendant was asked to give personalised instructions to a blind passenger. The flight attendant gently guided the passenger's hand to the controls above his seat: "Press this button to activate the call bell…and press this button to turn on the light if you wish to read."

Other common examples of being first position include all the situations where you would label people as inconsiderate in regular social interactions, e.g. the person who stops walking as they get to the end of the escalator, oblivious to the fact that people behind them have nowhere to go.

If you know someone who is always stuck in first position, I suspect that he or she is not a person you enjoy spending too much time with. However, first position has its place: when you need to figure out what your opinion is, what your needs are, or how you feel about a certain option. If we want to get someone back into their first position, all we have to do is ask questions that are focused on that person:

- "How do you feel about that option?"

- "How would you like it if we tried to implement that plan?"

All of us are capable of taking the first position, because this is where we feel hunger, fatigue and any other basic human survival indicators. But many of us struggle with or don't spend enough time in second and third position.

Second Position: "Other party's world"

Here we are associated with the other person and disassociated from ourselves. If I'm negotiating with you, then when I am in second position my attention is squarely on you. I don't just listen to what you say, but I do my best to put myself into your shoes and so truly understand you. By trying to mirror your thoughts and feelings, I will also start mirroring your body language, tonality, pace and volume. I try to understand how you feel, how you think, and all the external circumstances and concerns that are affecting you. Because it is all about you, I will predominantly listen. When I do talk I primarily ask questions. I will empathise, and I will be considerate. If I interrupt I am likely to do so between sentences.

If I at any point realise that I'm evaluating whether I agree or disagree with you, then I'm actually back in first position. If I have an internal dialogue trying to prepare my next answer, then I am in first position. And if am in first position I am no longer listening to understand. Think about it: if we have one dialogue in our head, and one with the other person, which one will we pay most attention to?

Second position obviously has its place. This is where we truly get to understand the other party's feelings, needs, and how they might feel about an option. Importantly it's also where we build rapport with the other party. People who spend most of their time in second position will present as selfless, and always paying attention to others, how they feel, and what they want.

To get someone into second position, again all we have to do is guide them with questions:

- "Let's for a second assume that you were me. What would you do in my position?"
- "How do you think that decision might come across from where I'm sitting?"

One extreme example of being temporarily stuck in second position is the cameraman who jumped out of a plane to film another skydiver. The cameraman was so focused on filming what the other skydiver did, gearing up, entering the plane, talking to the other divers before the jump, that it wasn't until he had jumped out of the plane along with his subject that the cameraman realised he had forgotten his own parachute.

Note that second position is when the attention is on someone else, not merely that it is not on us. If I'm speaking with you on the phone while I'm waiting in my car at the traffic lights, I could well be in second position in relation to you — truly listening. However, I'm not paying attention to the cars behind me. So in my interaction with *them* I am not in second position. As negotiators, we want to make sure that we take time to consider and integrate all stakeholders' perspectives, and that involves taking second position in relation to each of them.

Third Position: "The impartial and objective bystander"

This is my completely disassociated state. More specifically, I am disassociated from all individual perspectives including my own. In third position I am adopting the perspective that a perfectly neutral third party would have if he or she were observing the interaction between you and me. In third position I do not feel any of your or my emotions. I am observing what is happening without polluting this with judgements, assumptions or opinions. In third position I am not myopically focusing on my position, but rather looking at multiple possible options for satisfying everyone's needs. I consider the system, the whole and the collective goals.

Third position is perfect when we want to develop options that work for all parties, when we want to track the process of negotiation, when we want to understand the system, and when we want to avoid reacting emotionally. If we spend most of our time in third position then we increase our ability to make good negotiation process decisions. However, we also make it difficult for other people to connect with us on a personal level. To get people to adopt third position, we again use questions.

- "How might we look at this ten years from now?"

- "How might this appear to an impartial bystander?"

- "If your role was that of overall decision maker or architect, then what would seem like the best solution to you?"

INTENT | OBSERVATION | IMPACT

People who struggle to draw or paint often fail to recognise one important insight: "draw what you see, not what you know". Let's consider a five-year-old boy drawing a stick figure of his sister. The picture may include pigtails, a smile and a triangle for a dress. These are all features of his sister that the boy has identified. But the picture doesn't look like reality because the boy is struggling to convert the representation in his head to the canvas. For example, very few of the lines he draws actually appear as lines in the real world.

Someone who has mastered the art of painting will instead acutely observe what is in front of him or her. What does the artist observe?

Colour. Brightness. Darkness. That's it. There is no interpretation. By simply adding darkness to the canvas where reality is dark, brightness where it is light, and colour where there is colour, a picture starts to appear.

It sounds so obvious, yet so many of us don't realise the mistake we are making. And we make the same mistake in communication and negotiation. We don't objectively observe, but rather pollute what we observe with what is already in our mind. It is then no surprise that we miss (and misunderstand) much of what goes on in our interactions with people. Unfortunately our misunderstandings frequently result in incorrect perceptions, opinions and judgements that end up polluting the rest of the interaction.

In negotiation, and in communication, it is important for us to realise that we don't have all the facts. In fact (pun intended), we can bank on having access to fewer than fifty per cent of the facts in any communication. What do I mean by this? Good question.

Let's say that we are at a formal cocktail party and I greet you for the first time. I put my arm around you while introducing you to everyone else. This is the communication that you *observe*.

However, I predict that you will most likely start to interpret and add meaning to my behaviour. That meaning will be polluted by assumptions, guesses, beliefs, transference and more. You will probably end up with a mix of opinions, judgements and feelings. Perhaps you feel that I am a very friendly person who immediately demonstrated how much I value you. It is also possible that you interpret things differently and feel that I am invading your personal space, or that I'm fake for being so affectionate even though we don't yet know each other. This is the *impact* on you, and only you know exactly what this is.

Now, what did I *intend* by my behaviour? Perhaps I had heard that you didn't know anyone at the event and I really made an effort to include you. Or perhaps I recently had an argument with my girlfriend who said that I'm too cold and standoffish with people, and now I try to overcompensate. Only I know what my *intention* was.

This sounds very simple, right? Unfortunately, this disconnect between intent, observation and impact that we just described is a major cause of misunderstandings, conflict, unwarranted accusations and defensive behaviour — pollution.

When you later describe this evening to someone else, you might say that I was very forward. But is this what you observed? No, you just observed my arm around you and how I spoke to you and others. You may have felt as you normally feel when someone is forward. You may have assumed that my intent was to be forward. And all of this is conjecture. You simply have no way of knowing without further investigation.

In most interactions we (or the other party) will experience some form of impact long before we have the chance to clarify what the intent was. At this point we make a quick decision: do we think the intent was positive or negative? Some of us have a bias towards assuming that the intent is indeed negative. And if we already have negative perceptions or feelings towards the other party, then we are even more likely to assume negative intent.

One problem is that if the other party actually had positive intent, and we assume negative intent, then we *create* a problem; we accuse them of something they didn't do. This is pollution. They will predictably become defensive, and may even attack/accuse us right back. Many conflicts will start this way. As we will later see, the communication from the other party can be spoken words, or the location of one of their attack submarines. Regardless of what we observe, we consistently and incorrectly make assumptions about others' intent.

So what do negotiators do? Well, if faced with a choice of assuming positive intent or negative intent, we prefer to assume neither, but often lean towards assuming positive intent. The reason is simple; assuming positive intent has low risk of polluting the interaction, or damaging trust or the relationship. With the exception of situations that have already been established as hostile with danger to human life (e.g. war or armed robbery), there is usually little risk in assuming positive intent until something else is proven.

If the intent was indeed negative, then we will find out pretty soon. And even if intent was negative, it can still be very disarming to demonstrate that we think well of the other party. For instance, if two collaborating organisations have agreed to not compete against each by bidding on the same contracts, but suspect that the other party is still competing, then we can:

◆ act dumb: "Oh, it looks as if we accidentally forgot to tell each other that we are bidding for the same contract. Good we found out in time so that we don't end up accidentally competing with each other."

◆ or act curious: "You won't believe how surprised we were today when we learned that both our organisations have bid for the same contract. What a fluke! How do you think that happened?"

CUMULATIVE PERCEPTIONS

In his book *7 Habits of Highly Effective People* Steven R. Covey introduces the concept of the Emotional Bank Account. One interpretation is that the goodwill and investment by parties in a relationship (romantic or otherwise) can be represented as a bank account. When we do things for each other we make a deposit. When we hurt the relationship we make a withdrawal. The more we deposit, the more credits we have to draw upon in the event that we significantly damage the relationship in the future.

This is a very useful analogy, and as negotiators we can draw inspiration from it and apply it to several concepts detailed later in this book.

Because we are talking about perception, we will here emphasise that the parties will not actually see the same balance in the bank account. It is quite possible that I feel that I am making a deposit by taking my girlfriend out to a nice dinner. Actually, I make a big deposit because I have to cash in a favour from a friend to get a nice table at an exclusive restaurant. And oh, the dinner is very expensive which means I have to live on instant noodles for the rest of the week. So certainly a big deposit into the account!

But my girlfriend ends up being unhappy with the night. I accidentally forgot to ask if she was allergic to anything, and she was. The waiter was rude and it was raining and we couldn't find parking near the restaurant. Needless to say my girlfriend perceived that I had made a big withdrawal from the account.

Now, while this story is fictitious, it illustrates that even one simple transaction may be viewed completely differently by the two parties. Let us now consider a five-year relationship with such interactions. How different might the parties' view be of the balance of e.g. favours, support, trust, value created, sacrifices or transgressions?

HOW WE REACH CONCLUSIONS

We are negotiating, and currently we are discussing a point that we can't seem to agree on, the value of the company that is for sale. The seller says $20 million, but as the buyer we figure the company is worth $5 million, so what do we do?

One option is to realise that the two parties must have used different processes for arriving at their number. So rather than attacking the numbers directly, what if we instead sought clarity on what the two parties' processes looked like. Anything we can do to better align those two processes will help bring the final numbers closer.

So what process do we follow to reach a conclusion? There are a few simple but powerful models that can help us out. One is to view any process of reaching a conclusion as similar to using a mathematical or computer function. We use some form of reasoning (the function itself and the assumptions it is built on), we select what to input into that function (the data), and the function then spits out a result (the conclusion). So if we want two parties to reach the same conclusion, we may wish to align their reasoning, and the data that they apply that reasoning to.

I also recommend that you read up on the *Ladder of Inference*, which Peter Senge covers in his book *The Fifth Discipline Fieldbook: Strategies and Tools for Building a Learning Organization*. It is a simple yet powerful tool that negotiators use to identify, clarify and align diverging perceptions.

So how do we use such tools? We can start by breaking down how we reason and identify the data we deem relevant, how we interpret that data, what other assumptions and beliefs affect our conclusions, and share this with the other party. It is perfectly conceivable that we at this point discover that *we* don't have a good basis for the conclusion we have been pushing. And that is fine: skilled negotiators are open to persuasion.

We can also use the above tools to inform the questions that we ask of the other party, to help us understand how *they* reason, the data they deem relevant, how they interpret that data, and what other assumptions and beliefs influence their conclusions.

Note that we are not accusing anyone of being wrong. We are simply explaining what we did, and we are asking the other party to help us understand what they did. We have not yet decided who is right — we are just trying to understand where each party is coming from, and where the key differences in assumption, perception, logic or beliefs are. Thus one benefit of such tools is to help us manage a constructive dialogue.

With a clear understanding of how both parties arrived at their conclusions, we will now see the exact points where our thinking and perceptions diverged. In some instances such differences will be caused by inflexible and deeply held beliefs, and are therefore unlikely to change. But in many instances we will discover that differences are caused by trivial assumptions that neither party is attached to. In fact, when using these tools we will again and again discover that the other party has absolutely no rationale for their conclusions — they simply made them up! Helping a person come to this realisation is sometimes the only thing we need to do to make them change their mind.

Alternatively, instead of starting with our incompatible conclusions and working backwards, parties can start at the other end by seeking to jointly agree on how a conclusion should be reached. This is similar to changing the questions from "How did you arrive at the price for your car?" to "What process should we follow to price *any* car?" Because the conversation is removed from *your* car, we are more likely to remain objective. And once we agree on the process, we can apply it to our specific case.

Applying this thinking to the example of the business valued at $20 million (or $5 million, depending on where you stand), we may learn that the difference in valuation comes from any of these disconnections.

- Parties looked at different data when valuing the company. While one used multiples of comparable companies, the other considered free-cash flows.

- Parties looked at the same report that suggested drought for the next ten years, but did not agree on how that data will affect future profitability.

- The buyer feared that the business would lose customers when the owner leaves, and adjusted the price accordingly.

- The seller assumes the company will continue in its current form, but the buyer plans to integrate half of the business into its existing company, and discard the other half.

- The seller might have a personal need to sell at a certain price to look successful in the eyes of others, and is therefore asking for a higher price than his logic can support simply because he believes he deserves more.

The differences that were uncovered can now be dealt with one by one, and in a more constructive manner, and with more available solutions, than merely fighting over the final price. As just one example, perhaps a second buyer can be found who is willing to pay for the half of the business that the present buyer wishes to discard.

The more we clear up diverging perceptions, the better we will understand the problem, and the easier it will be to identify options for solving the problem.

PERCEPTION AND WORDS

Let us now discuss a couple examples of how we cause diverging perceptions and therefore unnecessarily add more pollution simply through our clumsy choice of words.

Universal statements

What do the following sentences have in common?

- You are <u>never</u> on time.

- You <u>always</u> do this to me.

- You <u>only</u> ever offer to help when you want something in return.

- <u>Everybody</u> agrees with me.

- <u>Nobody</u> in his or her right mind would do what you did.

- You ruined <u>everything</u>.

Chances are that these statements are never (!) true and therefore distort our message. Much of the time when we use so-called universal statements we actually intend to use a less extreme word, but we exaggerate for effect. The problem is that the other party will feel wrongly accused (and rightly so), and now we are likely to pollute our interaction with a debate over whether or not "always" was the right word to use, because the other party can certainly recall several times when he or she was on time. This debate was completely avoidable, but now we're stuck with it. And the emotions created by the debate are not going to dissipate in an instant, they are probably not going to help us achieve what we set out to achieve, and may be responsible for further pollution down the line.

Modal operators

Another group of words that frequently cause differences in perceptions are *modal operators.*

- have to

- must

- should

- ought to

- can't

- shouldn't

- need to

When I say something such as, "You can't be stuck in first position and expect good negotiation outcomes" I have (quite unintentionally) distorted the message. It is actually possible to still get the negotiation outcomes that you want regardless of what perspective you adopt. A more accurate description of what I meant would probably be: "There are several reasons that being stuck in first position will make it difficult for you to get the negotiation outcomes you want."

One potential problem caused by using modal operators is that we may unintentionally reduce the range of perceived available options. If you are my supplier and I tell you that you "must reduce the price of the product range by five per cent", I am effectively stating a demand, which tends to result in the least useful of available negotiation games (division). A different way of expressing the same need could be: "Our customers seem unwilling to pay the current list price for your products. We think one option could be to reduce the list price as long as we could keep our profit margin. One way of achieving that would be if we could reduce the price we pay you by five per cent."

This does not mean that you will give me the discount. But you now have a better understanding of what I am trying to achieve, and you may even help me find another way. You might for instance suggest that we instead optimise the supply chain from your company to my company, and try to find an opportunity to save there.

When negotiators hear the modal operators above, we may wish to check if we can substitute them with words or phrases that allow more choice, e.g. "might want to", "could", "can", "have the option to", etc.

Comparatives

The way we use comparatives also contributes to creating diverging perceptions. Comparatives are words we use to compare two or more things (larger, smaller, happier, hungrier, more intelligent, faster, less punctual, etc). However, we often leave out one of the two things being compared.

- We want *better* performance.
- Give us a proposal with *lower* risk.
- You need to work *more* efficiently.

Without the second half of the statement we as listeners are left to make assumptions, and that predictably lead to diverging perceptions and expectations. Instead we may wish to prompt the speaker to provide the omitted information:

- What type of performance? Specifically better by how much, and measured how?
- What type of risk? Specifically lower by what amount, and measured how?
- More efficiently than what or who? Specifically how much more efficiently, and measured how?

Words for measurements

We don't have to use the extreme versions of words in order to create misunderstanding. Have a think about what percentage you would replace the following expressions with:

- always

- often

- sometimes

- never

Now try to use one of the words in different sentences:

- I always lose my keys. (Hmm…five per cent of the time?)

- I'm always reading two or three different books at the same time. (Hmm…ten per cent of the time?)

- I'm always the one to take out the garbage. (Hmm…sixty-five per cent of the time?)

What we find is that these words are very context-dependent and up for interpretation. Thus using these words can result in the listener gaining a different understanding from the one we intended. Realising this, we may wish to use the actual number or percentage instead when referring to frequency, likelihood, amounts, and intensity.

Stereotypes

Do you ever stereotype or typecast people? Why? Perhaps you find that there may be some truth to stereotypes? Perhaps you find that "Germans are more punctual than Brazilians." While it is possible that the average German is more punctual than the average Brazilian due to cultural values or societal norms, there will still be a large number of Brazilians who are more punctual than a large number of Germans. Thus applying any stereotype involves a risk that we are wrong about the individual that we are dealing with. Furthermore, our individual traits are determined by numerous additional factors beyond broad attributes such as nationality, level of education, profession or sex.

Apart from increasing the risk that we misperceive the other party, our expectations of how someone (based on our stereotyped view of them) will act may create self-fulfilling prophesies. It can also result in loss of trust if we observe behaviour that doesn't fit the stereotype we assigned. Both self-fulfilling prophecies and trust will be covered in chapter 6.

Connotative | denotative

OK, so some words can have many interpretations. What if we just stick to the dictionary definition? Will we be safe? Sadly, and perhaps surprisingly, the answer is "no". It turns out that few of us learn a language by reading the dictionary. Rather we infer the meaning from how we hear the words used by others, and the contexts in which the words have been used. That means the *connotative* meanings that each of us associate with an individual word may vary dramatically.

> Please take a few minutes and draw a picture representing the word "marriage".

What is in your picture? A wedding cake? A house with a family of stick figures? A ring? What if I told you that my picture shows a prison? While I may have chosen my picture for comic effect, I hope it is also effective in demonstrating the very different meanings people associate with words. Now try the same exercise with the word "negotiation"…

So it is quite possible that we are entirely confident that the message we send to the other party simply can't be misunderstood. Yet, if the other party has attached different connotations to *any single word* the entire tone of the message may become distorted. Most often, we will have no awareness of the precise source of the misunderstanding, and as a result we typically resort to blaming the other person. In contrast, skilled negotiators appreciate how imprecise language is, and we will constantly monitor the language used, and check for understanding.

Level of abstraction

Picture a vertical line with the words *abstract, general* and *conceptual* at the top, and the words *concrete* and *specific* at the bottom. The way we communicate with words will fit somewhere on that vertical dimension. Different people will have different preferences for what level to have the conversation on. This is typically a reflection of how each individual thinks.

This concept is relevant for a number of reasons. We bring it up in the section on perception because discussing things at the most abstract, general or conceptual level is likely to result in very different perceptions. Please read the following paragraph:

> *We need to adopt a new strategy that embraces our core values. This will allow us to improve productivity and connect better with our stakeholders. We will achieve this by liaising with all parties, improving communication, innovating and collaborating.*

Now, imagine that you are the manager who will be in charge of implementing this strategy. Is everything clear to you? Probably not. You may have *some* understanding. And probably every single person who attended that board meeting will have a different understanding of what needs to be done and how.

At the abstract level it will be easy for us to get agreement, but difficult to get understanding. Perhaps this is exactly why it is easy to get agreement, because we have not yet discovered all the details where we disagree.

- Abstract: "Can we agree that we would like to pursue an outcome to this negotiation that is valuable and fair for all parties?" Yes.

- Concrete: "Do we know what that looks like?" No.

As we move down towards more concrete and specific language, all assumptions and different perceptions will need to be discussed if we wish to ensure understanding. Imagine that we at the general level agree to build a bridge. At the more specific levels we may discuss the material, size, type, cost, timeframe, who does what by when, where and how. We will need to discuss the specifics before we can feel confident that both parties share the same understanding of what the bridge project will look like.

So how do we know at which level of abstraction someone is presently communicating? One clue is look out for abstraction in both verbs (e.g. perform, improve, engage) and in nouns (e.g. performance, improvement, engagement). Note that we can move in three directions on the scale of abstraction: more abstract, less abstract, or sideways on the scale.

Yes, sideways. We can keep the dialogue at the same level of abstraction but talk about something different. For instance, we may use analogies to help explain the key aspects of a concept. We might also use examples that are similar, but separate from the current negotiation to reduce the likelihood of parties taking things personally, reacting, or getting caught up in (for the time being) irrelevant detail.

COGNITIVE BIASES, MENTAL TRAPS, AND PREDICTABLE IRRATIONALITY

This section provides a wide range of insights into how we are less rational than we would like to believe. Irrationality in itself it not necessarily a bad thing. The primary reason we hesitate to deal with irrational people is that we associate irrationality with unpredictability. However, if we can identify factors that explain how people are *predictably* irrational, then these factors also make people *predictable*. And the more predictable we find people, the more control we will have in influencing them.

Note that every symptom, syndrome and behavioural tic that explains why and how others are irrational, explains the same of us. Self-awareness stings! But we stand a greater chance of achieving change in another party by first admitting that we are also subject to the same sources of irrationality.

What follows is a superficial summary only, and our intent is to increase awareness rather than cover the depth of research available, or even cover all of the available cognitive biases and mental traps. The reader is encouraged to do further reading as these factors go to great lengths in explaining human behaviour that many of us find frustrating in negotiations. More importantly, these factors also explain why many of the negotiation insights in this book work.

(You will see some overlap between the different biases. That is fine. Different people researched them for different purposes. We are simply aggregating them here to help us gain more negotiation insights. The goal is not to be able to define all the biases, but rather to get a feel for how people think and behave.)

FACTOR	SUMMARY	EXAMPLE
TRANSFERENCE	This is where I take the emotions that I associate with another person or object, and transfer those feelings onto you. This typically happens because I already perceive some other similarity or link between the two.	The last time you bought a car you were swindled; now whenever you meet salespeople you feel that they are untrustworthy.
HALO EFFECT	Our perception of one person's (or object's) trait can be influenced by another trait of that same person (or object).	We are likely to assume that a healthy-looking person probably knows more about nutrition and exercise than an unhealthy-looking person.
PROJECTION BIAS	We believe we know how the other person thinks or feels based on how we think or feel.	A negotiator who is tempted to mislead the other party might then suspect or even accuse the other party of having an intention to mislead.

FACTOR	SUMMARY	EXAMPLE
HALLUCINATION	When we are convinced that we observed something that is not actually there, either because we have added assumptions and interpretations, or because our senses are inaccurate.	After seeing a police officer run after a young man we may be tempted to assume that the young man is an offender. But we didn't see an offence. In fact, the young man may have dropped his wallet, and the officer is seeking to return it.
SELF-SERVING BIAS	When explaining our successful outcomes we overestimate our own contribution, and when explaining our failures we overestimate external factors.	I am great at getting along with others. Well, of course not counting "difficult people".
ACTOR-OBSERVER BIAS	We overestimate the role of other people's personality in explaining their behaviour. But when explaining our own behaviour we are more likely to overestimate situational factors.	While your friend was late to her interview because she is unreliable, you missed your interview because of kids, traffic, traffic lights, bad luck, bad weather and/or your GPS running out of battery.
FUNDAMENTAL ATTRIBUTION ERROR	The first half of actor-observer: we hold other people more responsible for their outcomes, and we underestimate the role of external factors.	If a woman gets assaulted when walking home through the park, we may decide that she was partly responsible because she was wearing revealing clothes or because she was walking alone late at night.
PARTISAN PERCEPTIONS	Once we pick a side on an issue we tend to deem our side "the right side" and the other side "the wrong side".	Sports supporters of a losing team may deem that they deserved to win. But they are less likely to extend that courtesy to the other team if roles were reversed.

FACTOR	SUMMARY	EXAMPLE
CONFIRMATION BIAS	Once we form an opinion, we will actively seek data that supports our view, avoid or scrutinise data that challenges our view, and interpret ambiguous data to support our view.	Partisan news channels that carefully select stories, footage and sound bites to support their pre-existing political narratives.
SOCIAL UTILITY BIAS	We make our criteria for success relative to what other people get or achieve.	I may be very happy with negotiating a twenty per cent discount on my car. That is, until I discover that you got thirty per cent discount on the very same model.
RELATIVE GOAL TRAP	More general than the social utility bias, the relative goal trap suggests that we make our criteria for success relative to any arbitrary goal.	We feel good about buying an item at the FORTY PERCENT OFF SALE, despite everyone else also getting forty percent off, and despite perhaps no one else ever having paid the list price.
ANCHORING	When we don't know the true value of something, we place disproportionately too much weight on the first number that we hear.	A potential buyer making an insultingly low offer on your house, not with the expectation to pay that price, but with the expectation that this will focus the negotiation closer to that number.
SUNK-COST TRAP OR COMMITMENT BIAS	When we invest (e.g. time, money, effort) in anything (e.g. a project, a deal, a relationship, a negotiation), then we end up having a greater need to see returns from that investment. If that investment turns bad, we are likely to hold on to the investment and hope that our fortunes will change.	Halfway through a terrible show we may reason that we should at least stay until the end to get value for our money. But logic should make us realise that the money is already lost, and we should now choose how to spend the next two hours based on what will be most enjoyable from this point on.

FACTOR	SUMMARY	EXAMPLE
IRRATIONAL ESCALATION	When we escalate our commitment to an initial course of action that it is no longer beneficial to us.	Continuing to pursue the goal of winning a price war between companies after it becomes clear that the competition won't back down, and that the price war is eroding margins for all parties.

Referent point

Social utility bias, relative valuation, and anchoring all illustrated that we compare success to some kind of referent point. In these traps our referent points were: other people, perceived available value, and the first number mentioned. One cause of the sunk-cost trap is that we have our referent point in the past rather than in the present.

Most people pick their referent points arbitrarily and on autopilot, but we have complete freedom in how to chose our referent point. For instance, we could use the status quo as a referent point, and thereby view any improvement above today's performance is good (a "gain frame"). We can also set our referent point to be our first, most ambitious and most extreme opening position. In that case any outcome is likely to feel like a loss compared to our referent point (a "loss frame"). Thus our perception of success (and therefore our level of satisfaction) is quite separate from the content outcome we achieve, and can be simply influenced by selecting a different referent point.

So our referent points determine whether we perceive a gain or a loss frame. And the frame we perceive determines many aspects of how we negotiate. Negotiators thus seek to intentionally help all parties pick referent points that will lead to the negotiation we want to have. Specifically, if we want to play the integration or maximisation games, then a gain frame for all parties will typically be more helpful than a loss frame.

FACTOR	SUMMARY	EXAMPLE
CONTRAST PRINCIPLE	We adjust our evaluation of something based on what it is compared to.	To make a product seem cheaper we put it next to something more expensive, or to make a solution seem simpler we compare it with one that is more complex.
OMISSION BIAS	We hold ourselves much more accountable for what we do (actions) that for what we fail to do (omissions). We also consider harmful acts to be worse than harmful omissions.	We may choose to not vaccinate our child against a lethal disease if there is a small risk that the vaccine itself may kill the child. Statistically getting the vaccine may be the best outcome for the child, but we see ourselves as more responsible if our action contributed to the child's death.
STATUS QUO BIAS	When we have the choice of either changing circumstances or doing nothing, we often prefer doing nothing. The status quo carries certainty, and while we might expect that changing circumstances will leave us better off, we feel uncomfortable with the uncertainty that they could leave us worse off.	People who inherit shares typically keep those shares. If the same people had instead inherited the equivalent value in cash, they would be unlikely to choose to invest the money in those particular shares.

FACTOR	SUMMARY	EXAMPLE
ENDOWMENT EFFECT	Simply feeling that we already possess an item (or person, or pet, or deal) means that we will value it higher than if we don't yet deem that we possess it.	We may feel resistance to throwing out items when cleaning out our attic or wardrobe even if we would not pay money to acquire these items had they not already been in our possession.
ZERO-SUM BIAS OR FIXED-PIE MINDSET OR INCOMPATIBILITY BIAS	This bias states that we tend to assume that one party's gain has to be matched with an equal loss for another party.	Negotiators who engage in the division game!
REACTIVE DEVALUATION	If we are in disagreement, then you will value an option (or idea, or solution) less if I propose it than if you propose it.	Opposing political parties may at different times propose a solution to a problem, but reject an identical idea if it is proposed by the opposing party.
AVAILABILITY BIAS	When making decisions we give disproportionate weight to information that is most available, easiest to remember, or most vivid in nature.	A presidential candidate might elect to use dramatic exaggerations and even lies to smear the reputation of another candidate. Even if these allegations are rebutted, they may still influence voters.
ABOVE AVERAGE BIAS	On average, we believe we are more honest, capable, intelligent, insightful and fair than others.	When individuals in a group are asked whether they are more intelligent, or would be better at leading the country than the average person in the room, significantly more than half say "yes".

FACTOR	SUMMARY	EXAMPLE
COGNITIVE DISSONANCE	Cognitive dissonance describes the psychological discomfort we feel either when we have two conflicting beliefs, or when our actions conflict with our beliefs. To resolve the dissonance we have to change one of the two, or rationalise why we shouldn't feel the discomfort.	Believing that it is my responsibility to help people in need but refusing to give a donation to a beggar is likely to create cognitive dissonance. As a result I'll either change my belief, or my behaviour and thus give the money, or rationalise that this particular beggar didn't deserve my help.
POST-DECISION RATIONALISATION AND POST-OUTCOME RATIONALISATION	After we take an action, or make a decision, or an event occurs, we will seek or invent supporting reasons for why that was indeed the right thing to do, or the best outcome for us.	If I discover that I paid more for a camera than my friend did, then I might tell myself that I indeed need the camera a lot more than my friend, and that it probably creates more value for me than for him.
EFFORT JUSTIFICATION	Effort justification states that we justify our efforts in pursuing a goal by overstating to ourselves how desirable that goal is.	While or after taking part in a gruelling initiation process, military boot camp, or completing our degree, we are likely to overstate the benefit of that outcome to us.

FACTOR	SUMMARY	EXAMPLE
POST-DECISION RELIEF	The discomfort we feel when faced with difficult decisions tends to disappear once we make a decision. We run the risk of attributing that sense of relief to having made the right decision.	Faced with the choice between staying with our employer and accepting another offer we may feel overwhelmed. But once we pick either option the discomfort disappears and we tell ourselves that it is because we made the right choice.
PLURALISTIC IGNORANCE	The tendency to behave consistently with a group, even though each individual might have acted differently if alone.	While in the countryside, we might not think twice before helping an injured person at the side of the road; in the city we might not help because we assume someone else will.
FALSE CONSENSUS EFFECT	In contrast to pluralistic ignorance, the false consensus effect states that we overestimate the likelihood of other people sharing our outlook on the world, or that other people are in agreement with us.	We may walk into the negotiation assuming that the other party has the same needs and priorities as us.
DURABILITY BIAS	While we can fairly accurately predict how we will feel if something good or bad happens in the future, we overestimate how long our negative feelings will last.	We may not ask (for a date, for a raise, for a discount) because of our fear of rejection. But how long would the pain actually last if we asked and they said "no"?

As you will see such biases and traps crop up over and over again throughout the negotiation process. For instance, when we later discuss letting the other party do most of the talking when we seek to build rapport, this is because the other party is biased to assume that we agree and that we are similar until we signal otherwise.

EXPECTATION AND RECOLLECTION

By now we understand that limitations in perception means we only capture a fraction of what really happened. Further to this, our memory doesn't actually work like a computer hard drive, where we would recall the same information every time it is read. Rather our mind will recall different fragments each time, piece them together, and then make up the rest. What we actually remember each time will be influenced by a number of things, including the following.

- Our current emotional state. Have you noticed that when you are really happy with life all memories seem to be rather nice? And when you are really depressed then everything in your life feels negative? We may thus remember the same event completely differently simply based on how we currently feel.

- Information in the present. Giving information to people who are trying to recall something can cause the same people to incorporate that information into their memories.

- Current beliefs. Just as we saw that our beliefs may override all the logical steps in the process of arriving at conclusions, our current beliefs may override our memories. One predictable current belief is that we are in some way shape or form a "good" person, and our memory will selectively forget or edit instances that suggest otherwise.

- Rationalisation. Sometimes we don't remember but start to rationalise what we think *must* have happened, or what we think we *must* have done. Because memories are effectively constructed as we recall them, we may get confused and think we are *recalling* what we are actually *constructing*.

That is a lot of noise! And there is (at least) one more — our recollection is affected by what we expected to happen! If we spend time expecting a certain outcome, then something slightly better or worse happens, we may actually recall what we *expected* to happen. If we plan our one-week vacation one year in advance, and spend fifty-two weeks anticipating what the trip will be like, then in the future our memories of the trip may actually be tainted (for better or for worse) by our expectations of it.

As negotiators we can use such insights both to understand how someone's (including our own) recollection of "facts" may be inaccurate, but also to influence what someone will recall.

LEGITIMACY AND FAIRNESS

Importance of fairness

Is fairness important in negotiation? Well, it will depend on whom you ask and which negotiation game they want to play. Negotiators who say "No, it is not important" often envisage themselves playing the division game, envisage a one-off transaction, and envisage being the party having enough power to dictate an outcome.

In contrast, I would like to suggest that fairness is extremely important in negotiation. Specifically, we absolutely hate being treated unfairly. I don't want to be treated unfairly. And my bet is that the other party thinks exactly the same way. We resent it. We resist it. And if we are treated sufficiently unfairly we will start to feel an urge to get even. The desire to get back at whoever treated us unfairly may be so strong that we will go to great lengths and incur great costs to make it happen. Some people may even pursue mutual destruction because the emotions that drive revenge can be more persuasive than the logic that says we should do what is best for us.

A classic exercise that you may try with your friends or colleagues is to offer $2 (or a cake, chocolate bar, anything) for two people to share. One person is tasked with deciding how to split the value, and the other person will decide whether to accept or reject the deal. If the deal is rejected then neither party gets anything.

So how important is fairness? Well it turns out that if the first party insists on much more than $1 for him- or herself (what we could argue is *fair*), the second party is likely to reject the deal. If, for example, the first party insists on $1.50 for him- or herself and $0.50 for the second party, the second party is not very likely to accept the deal.

Now think about this for a minute. The second party has the choice between getting $0.50 and getting nothing, and he/she chooses nothing! How come? The second party feels unfairly treated (i.e. feels resentment) and chooses to punish (i.e. take revenge on) the first party, even though this incurs a cost for both parties (i.e. mutual destruction)!

This effect becomes smaller as the absolute value of our share increases. For example, say that you bought two lottery tickets together with your spouse, and then you divided the tickets between you. If your spouse's ticket later won $100 million but he or she decided to only give you $5 million and keep $95 million, then it is still not very likely that you would tear up the winning ticket out of spite.

Subjective fairness of content

So what is fair? Well, it turns out that fairness is a rather subjective concept. Let's see if we can illustrate with an example. Imagine two parties, and you are tasked with determining the fair way for them to split $100.

Let me guess, $50/$50? OK, that's a good start. Let's now create a few more difficult scenarios.

- The two parties have together generated the $100. One of the parties is very rich and the other is very poor. So the poor person needs the money more, and the money would hardly make a dent in the rich person's wallet. Could it be fair that the poorer person gets more of the money because it makes a bigger difference to him or her?

- Could it be fair that the richer person gets more money, because he or she is taxed fifty per cent on every dollar, whereas the poor person doesn't have to pay tax? So to be fair perhaps we should consider post-tax money, so that both parties have the same amount to buy things with?

- What if the two parties had different roles in the venture, e.g. one did IP and one did sales? Let's say that the party doing the sales is actually a team of two people but there was only one person doing IP. Should the money be split half and half between the two functions/departments, or one third each for all the people in the company?

- What if with just two parties there is a precedent, where last year one person got seventy dollars and the other person got thirty?

- What if the two parties have struggled for a long time to make any money, so one of the parties got his mother to buy services for $10 to help out. Could that qualify him to get a bigger share?

- What if one party has the power to take all the money for himself and could fire the other party if he wanted, but agrees to *only* take ninety per cent to be *fair*?

- What if the $100 is actually four single meal dinner vouchers, two for vegetarian and two for meat-only restaurants. Assume only one person is vegetarian but both parties prefer vegetarian to meat?

This is still a rather trivial example, but we can already see that there are multiple ways of defining what is fair. With some creativity we can come up with rationales for why every conceivable split from \$100/\$0 to \$0/\$100 between the parties could be fair.

Now imagine that instead of you as a neutral party deciding what is fair for the parties, the two parties have to themselves agree on what is fair. Is there a risk that partisan perceptions and confirmation bias will ensure that parties will disagree on which criteria is fair? Absolutely. Similarly we can predict that a buyer and a seller will each self-servingly seek out the criteria for fairness that favours that party.

Fairness is *not* an absolute or objective concept, but rather an inherently subjective one.

Fairness of process

When I ask my participants, "What is more important for fairness, the process or the outcome?" I often get the answer, "The outcome!" The most common argument is that if the outcome is not good, then we don't care about the process.

But it is actually the other way around. We can accept a less than perfect outcome, because we understand that the other party is not likely to be in perfect control of all the constraints that limit the outcome. It might be negatively affected by time pressures, orders from superiors, limited resources or restrictive company policy. In contrast, we *do* feel that the other party is in complete control over how he or she negotiates with us. Thus we are much less accepting of an unfair process than an unfair outcome.

To illustrate this, imagine that you are looking to negotiate employee salary levels with me (the CEO) on behalf of a union. Your stakeholders hope for a three per cent increase this year. Picture a process whereby you and I sit down together, analyse all parties' needs, work out a way to align our interests, realise the joint challenges we face to make our business profitable, create a plan for the future, etc. You walk away with a 0.5 percent increase in salary levels, but you also understand that this approach will allow the company to grow, all employees to remain employed, as well as allow for bigger increases each year for the next ten years. You have seen all the numbers and know that I'm not trying to cheat you — I simply can't find a way fund a three percent increase this year.

Contrast this with an approach where I say: "I'm not going to negotiate with you. You're all replaceable so I'm not going to waste my time with you. I'll decide what is fair and you will get a one percent increase this year. Take it or leave it."

When only presented with one of these scenarios, participants overwhelmingly rate the *outcome* in the first scenario as more fair, and easier to agree to. What they don't realise is that they are actually evaluating the *process* as being fair.

Relationship and fairness

Let us revisit the example of winning money in the lottery. If you buy the winning ticket in the presence of another person, how much would you give them? They bought their ticket just before you and it could just as well have been they who won.

How much would you give if it were a loved one? Half of the winnings? More than half? Is it conceivable that a grandmother buying the ticket with her grandson might actually voluntarily give away *more* than half? Of course.

But how much would you give to an acquaintance? Colleague? Stranger? How much would you give to someone you actively dislike?

The only thing we've changed in this scenario is the relationship with the other party. Yet, it has a dramatic effect on what you feel is a fair split of the newly acquired value.

This is an important insight. We mentioned earlier that we can come up with an endless array of arguments that could all be considered fair. So which one do we pick? Well, that depends on how much we like the other party! The more we like the other party, the more likely we are to choose a criterion that favours both parties equally (or favours them more!). But the weaker our relationship is with the other party, the more likely that we will choose a criterion that favours us.

While the integration and maximisation games focus on creating new value, all games can reach a point where parties have to agree on what is a fair split of value. If we understand the importance of fairness, and we understand how the perception of the relationship affects the perception of fairness, then we also understand how important strong and positive relationships are to influencing outcomes in negotiation.

Objective standards

A common concept taught in negotiation is that of encouraging parties to agree on objective standards to determine how to split perceived conflicting value. In practice this sometimes fails because:

- as we have discussed, fairness is inherently subjective;

- after covering perception in this book we know there are no objective facts in negotiation;

- objective standards, e.g. prevailing market rates, are often little more than arbitrary precedent, or social utility bias in action, and are rarely aligned with the needs parties seek to satisfy; and

- if parties have to negotiate and agree on what is objective, they will still do so in a self-serving manner, subject to partisan perceptions and confirmation bias. In other words, they will play division in their negotiation about which criteria or standards to use!

The last point is worth repeating: we often see negotiators initially playing integration to create value, only to resort to division when it is time to agree on how to split that value. And if the game will end up with division, then parties have a strong incentive to use division tactics throughout the entire negotiation!

But what if we could use a third party, e.g. a judge, to decide what constitutes right and wrong, what is objective and what is fact? Yes it will certainly limit the extent to which either party can influence the criteria used. But can a judge's decision feel unfair to you? Of course it can. You can resent a judge's decision for being unfair just as you can resent another party for negotiating unfairly. And we already know the risks of leaving a party resenting an unfair outcome. Also, if a third party dictates the outcome we have to comply with then perhaps we are no longer in a negotiation, or at least not in a negotiation where we have sufficient influence.

So what can we do instead? We can learn from the above and accept that fairness is a subjective perception that we can influence through strong relationships and a fair process. We can also do one more thing, and that is to create an abundance of value; parties find it much easier to share when each party can get enough. And how to create more value is a main focus of this book.

GOOD AND BAD ARGUMENTS

How many arguments should we use to convince the other party? All of them? Interestingly, having more arguments to support our view is not always better than having few arguments. Some of our arguments will inevitably be weaker than others, and there is a risk that the other party will selectively focus on the weakest argument. Thus bad arguments effectively undermine good arguments.

Additionally, when we feel that the other party is trying too hard to convince us we tend to get suspicious. This is an appropriate reaction. Usually people who are truthful will expect to be believed. However, people who (consciously) lie expect to *not* be believed, and therefore tend to overcompensate with *too* much evidence. We tend to pick up on this eagerness unconsciously and it can reduce our trust in the other party. Of course, this applies as much to us as it does to the other party.

LOGIC, PERCEPTION, EMOTIONS

Are we persuaded by logic? Well, the short answer is that the most rational and logical of us would like to believe so. And in some instances we are. Typically this is limited to the domain of topics that we are not emotionally attached to, and where we don't have strong opinions, and that don't relate to our ego, and that aren't tied to our values, and… Well, let's just say that there are *some* instances where we are persuaded by logic. Some.

We can pick two scientists with opposing views, have them run a research study together, and in the end one of them may very well look at the outcome and say: "Wow, I had no idea. But I guess the facts speak for themselves!"

The astute reader will pick up on the fact that this result was not limited to facts. We also ensured a process of involvement. If we exclude that scientist from having input into the research, then we would reduce the likelihood that he or she will be persuaded by the results. Instead we increase the likelihood that he or she will rationalise the results as being the fruit of a flawed process, based on flawed assumptions, and perhaps by flawed scientists.

While we would probably like to view ourselves as objective, rational, scientific people, we aren't. Yes, we do love facts, logic, and rational arguments…when they support our view. And if we can't find ways to rationally support our view, then we will resort to creating arguments based on logical fallacies (the reader is encouraged to familiarise him- or herself with these on the web). Unfortunately neither approach does a good job of persuading the other party.

So what does persuade us? Emotion. Perceptions. Psychological biases. Needs. These are the tools skilled negotiators work with.

SUMMARY: PERCEPTION OF WHAT?

Perception of everything! Perception is reality for both us and the other party, and the other party are likely to have different perceptions of every single aspect of the interaction.

- What we are negotiating about.

- What we said, what they said.

- The history between parties and what has happened in the past.

- Who to blame.

- What the negotiation process is.

- What the negotiation process should be.

- The relationship.

- And just about everything else…

To reiterate, if we want to be skilled negotiators, we are well advised to leave our ego at home (unless we negotiate at home, in which case we need to find another place to store our ego temporarily). We may achieve greater success if we:

- appreciate the limitations of our perception and of how we think;

- stop assuming that we are "right";

- seek to predict and prevent and clear up misunderstandings and diverging perceptions; and

- double-check or triple-check all parties' understanding and perceptions throughout the negotiation.

4

BECOME A NEGOTIATOR

IN CONTROL

Are you in control of your life? OK, perhaps that question is a bit too broad; you are probably in control of some things and not in control of other things. Perhaps a better question is how much control do you have over your life? Different people will give very different answers to this question.

Specifically, some of us have a bias towards believing that we have much control over our lives, and some of us have a bias towards thinking that life mostly happens to us. Management literature is often generous and says that neither of these traits is better or worse.

However, in negotiation it is helpful to assume that we are indeed in control of outcomes. This assumption tends to lead to a more curious and proactive approach. It also makes it more likely that we take responsibility when things don't go well. That sinking feeling of responsibility for failures is often useful in providing us with the motivation to change and improve going forwards.

Of course, sometimes there is very little we can do to affect what happens to us. A hurricane may strike the town where we live, and there is nothing we could have done to stop it. Still, if we look carefully at this scenario, we will find that we have more influence over what happened than we initially thought.

- With practice, we can always be in control over how we react to something.

- We are always in control over how we choose to respond to something.

- With foresight and awareness, we can often choose how we prepare for something happening.

- The same foresight and awareness may help us avoid or prevent that "something" from affecting us.

For instance:

- Our reaction to a hurricane wiping out our house might be one of anger or sadness, and asking ourselves why this happened to us. Our reaction could also be to appreciate the future pleasure, growth and character building that will come from having overcome significant challenges in our life; once we overcome significant challenges we often value having had that experience.

- Our response may be to give up. Our response can also be to make a list of the most important things to do from this point on, reflect on what mistakes we don't want to repeat again, and then get busy moving forwards.

- Knowing that we live in a region that regularly gets hit by hurricanes, we may choose to build a storm shelter, buy hurricane insurance or even consider moving somewhere else.

At this point I would expect my more cynical readers to raise the fact that some outcomes and circumstances are indeed out of our control, e.g. getting crashed into by a drink driver or being genetically prone to a certain disease. That is true and I agree. However, the emphasis is on the word *some*. The vast majority of outcomes and circumstances we face can be within our circle of influence and control, if we take control.

FOUR STEPS TO ELITE NEGOTIATION PERFORMANCE

Step 2. Acquire knowledge

Quite predictably, a large number of unskilled negotiators lack knowledge about negotiation. Does that mean that knowledge is the key to becoming a skilled negotiator? Well, it is *one* key. Just like understanding a sport is *one* key to becoming a skilled player in that sport.

Acquiring knowledge increases our awareness of what is going on in the negotiation, it helps us know what to look for, and it helps us understand the impact of our actions. One could argue that having only knowledge about negotiation is sufficient if we wish to teach others, although I would recommend that even teachers lead by example and demonstrate desired behaviour in every interaction with participants.

Step 3. Change behaviour

But having knowledge alone does not result in improved negotiation behaviour. If this were the case then every MBA student who attended a negotiation course, every PhD student who specialised in negotiation, and every lecturer and trainer in negotiation would be outstanding negotiators (and every soccer coach, supporter or commentator would be a skilled soccer player). This is not what we observe. Being able to reason about negotiation and applying negotiation skills are two different things.

If we wish to become highly performing negotiators then we absolutely need to instil this knowledge into our behaviour. Our negotiation performance is determined by what we actually *do*; e.g. it does us little good to *know* how to build rapport if the behaviour we exhibit results in breaking rapport. How do we instil the knowledge into our behaviour? We practise. Diligently!

Step 4. Evaluate and adjust

We also need to review our results and solicit feedback on our performance. This allows us to identify what is working for us, and what is not. And if something is not working for us, then we keep changing our approach until it *does* work. This is very much related to self-awareness, which we discussed earlier.

A typical process is to repeatedly ask what you're doing well and what isn't working, keeping the former and changing the latter. Understanding what not to do is important, but it has the drawback of not telling us what we should do instead. So we specifically want to consider what else we want to try. And if we don't know what that should be, then sometimes trying *anything* else is better than repeating what clearly doesn't work.

You may also wish to solicit feedback from your co-negotiator, if you have one, your negotiation coach, or anyone who observed your negotiation. Their view will often be more valuable than yours, partially because they will find it easier to perceive you as the other party does, and partially because their opinion is not distorted by your ego. In fact, you may even wish to consider asking the other party for feedback!

...Step 1. Adopt a healthy mindset

No, putting this last is not a typo. Once all the knowledge and skill are installed and honed through practice and feedback, you are equipped to influence the negotiation in any direction. And that direction will be guided by your mindset. This is the set of assumptions and beliefs that you hold about negotiation. A healthy mindset tends to guide a negotiator towards creating maximum value for all. In contrast, an unhealthy mindset, e.g. believing that winning is important, or that protecting one's own ego is important, will typically bring about suboptimal outcomes, regardless of what the negotiator is actually capable of.

Your mindset will also affect how you approach the learning process of becoming a skilled negotiator. If you already rate yourself as proficient you probably won't see the need to improve. But if you instead appreciate that there is always a next level, and a level after that, then you are more likely to commit to a lifelong journey of continual improvement. Thus adopting a healthy mindset may actually be the first step for any aspiring negotiator.

LIMITATIONS OF EXPERIENCE

"You only learn negotiation through experience." Is this statement true? Of course not — it completely runs against our previous insights about the autopilot and the four steps to achieving elite negotiation performance.

But it happens to be a statement that I hear quite often, so I think it is important to allocate some space in this book to explaining why we might want to look beyond our own experience.

- We are the ones evaluating our own experience, and we have a deep psychological need to feel good about ourselves.

- As part of needing to feel good about ourselves, we also have a tendency to forget the bad experiences, and only count the good ones.

- We look at our own experience and realise that others don't have the same experience as us. We assume this means they know less or are less skilled. However, we conveniently fail to acknowledge that others will have, and can draw upon, experiences that we don't have.

- The real world is very complex and multiple variables affect any single outcome. By just viewing one specific experience we have no way of gaining certainty on specifically which variable had a positive or a negative affect on the outcome. In contrast, systematic research will replicate such events many times, where only a single variable is changed, and thus give more conclusive evidence of what cause/effect patterns exist. This research then informs the theories and concepts we learn.

- Along the same line, real-world experiences typically don't occur exactly the same way again. This point can be remembered with the quote: "Generals always prepare to fight the last war." The next situation will be at least slightly different, thus reducing the likelihood that the approach that worked last time is replicable without modification.

- In the real world there is often a lag between the action we take, and the final outcome. In that period multiple other variables may contribute to making the outcome better or worse but we fail to acknowledge them.

- We typically fail to account for the element of chance, particularly for positive outcomes. So when we make a bet that a stock will go up, and it does, we gladly take credit for an excellent decision. Of course, there may be hundreds or thousands of factors affecting the stock price, and the result could be due to one (or all) of the factors we didn't even think of.

On its own, experience is a comparatively slow and noisy way to acquire negotiation insights. It also requires us to make all the (often expensive) mistakes ourselves. And when the mistakes *do* happen, we risk blaming someone else or something else in order to protect our ego, thus effectively missing the learning opportunity.

Don't get me wrong — experience is a very important part of becoming a better negotiator. But first we need to adopt a healthy mindset. We then jump up on the shoulders of giants — there are plenty of people who have paved the way for us so we might as well learn from them. And when we practise these insights we will inevitably build experience. And that will be experience of thinking like a negotiator, as opposed to more experience of running on autopilot.

AN INTENTIONAL, INFORMED, COMPREHENSIVE, FLEXIBLE, ADAPTABLE, AGILE, PRECISE AND SITUATIONAL APPROACH

Let's share two hypothetical negotiation approaches. One presents insights that supposedly work in every single situation. Another says that every negotiation is different and needs to be considered on a case-by-case basis. Which is the right one? Well, neither.

Both perspectives have merit. We can certainly identify insights and patterns that are applicable and common to virtually all negotiations. We can also identify aspects of each negotiation that make them unique. So a robust approach would surely include both perspectives.

Skilled negotiators adopt a deliberate and intentional approach to negotiation. This means they consciously decide how to negotiate, as opposed to running on autopilot. Skilled negotiators recognise the value of a comprehensive and informed approach, as opposed to relying on oversimplified models or tricks. Their approach is also flexible enough that it can be adapted and delivered with agility and precision, given the current situation or context.

Another way of saying it: first figure out how influence works, then devise the most useful approach given the current context.

AWAY FROM RECIPES AND TOWARDS SKILLS

The most common questions I get from unskilled negotiators are typically along the lines of: "Can you teach me some tricks for buying a car?", "What are the three steps for fixing a relationship?", "How do I negotiate my salary?" or "What are your top tips for negotiating in my industry?" The focus tends to be on quick fixes, or at least on recipes that can be followed step-by-step for identical and repeatable results every time.

Rather than looking at negotiation as a set of recipes, I would encourage a slightly different mindset. Sticking with the cooking analogy, a skilled negotiator is like a chef who:

- understands all the ingredients that are available for cooking;

- understands the characteristics (flavour, consistency, etc) of those ingredients;

- understands the different processes by which they can be cooked and combined;

- understands what all the people at the table would prefer to eat and restrictions such as allergies and budgets; and

- understands the relationships and social preferences of all the guests.

Then, no matter what ingredients are available, no matter what preferences the guests have, the chef will be in a position to find the best available solution (i.e. the best possible dinner and evening for all guests). This chef follows a very intentional, informed, comprehensive, flexible, adaptable, agile, precise, and situational approach.

Now *that* is a level of skill a chef should be happy to aspire to. And the analogy holds very well for negotiation as well. So out with the dust-covered box of recipes — any recipe is unlikely to be the best available solution given the complex parameters of the current negotiation.

SEPARATE PEOPLE FROM BEHAVIOURS

Is a person's behaviour a reflection of their personality? Does our personality determine the way we behave in negotiations? Some negotiators answer yes to these questions and this has led to a number of personality-driven approaches to negotiation. And yes, it would be *very* convenient if these approaches actually worked, because then we would have a recipe for how to negotiate with every single person on the planet.

I agree that our personality plays one part in influencing our behaviour. I would like to add that our behaviour is also influenced by our emotional state, the current context we find ourselves in, and the process we either consciously or unconsciously try to follow. Many of the behaviours individuals exhibit have no relation to their personalities. Thus we cannot reasonably expect to draw accurate conclusions about people's personality merely by observing individual behaviours. And if we don't know the other person's personality, then a purely personality-driven approach to negotiation will not be very helpful to us.

In general I would suggest that considering emotional state, context and process will provide more insight and control over the negotiation process than diagnosing a negotiator's personality. The main exception would be when psychological disorders are present or parties are influenced by drugs or medication or have failed to take their medication. In these cases negotiators are well advised to seek advice from qualified psychologists or psychiatrists.

Personality, emotional state, context, process

A range of factors already influences human behaviour: our personality, our emotional state, the context of the situation, and the learned process or pattern of behaviour that we follow. So one way to influence people is to influence these factors.

Note that while *personality* also explains people's behaviour, there is typically little we can do to influence it — another drawback with purely personality driven approaches to negotiation. Few of us are qualified to assess other people's personalities. We rarely have enough exposure to another party to get a sense of their default behaviour, or the opportunity to give the other person a written psychological test. And we have a tendency to make wild assumptions about other people's personality based on the behaviour we observe.

What about assessing our own personality? In the earlier section on self-awareness we discussed how we have a strong need for a healthy self-image. This makes us rather self-serving and not very objective when assessing ourselves.

However, we *can* identify *individual* aspects of people's (and our own) personalities and the way they think. In particular, the way we communicate gives away a lot of information about how we think: do we think in pictures, words or feelings? Do we think in abstract or concrete terms? Such insights can certainly help a negotiator build better rapport, improve understanding, and ultimately be instrumental in influencing the other party.

Human behaviour can also be significantly affected by a person's present emotional state. In fact, our emotional state has a physical effect on how our brain and body works and vice versa. For instance, we are likely to slouch when depressed, and more likely to feel depressed when slouching.

Compared to personality, emotional states are often easier to recognise, easier to influence, and they provide more predictable consequences for the rest of the negotiation. All we have to consider is how easy it is to get a child to stop crying by merely getting him or her to focus on something else. So incorporating an understanding of emotions is a fundamental part of our negotiation approach.

Let's also consider how the context influences our behaviour. As it turns out, we change our behaviours based on the person we are dealing with, the role we assume, who else is observing the interaction, time pressure, and many other reasons we can group as the context or the situation. For instance, a person working as a business executive or prison guard might behave in a dominating and controlling manner at work, and still behave in the most caring, gentle and understanding manner with friends and loved ones.

What if we changed other aspects of the context? What would you do if you could be invisible for a day? How would your behaviour be different from any other day? Without knowing anything about your personality, I believe the chances are high that you would do things while invisible that you would otherwise not do.

The field of social psychology helps negotiators by offering insights about how human behaviour changes in response to specific changes in the context. These insights often work irrespective of people's personalities!

- The classic Milgram experiment demonstrated that as long as an authority figure was present and claimed responsibility for the consequences, sixty-five per cent of average individuals would administer (what they believed were) the maximum available and possibly lethal shock of 450 volts to another person as punishment for answering test questions incorrectly.

- The percentage of individuals who administered 450-volt shocks *did not* change in response to whether or not the "victim" claimed to have a heart condition.

- The percentage of individuals who administered 450-volt shocks jumped to ninety per cent by changing one parameter; by leading the individuals to believe that they had observed the end of a previous experiment where 450-volt shocks had been administered.

We can apply such insights to negotiation for increased control over outcomes. For instance, the third version of the Milgram experiment above highlights the persuasive power of introducing a precedent, which is one of many ubiquitous tactics used in negotiation.

Note that in addition to driving some of our behaviour, the *context* also influences how we interpret those behaviours: avoiding eye contact may be interpreted as shifty in some western cultures and as a sign of respect in some eastern cultures.

Finally, as we discussed in the section on autopilot, some of our behaviour is driven by learned processes of interaction, i.e. patterns of behaviour. We may have made a conscious decision to learn some of these processes, e.g. by taking a negotiation course. We may also simply have copied, imitated or modelled other people's behaviour without having had any intention to do so. We may intentionally try to follow these processes, e.g. applying knowledge from the negotiation course. We may also follow these processes unintentionally (on autopilot), e.g. because of habit or in response to some emotional trigger during the interaction.

This is an important insight for negotiators. It means that any behaviour we observe may be intentional or unintentional. We simply do not know. This highlights the importance of withholding judgement and considering multiple available explanations for people's behaviour.

As an example, I once worked with a negotiator who is still one of the most rational, cerebral, measured people I've ever met. He once shared that he was trying to improve his skill in using power and aggression to coerce people into giving in. Soon enough I found myself in a negotiation with this same negotiator! At one point in the conversation he became uncontrollably angry with me. I called the bluff and shared that I would not negotiate with him when he is angry, at which point his anger disappeared in about one second (in a future book on interrogation we'll discuss why this suggests that the emotion was faked). Had I not been aware of the intentionality behind this negotiator's process, then I would have been likely to assume the emotional outburst was genuine, and I might have felt pressured to give in as a way to protect the relationship.

Now that we have shared four factors that influence our behaviour, how about we try it out? Please begin by writing down the key traits that define you as a person. Then, for each of these traits, list a situation where you demonstrated the opposite behaviour. Please categorise the explanation for your behaviour as *state*, *context* or *process*.

Note that neither of these behaviours was caused by your personality since the behaviour was contrary to what you said your personality is! Or *are* they part of your personality? In which case you may wish to alter your perception of what your personality is!

EDUCATE YOUR AUTOPILOT

We previously recommended turning off our autopilot. This doesn't mean the autopilot is an inherently bad feature — we will here see that is a key tool for achieving a dramatically improved level of negotiation performance.

The main concern with the autopilot is that for many of us it is exceptionally poorly educated about the negotiation process. Also, we tend to drop into autopilot indiscriminately throughout the negotiation. It can do a lot, but it can't do everything.

So leaves us with at least two questions; what is the autopilot good for, and how do we educate it?

In answering these questions, let's first imagine that our minds are divided into a conscious mind and an unconscious mind. This is not an exact representation, but it is nevertheless a useful model. It turns out that we can consciously do things that are very complex, but we do them fairly slowly and one at a time. If we try to do several things at once with our conscious mind, then we actually end up switching our attention between the tasks. Those of us who claim to be poor at multi-tasking tend to consider the things we do consciously: reading a book and listening to a conversation may already be more than we can handle.

In contrast, our unconscious mind is very capable of performing multiple tasks in parallel. These tasks typically have to be fairly simple individually, but they can also be *combined* to form tasks of tremendous complexity, much like an object-oriented computer program. If we consider the complexities of an activity such as speaking a language, we realise the extraordinary complexity involved in finding the right words and structuring them into sentences according to grammatical rules. And we do this in real time, while having spare processing capacity to think of what next to say, and while coordinating the movement of our limbs and keeping balance as we walk down the street with our phone in our hand.

Our focus on an intentional, situational and agile approach to negotiation suggests that we would want to think about negotiation consciously, rather than running it on autopilot. However there are so many factors a negotiator needs to keep in mind and apply at any point in time. There are simply too many insights for us to be able to do this consciously. Fortunately we can offload many of them to our unconscious mind, our autopilot.

For example, we can educate our autopilot to constantly track the type of questions we hear, and ensure that we use questions with a low likelihood of creating disagreement. Our autopilot can also be responsible for executing non-verbal behaviour that is conducive to rapport and trust building. Our autopilot can keep track of whether the parties are in agreement or disagreement, what category of needs are being surfaced, parties' emotional states, tactics used, what process the negotiation follows, whether ideas are converging or diverging, whether the communication needs of the parties are being matched, and ensure that we use language that regularly checks for alignment of expectations and availability of time. Our autopilot may also be educated to run constructive patterns even when we find ourselves in a crisis, or when our emotions are high.

So how do we educate our autopilot to take over this workload and free up our conscious mind to manage our negotiation strategy? We practise! Whether we acquire the knowledge from concepts, whether we are just experimenting, or whether we are imitating someone else, we educate our autopilot through practice, practice and more practice.

One standard framework[2] that is helpful for explaining the process we follow to educate our autopilot follows.

- We begin as *unconsciously incompetent*, a state where we are unaware of what we don't know.

- We then progress to becoming *consciously incompetent*, the point where we realise that a skill can be developed, but we haven't mastered that skill yet.

- After sufficient practice, we become *consciously competent*. We now have a good command of the skills, and we can explain to others what we are doing. However, we still need to think consciously about what we are doing.

- At some point be become *unconsciously competent*. This is where our autopilot is fully capable. We no longer have to think about what we are doing, and we might even forget the theory and concepts — our behaviour is just doing the right thing. Just like a true autopilot.

I would also like to emphasise several insights that are not necessarily captured in this representation.

- It is possible to consciously or unconsciously move from any of the first three states to the unconscious competence state by merely modelling someone who is already competent. However, this doesn't provide the meta-cognition (conscious understanding of what we are doing or why it works), and thus it doesn't lead to ongoing reflection and development on our own. This is a contributing reason why we shared reservations about learning through experience alone.

- While we might assume the fourth state is the one to strive for, I would like to suggest that we actually want to strive to attain both the third and fourth state at the same time. This allows us to execute flawlessly, while retaining the meta-cognition we need in order to teach others and to continue our development.

♦ Finally, rather than applying this model to the giant topic of negotiation skills, it makes more sense to apply it to each of the individual skills that a negotiator would like to master. We might currently be unconsciously competent at competitive negotiation, while at the same time realising that we are consciously incompetent at a sustainable approach to negotiation.

AN ETHICAL APPROACH TO NEGOTIATION

Is negotiation ethical? As we progress through this book we will come across ideas and practices that are clearly ethical and some that are clearly unethical. Many of them are quite independent and can be used by either ethical or unethical negotiators. Some could be used to influence parties towards mutually beneficial outcomes, or they could be misused to manipulate and take advantage of the other party.

Participants often ask whether negotiation or influence is the same as manipulation. To this I reply that the desired outcome is the same, i.e. to get the other party to change their thoughts, feelings, perceptions, beliefs or behaviour. However, the mindset driving the interaction is ethical in the case of influence, and unethical in the case of manipulation.

Some negotiators deliberately sit on the fence on this issue. They realise that many clients would want to know all the juicy insights for getting an unfair advantage over their perceived opponents. These negotiators will often make the argument that they simply share ethical and unethical insights, and that it is up to the client to negotiate in the manner they feel comfortable with. In these situations the client's moral compass will drive the negotiation behaviour. Unfortunately our moral compass knows just as little about negotiation as our personality or autopilot, and none of them is a good driver for our negotiation approach.

I will take a different approach. I firmly recommend that we adopt an ethical approach to negotiation. The reason is simple: an ethical approach is more sustainable, and has higher potential for value creation than the alternative. Now, I will still share all the insights, whether ethical or not. And the reason for this is also simple: awareness is the first step towards control in negotiations, and if we want to become elite negotiators then we absolutely benefit from being familiar with anything the other party may throw at us.

"But Filip, how can you negotiate ethically when the other party is inherently unethical?" is the question that I would expect at this point. In many instances, the best option will actually still be to negotiate in an ethical manner.

To illustrate my point, let's pick a negotiation scenario with a clearly unethical criminal who has barricaded himself with a hostage. This individual will probably not let morals stand in the way of himself and freedom. Assume that we lie to the perpetrator and tell him that if he surrenders he'll be free to go. Let's say that he believes us, surrenders, and then to his dismay he is put in prison. He serves his time, and then he joins the statistics of repeat offenders.

How much will the perpetrator trust the hostage negotiator next time around? The perpetrator may not even engage with the negotiator at all! Add to this that while the perpetrator was in prison, he potentially told every single inmate about the police tactic of lying. Thus that one instance of unethical negotiation (lying or not keeping a promise) may have made thousands of future negotiations considerably more difficult.

Unethical behaviour in negotiation translates to considerable risk. No matter where our moral compass points, the ethical approach will be a lower-risk approach with higher potential for satisfying our needs over the long term.

Finally, as with any insight, we can of course paint up an extreme counter-example. If we are negotiating with a terrorist who has his finger on the button of a bomb, then the risk of casualties may outweigh the risk of lying. And that is exactly the way the negotiator would reason: by comparing risk and reward. Our main insight remains unchanged;

unethical negotiation practices are inherently risky, and there will be very few instances where they are the best available option.

5

TAKE CONTROL OF
THE NEGOTIATION PROCESS

——— ——

Process encapsulates pretty much everything in this book. Deciding what game to play is a process decision. Deciding how to present options to create commitment is a process decision. Deciding how to ask questions is a process decision. And so on. If you manage to do everything in this book, then you are doing a good job of managing the process. In this section we have grouped a number of overarching process choices available to us.

A PROCESS VIEW OF NEGOTIATION

Negotiation as an ongoing process

When does a negotiation start? The answers in my seminars range from the first time the parties meet to the point where the parties start the formal negotiation meetings.

In contrast, I would like to suggest that a healthy mindset is to assume that all of your future negotiations have already started! By that I mean what you do today can influence any of your future negotiations.

Let's look at a concrete example. Imagine that you are recruiting a new employee. The interview is the first time the two of you meet. Might the business school that the applicant attended influence your decision to hire? Absolutely! Might a negative experience a close friend of yours had with this particular applicant ten years ago influence your decision? Again, absolutely!

If you realise the gravity of this insight, then that should reinforce why skilled negotiators put so much emphasis on relationships and mutually beneficial outcomes, and shy away from destructive behaviours that negatively affect the relationship or one's reputation.

So when does a negotiation end? Seminar participants' answers typically range from "when we agree" to "when all that was agreed has been delivered".

Again I would suggest that we challenge our assumptions. Do we know for certain that this is the last time we will negotiate with this party? Well, no. The negotiation might be recurring on a yearly basis. Any of the parties may change jobs and in the future cross paths again. We may in the future negotiate with this negotiator's wife, family, friends, or ex-colleagues. Will our behaviour in today's negotiation affect these future negotiations? You betcha!

Years ago I attended a crisis negotiation course held by Steve York. In my notes from the class I jotted down the following quote from Steve: "It is remarkable how often people whom you hoped to never have to deal with again, insist on popping up in your life over…and over…and over again."

If negotiations don't have beginnings or ends, then they aren't events. Rather they are processes. Specifically, they are ongoing processes.

A process that spawns other processes

During the negotiation we constantly spawn additional negotiations. This becomes particularly clear in arguments. You may ask me to take out the garbage, and then I start a new negotiation process about what is a fair balance of work. You may bring up that you have taken out the garbage ninety per cent of the time in the last few months, at which point I start a new negotiation process about the validity of that number. At this point you mention that I always argue with you, and I in response spawn three new negotiations: one about how often we argue, one about what constitutes an argument, and one about whether you or I started the present argument. And ideally I wish to "win" each of these negotiations.

This spawning of new processes takes place in virtually all negotiations. I may accidentally bruise your ego, and unbeknownst to me you now create a parallel negotiation where you try to boost your ego, or hurt my ego in return. If I'm not aware of what is going on, then your behaviour will suddenly strike me as more difficult, unreasonable and unpredictable.

A process within a complex system

Negotiations, particularly larger scale ones, rarely exist on their own. Rather they are simply one out of many concurrent negotiations in a larger system.

We have to ask ourselves: "Is the current negotiation the most appropriate negotiation to have given the outcome we wish to achieve?"

Consider a supplier that found itself in constant price negotiations with its client, a giant retailer. Before buying the products from the supplier, the retailer would first see if it could source the products more cheaply from overseas. The supplier was part of an international brand that had different price levels in each country. As a result the retailer could often find the same product much cheaper from other countries, and would bypass the local supplier.

In this negotiation the system was set up to always give the retailer the temptation to import from overseas. In negotiations we sometimes find it impossible to influence other people because other parts of the system are influencing these people to think, feel or behave differently. Here we may be well advised to change games to maximisation and attempt to negotiate the system instead.

For instance, the local supplier, recognising the problem, could consider instead negotiating with its international head office to set up mechanisms that would prevent products in one country from being exported into another country.

A process within many systems

While we ultimately wish to understand the entire system we operate within, this can be a daunting task. To make things more manageable we can take short cuts and consider the specific sub-systems that our negotiation process is part of. For example our negotiation may be affected by the dynamics of the economy, influenced by politics and news, and it may need to comply with the constraints of laws and cultural norms. As these systems can and do influence our negotiations, we may also wish to consider how we can influence each of these systems.

A dynamic process within a dynamic system

Very few elements in a negotiation are static. We certainly do not make our decisions in a vacuum. Rather every action we take will have consequences that change the system we negotiate in. Many actions we take will be met with a reaction by the other party, which also changes the system we negotiate in.

We are unlikely to be successful negotiators if we only think one step ahead. As negotiators we certainly want to think of what to do next, but what drives that decision is our analysis of the future scenarios that take place *after* what we do next.

If you drop a pebble in an aquarium with two rubber ducks floating on the water, the initial ripples created by the pebble will traverse through the aquarium. The ducks will move slightly as a result. The ripples will then bounce on stationary objects such as the walls and the water pump. Once the ripples change direction they start intersecting with other ripples, and will then affect the floating objects again. At this point what started as a clean pattern of concentric ripples around the pebble has now turned into a messy pattern covering the entire water surface. And we may have very little control over what these ripples do next.

Remarkably often I observe negotiators who suggest actions with total conviction that there will be one clear and certain outcome, e.g.: "We'll threaten to walk away and then the other party will come back to the table and agree with our demands."

This is not how negotiation works. So this is probably not the way we should make decisions about the negotiation process. Instead we need to consider the consequences and reactions before we take any action.

- If we do ABC (or get XYZ), what will happen?

- If we do ABC (or get XYZ), what will specifically not happen, or no longer happen?

- If we don't do ABC (or don't get XYZ), what will happen?

- If we don't do ABC (or don't get XYZ), what will specifically not happen?

For example, when two companies were in competition to acquire a target company, the target company could simply play the two bidders against each other and thereby increase the price. Simple as that? No.

One of the bidding companies, thinking strategically like a chess player, analysed the possible actions and reactions several steps ahead. As a result it chose to remove itself from the negotiation. The remaining bidder overestimated its newfound power and bargained too aggressively until the target company eventually broke off negotiations. At this point, with no bidders and desperate to sell, the target company approached the bidder that had previously voluntarily exited. And having someone effectively beg you, as the sole bidder, to acquire his or her company is a very powerful position to be in. Thus by analysing actions, reactions and consequences several steps ahead, this bidding company changed the distribution of power in the system.

Separate people from problems

> I'd like you to think of a person you find difficult to deal with.
>
> Are they the problem, or are you?

It turns out that we are not too keen to accept we might be the problem. So why do we think the other party will ever agree to be the problem?

If we take the systems view of negotiation, then we realise that each action has a reaction. A small action (an unintentional insult) may have a bigger reaction (a defensive argument), which may have an even bigger reaction (an accusation of the other party being defensive for no reason), and so on. Often there may be no single cause of the problem!

I suggest that it is more helpful to realise that there are multiple potential sources of problems, and we simply don't know which one it is until we investigate. It could be something we did or failed to do, something the other party did, the combination of our respective approaches to negotiation, or some other element of the system. To illustrate the latter: I was swimming in an ocean pool, following the circuit laid out so that all swimmers in a lane are going in the same direction. When I collided with another swimmer my initial reaction was one of anger, until I realised that the waves crashing in over the wall — forces in the system — had moved me sideways into the wrong lane!

While separating people from problems is a concept that is frequently mentioned in negotiation books (and for good reason), few books share the option of doing this non-verbally. We can spend time understanding the importance of separating people from problems, and then improve our negotiation behaviour towards the other party, but what do we do when the other party relentlessly insists on mixing us up with the problem?

One option available to us is to use gestures, posture or movement to physically separate ourselves from the problem. We might use a prop, e.g.

a pen or glass on the table, to represent the problem: "So I guess we have a problem here, what can we do about it?" We might also gesture as if we placed the problem in our hand, and we now extend our hand to the side to create space between the problem and us. We may even put the problem on a whiteboard and stand next to the other party while we both together look at the whiteboard.

No matter what specific approach we pick, our intention is to create a clear separation between the problem and us. If the other party is looking at the problem, they are not looking at us, and we reduce the likelihood of the two getting confused subconsciously.

TIME

Time is a depreciating commodity. One of the first things we need to do is figure out how much time we have, and the best way to use that time. That is true for negotiation. More importantly, it is also true for life.

Pre-negotiation time has already started

If all future negotiations have already started, then that means that we are already in pre-negotiation time for all those negotiations. Might it be beneficial for us to in the meantime build a great reputation as someone who creates value for everyone we work with? Might it help to build strong relationships with everyone we interact with? Could it be beneficial to put effort into building a large network of contacts? Would it serve us well to avoid creating enemies? Can practising all the negotiation insights in this book ensure that we are proficient by the time we face that critical high-stakes negotiation? The answer to all of these questions is "yes".

Let's say we just found out about a specific negotiation coming up. What decisions do we now wish to make in relation to time? How about we start by answering the following questions.

- How much time do we need to prepare for the negotiation?

- How much time do we have to prepare?

- How much time do we think we will need for the negotiation?

- How much time do we have to negotiate?

- By when do we need an outcome?

- Who decides how much time is available for all of this?

- How can we negotiate for more time?

- How can we start influencing outcomes *now*?

- What happens if either party runs out of time?

A key point is to realise that there is no actual difference between the time when the formal negotiation is scheduled, and the time leading up to that negotiation. It is all negotiation! However, we tend to perceive a difference. Changing our own perception of time provides many opportunities to improve negotiated outcomes.

- While parties are often guarded when the formal negotiations begin, in the time leading up to those negotiation parties can be open to meeting in more informal circumstances, and it can be easier then to keep options creative and hypothetical than later in the process.

- When we hear a suggestion that we do not like, our initial response may be to reject, defend, fight back or ignore, but with time we may come to evaluate that idea more objectively (and favourably). The earlier we can test our ideas with the other party, the more likely that we will have time to influence his or her mind.

- The more complete an idea is when we propose it, the higher likelihood that the other party will reject it based on reactive devaluation. Thus we want to allow time for the other party to build the ideas that we seed.

- In some cultures, e.g. the Japanese, the negotiation team is more likely to have reached consensus internally before formal negotiations begin. In this case we may have no other option than to influence early before consensus is reached.

- Our reputation is most often (not counting political smear campaigns and the like) a direct result of (other people's perception of) how we have spent our pre-negotiation time.

- The more exposure we have to a negotiator in an informal negotiation environment, the more able we will be to identify his or her normal mode of behaviour. This calibration improves our ability to detect tactics, lies and deceit, and also to build rapport.

Given all of this, I would like to put to you that a skilled negotiator would aim to do most of the influencing in the pre-negotiation time. I would even go as far as suggesting that a skilled negotiator will aspire to reach agreement before the formal negotiations ever take place.

If, on the other hand, we are unaware that the negotiation has already started, we might (unintentionally on autopilot) negatively affect the process. Remember, we influence all the time whether we want to or not. It is very common that negotiators miss the entire pre-negotiation time, and by the time the negotiation starts it already has significant momentum… in an undesirable direction! And let's not forget the possibility that the other party understands the concept of pre-negotiation time and is already intentionally influencing you.

Post-negotiation time

Given our insight about negotiations as ongoing processes with no beginning or end, this section should perhaps be more appropriately named *post-agreement time*.

Despite having agreed, we still have more to negotiate. It is rare that negotiators at the agreement phase will have considered all details that need to be agreed upon for the outcome to be realised. For instance, in a negotiation between an operator and a coalmine, parties may agree to lease X number of trucks by day Y. But some of these trucks may in the end not be available on day Y because another customer presently leasing them had the option to extend their lease. These details may need to be re-negotiated later, and perhaps by different people. Even once every single detail is agreed, any part of the system might still change and trigger the need for more negotiation. Furthermore, the agreement might not be fully honoured by either or both parties, and that can certainly lead to more negotiation.

The insight that negotiators in the agreement phase often fail to consider all details of implementation was (unintentionally but succinctly) summarised by the instructor of a first-aid course that I attended. After he had explained the instructions for administering an auto-injector of Epinephrine to children he added: "…but whomever came up with these instructions has probably never tried to restrain a five-year-old child with anaphylaxis for ten seconds while jabbing him or her in the thigh with a giant needle."

Note that while we are focusing our attention on closing all the loops of the current deal or negotiation in post-negotiation time, we are at the same time in pre-negotiation time for all our future negotiations. Forgetting this can be detrimental.

Let me illustrate with an anecdote. When I paid for my first motorbike, the dealership assumed the negotiation was over and they had got away with selling me a dud. The bike had serious engine problems and some of the documentation relating to the bike had been forged by the dealership. When I later upgraded my bike to a more expensive model, I chose to do so at a different dealership, one that was willing to engage in a win/win negotiation.

I sometimes mention this anecdote, using the names of the companies, in response to participants' questions about secondhand-vehicle sales and tactics. Maybe one thousand of my participants every year fit the profile of a first-time motorbike customer. Is it possible that this anecdote might sway participants to prefer the second dealership over the first one? Of course.

So was the first dealership's assumption correct that the negotiation ended when I paid for the motorbike? Or is that negotiation perhaps still going today?

Establish a timeline

The ongoing nature of negotiation becomes particularly clear when we acknowledge that such interactions often involve many different people along the way. A crisis negotiator may get involved after parties have neglected their preparation time, ruined the relationship, irrevocably destroyed value, and when trust is merely a faint memory.

When I enter the negotiation I need to first understand what has happened prior to me entering. Briefing the new negotiator may seem obvious. However, I'd like to illustrate that sometimes we don't realise how much of the total timeline is relevant.

In negotiations between two married people, it is quite possible that a mishap from years or even decades ago may still affect the current negotiation. In international disputes between countries or groups of people, parties may base their decisions on what may have happened hundreds or even thousands of years ago.

When we plot the timeline of events leading up to the present state we may wish to track other aspects too. Some of these aspects will make more sense after we have covered them in the book. For now, just entertain the view that it might be useful to understand how perceptions of the following have changed over time (the past), the cumulative effect (the present), and how we want them to be (the future). Aspects to consider include:

- quality of the relationship
- level of trust

- level of interaction

- amount of communication

- amount of value created

- level of cooperation

- level of understanding

- level of reliability

If these are positive, then it may be a great idea to share that with the other party, particularly at difficult parts of the negotiation: "Look, we have had this great working relationship for years and years. How about we see if we can continue and build on that rather than making things worse?" And if the history is terrible, then it might also be strategic to acknowledge that and focus on the positive change or trend: "We can probably acknowledge that we have had trying times in the past, and with this new option on the table I hope that we all feel that things are moving rapidly in the right direction."

Particularly in negotiations where parties have a history of destructive behaviour, it may be valuable to raise this as a lesson about consequences: "Where we are today is a direct result of our respective behaviour. Is this where we want to be? What would be a more constructive process for us to follow going forward?"

Agree on time

Agreeing on time can help ensure that it does not become an obstacle to value creation or agreement. And if the other party does not wish to agree on time (e.g. because they want to use time pressure against us in a competitive negotiation), then we at least want to know that. Recall the questions we asked ourselves in pre-negotiation time. What is the other party's view on the same questions? Can we agree?

Deadlines

Is it always in our interest to meet deadlines? In general this is the preferred negotiation behaviour as it gives us a track record of reliability, which signals predictability, which (if positive) signals trust. By meeting deadlines we also model desired behaviour, and may influence the other party to do the same.

However, meeting deadlines is not a goal in itself. Skilled negotiators are careful not to submit to time pressure if it negatively affects our negotiation outcomes. As time pressure rises, the rate at which we give concessions goes up, we make more mistakes, we feel more stressed, we stop thinking of creative solutions, we evaluate prematurely, we make more statements which means we learn less about others, and we make rushed decisions. Giving in at a deadline can also encourage the other party to continue using deadlines to get more from us.

Hostage negotiators know this and instead use time to their advantage. This means they love the perpetrator to have deadlines, but they never put deadlines on themselves. They may purposefully miss deadlines the perpetrator sets in order to signal that the perpetrator is not in control. This is usually a big step towards weakening the perpetrator's resolve.

Of course, missing deadlines can also have negative consequences, including missing out on a deal, and signalling unreliability, which tends to damage trust and relationships. As with any decision in negotiation, we seek to assess the risk and reward of any decision we make.

Using the 80/20 rule, negotiators often suggest that eighty per cent of deadlines are false and the remaining twenty per cent are negotiable. I tend to agree. We want to remind ourselves that deadlines are rules, rules are set by people, and people can be influenced to change their minds.

When considering deadlines, we may wish to understand who has them. What are they? Where do they come from? What are both the positive and negative consequences for either party if deadlines are missed? How do we feel about the deadlines? What are the available options for negotiating them? Might *we* even want to introduce a deadline?

Cost of time

Deadlines may seem like binary events; either we have reached the deadline, or we haven't. However, in many instances in negotiations cost will be incurred continually as time progresses, not just at the deadline.

In the case of a strike this is obvious: both the union and the company will incur costs for every minute the strike continues. Of course, that is the point — the hope that the pain and costs will motivate the other party to give in first.

In other circumstances we might fail to consciously account for the cost of time. For instance, inmates who take over a prison may feel a temporary sense of unity from the victory of finally experiencing some power and control. And the illusion of optimism may inflate inmates' expectations of the final outcomes.

However, as time passes the momentum and excitement among inmates will drop. Unity will start to break down as different factions remember they don't actually like each other very much. Eventually boredom, hunger and fatigue will kick in. The longer the siege continues, the less power the inmates will have.

While the inmates may be unaware of this cost until it is too late, law enforcement thoroughly understands this insight and uses it to its advantage by simply stalling for time.

Past | present | future

Successful negotiations tend to follow a pattern where the discussion broadly progresses in one direction, from the *past*, to the *present*, to the *future*.

If we are negotiating to resolve a problem, that problem typically occurred or was caused in the past (although sometimes the problem is occurring as we speak, or is one that we anticipate happening in the future). We are probably negotiating because there are specific needs that are unsatisfied as a result of the problem. In the past we will also find the patterns of behaviour that led to the problem. The past holds the history and experience we share with the other party, whether positive or negative. And the reader is reminded here about transference, i.e. that we are likely to pollute negotiations with aspects of our own past that have nothing at all to do with the current interaction.

The past is also a resource that we can draw upon to improve the negotiation process. We can revisit the things we have already agreed to emphasise that we are making progress. No matter how situations turned out, we can share and emphasise the positive intent we had. In contentious negotiations we may also emphasise the negative things we have not done (e.g. refrained from using negative attack ads in a political election process, or refrained from launching an assault on the hostage taker). Finally, the past also holds experiences and lessons that we may draw upon as resources for finding a solution.

The present is where our current needs are. Negotiation is all about satisfying needs, and in order to identify all the needs we need to consider the present. Interestingly, whether we recall needs that were satisfied or unsatisfied in the past, or we anticipate having these needs met in the future, we can still experience the associated feelings and emotions in the present. When I ask you how you felt about a certain past experience, or if I ask you how you would feel about achieving a future goal, you can instantly put yourself in the associated emotional state. This is a key tool for influencing human behaviour.

The future will hold options, solutions and outcomes to the current negotiation. The future will also include all possible scenarios, whether desirable or undesirable.

A dysfunctional pattern in negotiation is where parties are not discussing the same thing. One party might be talking about what they need (the present) whereas the other party is talking about the problem (the past). Occasionally both parties are stuck discussing the problems (the past) and never make the transition to the present and the future.

As a means of building rapport, we will aim to match where the other party has his or her focus. If he or she is talking about the past, then we may wish to match this by staying with that conversation, and then gently try to shift the conversation to the present, and then to the future. One way to do this is by use use of appropriate questions.

- What caused that to happen (past)?

- How did you feel about that (past → present)?

- What is important to you now (present)?

- What would be the ideal outcome for you (future)?

- What does success look like to you (future)?

- How could we achieve that (future)?

- How do you feel about the current suggestion (present → future)?

Selected insights from neuro-linguistic programming (NLP) can provide us with tools to achieve some of this non-verbally. For instance, people will consistently look and/or gesture in one direction when discussing the past, and another direction when discussing the future. So in addition to using questions to shift the time focus, we can further influence the desired shift through congruent use of gestures, or the placement of various props, and even through deciding where we stand in relation to the other party when we discuss problems and solutions.

FIVE APPROACHES TO INFLUENCE

We have organised all negotiations into four distinct games. Let us now have a look at how we can similarly identify five broad approaches to influencing others to change their behaviour.

Rewards

Giving rewards is a tool for getting people to do what they don't want to do by offering them an *extrinsic* reward. Rewards can be either ethical (positive encouragement) or unethical (bribes). We can motivate people to do almost anything using rewards. For instance, I typically share with my participants the (fictitious and hypothetical) request that they run around the building naked on a day when all their friends and family are present. Typically this offer only appeals to a microscopic number of daring participants.

Then I ask who would do it for $1000? For $1 million? $100 million? For $100 million that will go to charity? Gradually I get almost all participants to accept. I have put this scenario to a couple of thousand participants, and I would estimate about only one to two per cent say they wouldn't accept the offer no matter how big the reward is.

So we can get almost anyone to do almost anything using rewards, but there are limitations.

- It is an expensive way to influence people.

- It does not result in motivation or commitment. If I want you to run a second time, I will probably have to pay you again.

- And if you come to expect the reward but don't get it, you may feel resentment and we have unintentionally undermined the intrinsic motivation you had.

- It encourages people to ask for more. After I've raised the amount a couple of times, the last few participants still declining the offer often cite "We want to see how high you will go" as the reason for not accepting. And this is a real risk with extrinsic rewards; they motivate people to ask for more extrinsic rewards!

- If extrinsic rewards are sufficiently high, we may rationalise self-serving, immoral and unethical behaviour, and we are incentivised to game the system for personal gain. For examples we don't have to look further than Enron or the Global Financial Crisis.

Punishment

Replace the reward with a $500 gun, and a credible threat that I will shoot anyone who does not run naked around the building, and almost every participant would comply. A few very proud participants still decline, but everyone changes their mind if the threat is modified so that the gun is pointed at a loved one instead.

And this approach would only cost $500 for one gun instead of potentially millions or billions of dollars in bribes. And we had a higher rate of compliance? So is the recommendation from reading this book that we should use threats, power, force and coercion? They're cheap *and* effective.

Of course not. What we haven't accounted for is the predictable and negative by-product of this approach, namely resentment. And as we reinforce throughout this book, resentment can turn into resistance, revenge or even mutual destruction. For instance, in our fictitious scenario we can expect that participants will bring their own guns next time they expect to negotiate with me.

Unfortunately, coercion is one of the more common approaches to influence and typically results in the division game. We are so used to this game that we often don't even realise that we are using threats. A common threat is that of walking away. Typically this is phrased as "My way or the highway"; "I'm sorry, this is what I want, and unless you change your demands we won't have a deal"; or less overtly, "Do what I ask of you, or I will be angry, sad or grumpy in order to damage the relationship as punishment for your lack of compliance."

Because we are still trying to get people to do what they don't want to do (punishment is really just a negative extrinsic reward), we don't build commitment or motivation. Specifically, even if you agree to do the run in response to my threat, chances are that as soon as you are out the door you will change course and run to the police station instead.

Align needs with options

The approach recommended in this book is to figure out what parties' real needs are, and invent options for satisfying those needs. Thus we seek to get people to *want* to do something. This approach is typically cheaper than rewards, and builds stronger intrinsic motivation and commitment than rewards or punishment. Note that what parties say they want will be subject to generalisation, distortion and omission and we will have to do quite a bit of investigation to uncover the real needs. The good news is that many of these needs are predictable, so skilled negotiators already have an idea what to look for.

"Discovering needs" is only part of the process. The other part is finding ways to satisfy these needs. Straightforward approaches involve parties helping each other out, which typically results in the integration game. More advanced approaches such as the maximisation game seek to change the system we operate within to better cater to all parties' needs.

Misrepresentation

The first three approaches have illustrated that it is more powerful (and often cheaper, and more sustainable) to get people to want to do something, than to get them to do something they don't want to do.

Unfortunately unethical manipulators have worked out a fourth alternative: to trick you into believing that you are going to get what you want, when in fact you won't. Yes, this approach involves deceiving, misrepresenting or lying. And yes, this is often how sales and marketing departments choose to influence you.

Recently I found a beautiful (or sad) example of this. 7-Eleven ran an advertising campaign on Sydney buses for "Slurpees" with new flavours: *Slurpee season. 13 flavours, 13 weeks.* The poster I saw had a huge headline saying: *NEW PINEAPPLE.* The poster also included a picture of half a Slurpee on top of half a pineapple. At the very bottom of the poster, in the smallest font on the poster, one sentence read: *Fruit shown is illustrative of flavour only and is not an ingredient of the product.*

Our society is full of misrepresentation. Why? Because it is perceived to be easier to lie about satisfying people's needs rather than actually satisfying those needs. And like any tactic, misrepresentation works — at least until people discover that they have been duped, at which point they are likely to experience the usual negative by-products.

Manipulation of perception and feelings

The last approach of influence has less distinct boundaries, and can overlap with all the previous four. It can be ethical and unethical. It can be intrinsic and extrinsic. This approach focuses on changing the extent that parties *perceive* that they will get their needs satisfied, without actually changing what parties get or think they will get. In other words, it is about manipulation of perception and feelings.

Many of the tactics used in the division game are unethical applications of this. Often these tactics exploit the predictable nature of our behaviour on autopilot due to cognitive biases and mental traps.

But manipulating perception can also be used with ethical intent. Perhaps we know that the deal is in fact very good for the other party, but they have unfounded fears, negative behavioural patterns or other reasons that could cause them to miss out on something that is good for them. For instance, we may wish to help a friend beat her addiction to illegal drugs. Or we may wish to motivate someone to leave a history of crime behind him and instead go to university or pick up a trade. By overstating the expected results of the desired path we may motivate them to make the right choice, and own that choice. Is this ethical? I don't have a clear answer for you. But would I judge you for tricking a loved one in trouble to get back onto an ethical and healthy path that is better for all? Of course not.

PROBLEM | OUTCOME

When we review a large number of negotiations, one of the distinguishing patterns we observe is related to whether the process is problem or outcome focused.

In *problem/solution-focused negotiation* we believe that we negotiate in order to solve a problem. If that problem is complex we typically break it down into "issues". If we are playing the division game, each party will go through the list of issues and establish their opening position, expected outcome, and walk-away points. Then the positional bargaining or tug of war starts. If we are playing the integration game, we instead use the problem or the issues as starting points for figuring out underlying needs. "If we get our desired delivery date, what will that mean for us? What will it allow us to do? What if we don't get it?" Regardless of which game we are playing, we start with the problem and the needs it leaves unmet. The negotiation process is set up to produce a solution to that problem, and satisfy the unmet needs.

However, we don't just have needs that are unmet by a specific problem. We also have other unmet needs, needs that are somewhat met, and needs that are currently met completely. *Outcome-focused negotiation* considers all the needs we want satisfied. The process then becomes focused on how to satisfy all those needs, and hopefully for all parties. Note that with the outcome-focused process we don't need to have a problem in order to start negotiating. All we need is an interest in creating better outcomes. And better could simply mean an improvement from the status quo. Outcome-focused negotiation frequently has a gain frame and tends to more naturally lead to the integration or maximisation games.

A simple way to contrast the two approaches is to consider our own physical and mental health. With a problem/solution-focused approach we ask ourselves "What is broken and how do I fix that (and only that)?" With an outcome-focused approach we instead ask ourselves "How do I want to feel? What do I want to be able to do physically? Why are those things important to me? And how can I achieve a level of health that allows me to feel and do all of that?"

TRADE | SATISFY

I often get the question: "How do you negotiate when you have nothing to give?" This question highlights an underlying assumption that negotiation is about trading — one item of value for another item of similar value.

It is common for people to approach negotiation as a process of trades, tit-for-tat or quid pro quo: I will only do something for you if you do something of equal value for me. The main driver is to protect us from being taken advantage of. But equal trades also limit value creation potential. Imagine that you can do something for me and I can do something for you. We trade and we're happy. Great!

Now instead imagine that you can do something for me, and I can do ninety-nine things for you. We trade one-for-one, and then we part ways. But hold on...you have now missed out on having a ninety-nine times more desirable outcome. If I can help you satisfy your needs, why wouldn't I? And what if I have something I can do for you and you have nothing you can do for me? If we think in terms of trades then there won't be any negotiation, and no value will be created.

This is not to say that we should always use the satisfy strategy. Like most insights in this book, the choice of trade vs. satisfy needs to be made given the context of the negotiation. Here, we are simply increasing awareness of two strategies, and demonstrating that the satisfy strategy can create more value and stronger relationships.

Let me illustrate with an example. A friend of mine is an absolute master of relationship building. No matter how you treat her, she will remain open, honest, friendly, caring and respectful. And she will actively bombard you with friendliness and kindness until you simply give in and start reciprocating that positive behaviour. Yes, sometimes people don't reciprocate and instead exploit her kindness. But the vast majority of people just love her and eagerly try to maximise value for her. If we understand the importance of rapport, trust, relationship and reputation, then we understand that she is a truly outstanding negotiator.

Sadly, many of us instead apply the trade and tit-for-tat strategies to our relationships. If someone treats us well we treat him or her well. But if someone treats us badly then we reciprocate the negative attitude. And if we have done someone a favour and they don't reciprocate, then we stop doing them favours. We do this to protect ourselves from being exploited and from feeling rejected.

But pause here for a second and ponder on the result of our process choice. How much value do we miss out on in the long term compared to my friend? Perhaps the fearful, suspicious and defensive attitudes that fuel the trade strategy actually restrict our value creation potential?

We will revisit the satisfy strategy when discussing relationships and options for value creation.

CONTROL | TRACK | MATCH | SHIFT

Throughout this book we cover a range of concepts that illustrate how we have different preferences for how to think, communicate and act. If unmanaged, these differences can lead to pollution in the form of reduced rapport, friction in communication, and poor understanding.

As skilled negotiators we seek to *match* attributes of the other party. This will increase the likelihood that the other party will see us as similar, which helps create rapport, which contributes to building trust. Matching how the other party thinks and communicates also helps the other party understand us.

Matching, however, is not the end game. We may then wish to influence (or shift) how the other party thinks, feels, perceives, communicates and behaves in order to lead them to the outcomes we seek. Our ability to influence (or shift) is much stronger once we have rapport and understanding, which is why we begin by matching. We may also attempt to shift merely to test whether we have rapport. If the other party matches us when we shift then that is an indicator that we have non-verbal rapport.

But before getting to matching and shifting we have to do two other things. The first is to control our own thinking process, feelings, perceptions, communication style and behaviour. We stand little chance of influencing someone else if we can't influence ourselves! The second is to track (or observe) what the other party is doing. Hopefully it is obvious that we can't match the other party unless we understand what it is that he or she is doing.

Thus the technique is control | track | match | shift, and we may for instance wish to apply it to:

- visual, auditory and kinaesthetic oriented words;

- visual parameters such as posture, body language, eye contact, gestures and clothes;

- auditory parameters such as tonality, pitch, volume, pace, pauses, speed, length of sentences, and colloquial expressions;

- kinaesthetic parameters such as touch, proximity, height, angle, location, energy levels and breathing patterns;

- belief systems, behaviours, thinking processes, level of abstraction;

- first |second | third perspectives; and/or

- past | present | future words, focus and gestures.

Note that for each of these we have a preference, and we have a range in which we are comfortable or capable of operating. As negotiators we do well to practise and expand our ability to cover the entire range, as this will give us maximum flexibility to adapt to other people.

Let us also emphasise that we typically wish to match positive, or at least neutral behaviours. If the other party is polluting his or her language with accusations, blame, threats, distortions, interruptions, then matching those behaviours could risk polluting our interaction further. Remember, matching is not a goal in itself, but rather a tool to increase rapport, understanding and our ability to influence. Thus we want to match the positive behaviours. If the other party is guilty of negative behaviours we may instead wish to reframe those into something more positive and constructive.

We also caution against taking this concept too literally and matching the other party in a monkey-say-monkey-do fashion. Our task is not to be identical but rather to be sufficiently similar.

Recently I had my first face-to-face meeting with a negotiator whom I met briefly a year ago. He leant back in his chair and started talking, and I leant back in my chair and started listening. He would clearly lean and gesture to my left when talking about pasts and problems, and clearly gesture to my right when discussing options. I mirrored his gestures. He spent most of his effort on discussing problems and obstacles, so I let him talk about this for a while. He used very concrete examples, which suggested to me that he was a concrete thinker. To work with this I used props on the table (a glass, the table salt) to represent the different parties in the example we were discussing. When he later wanted to add his opinion he *also* used the props on the table. As the conversation became more exciting I decided to test the level of rapport. I leant forwards. Within a few seconds he leant forwards. I gestured to my right while suggesting an option, and he continued talking about that option. To get him to snap out of first perceptual position and consider other perspectives, I simply asked him to assume the perspective of other collaborators, of me, and of other stakeholders.

I had tracked what he was doing, I matched it until we had rapport, and then I tried to shift to see if he would follow. And he did. This gave me a strong non-verbal indicator that we were in rapport.

Note while we have *more* options available for us to build (and break) rapport face to face than for example over the phone or via email, we always have options. For instance, if we are negotiating via email, then we may want to match the length of our emails, presence or absence of emoticons, capitalisation and punctuation, presence or absence of salutation, formality of sentences, time between receipt and response, and so on.

THE FORMAL TOPIC IS OFTEN A PROXY FOR THE REAL ISSUES BEING NEGOTIATED

Opening today's newspaper I see that the Republicans and Democrats in the US can't agree on a bill that imposes further restrictions on mercury and arsenic emissions. Perhaps the rest of us look at this and think: Isn't this a simple issue? Surely less mercury in the environment can only be a good thing? And if this negotiation existed in a vacuum by itself then I reckon reaching agreement would not be that difficult.

But as we've discussed the negotiation is part of a system. The outcome of this negotiation will send ripple effects through the system and that will affect other negotiations. It is quite possible that these completely separate negotiations are affecting the current negotiation.

In this scenario, the Republican Party's other interests included saving jobs, specifically in domestic cement factories. The Republicans anticipated that more stringent environmental controls would add cost to domestic manufacturing, which could in turn make the US less competitive with China. The Republicans also have a stated interest in seeing a smaller government. Thus Republican resistance to the above bill was not necessarily related to the environment at all, but was a proxy for a broader, separate negotiation of reducing the government's influence.

As we will see later in this book, such differences can often easily be turned into mutually beneficial outcomes. In this case the negotiations could for instance be reframed to multiple separate topics.

- How can we reduce damage to the environment?

- How can we save/add jobs?

123

- How can we stay competitive with China?

- How can we ensure that we have a government that does all the things a government should arguably do, and at the same time address all the inefficiencies and waste that we see in government today?

- And if responsibilities were to be moved from the government to other parties, how do we ensure the same level of representation and accountability for those responsibilities?

It is quite possible that the parties could find ways to agree on all of these points, and that their aspirations would be achieved. For example, perhaps increased pollution controls would create more jobs in the manufacturing of pollution control and monitoring instruments than could be saved in the domestic cement factories. Perhaps those jobs could be more valuable for the country in terms of tax revenue. And perhaps this industry is one where there is less head-on competition from China and the US could therefore get access to a big chunk of the global market? And perhaps the system could be set up so that the bulk of these jobs are in the private sector? As I've said before, a key reason that we don't find mutually beneficial outcomes is because we assume they don't exist, and therefore we don't look for them.

It is also important for us to regularly check that we are in focusing on the real issues and not the proxy. For instance, in negotiations between the FBI and David Koresh near Waco, Texas in 1993, Koresh repeatedly broke promises made to authorities about his intentions to leave the premises. Parts of the FBI were upset about being lied to. However, in the process Koresh kept releasing a steady flow of persons from the premises. By that measure the negotiations were arguably successful.

NEGOTIATE THE PROCESS

Much of our negotiation success relies on our ability to influence what process parties should follow. In many circumstances, we may wish to have this negotiation completely separate from the content negotiation. E.g. "It seems to me that we are struggling to understand each other. How about we take a minute and figure out why that is and what we can do about it?"

If we look at a large number of negotiations, we start to see patterns of where in the process the interactions go off track. With this foresight we may seek to prevent such patterns by negotiating and agreeing on the process upfront. Allan Parker creatively refers to this as "agreeing on the frames around the negotiation", based on the analogy that just as a frame can enhance a painting, one can enhance a negotiation.

Ideally we agree on these frames before we launch into the content. We can also revisit these frames during the negotiation if either party is acting in violation of them. Our desire to avoid cognitive dissonance will result in psychological pressure for us to act consistently with what we have already agreed to. We will also be able to apply any insights from the section on building commitment (later in the book) to increase the likelihood that both parties will in fact negotiate according to the agreed frames.

Next we will introduce a couple of broad groups of process frames that can be useful for most negotiations.

The "why" frames

What would be the value of agreeing on *why* we are having this negotiation? The short answer is that discussing the purpose of the negotiation will help us reveal what we want and the needs that we are trying to satisfy.

Also, it may also be valuable to understand and agree what specifically triggered the need for the negotiation. What is the background information that led us here (history frame)? Did the commercial circumstances change? Did the system change? Did parties exhibit undesirable patterns of behaviour towards each other? Knowing this will help us to identify whether this is the right negotiation to have, or whether we even wish to negotiate.

Finally, agreeing on the purpose (purpose frame) tends to put all parties on the same page. An agreed purpose is a shared purpose, and therefore opens up the potential for mutually beneficial outcomes.

The "what" frames

What do we want from this negotiation? Do we want an outcome (outcome frame)? Do we want agreement (agreement frame)? Do we only want the complete outcome or can we also agree on any incremental improvement on the status quo (improvement frame)? Do we want to search for mutually beneficial outcomes? Sometimes we find ourselves in negotiations where the other party doesn't want an agreed outcome, but rather just want the negotiation (and us) to go away! Knowing this can save us a lot of time and frustration.

Note that we are not discussing what the outcome should be — we are simply agreeing that we want one. What might be the benefit of this? Well, at a few places in this book we mention that we are more likely to find what we are actively looking for, so agreeing that we want agreement and/or an outcome will help steer the negotiation in that direction.

The "how" frames

If we do not discuss how we wish to negotiate, then the likely scenario is that parties bring their own expectations and assumptions about this. Chances are that the parties' respective models won't be entirely compatible.

I recall one interaction with a negotiation company that promoted a sequential step-by-step model. During a meeting the other party suddenly became visibly irritated and said: "No! You're not following our process! Don't try to find agreement until we have listed all the disagreements!" We obviously had very different ideas about what we wanted the process to look like and at this point realised that we needed to spend some time agreeing on how we should negotiate (process frame).

In theory most insights covered in this book could be raised when agreeing on the how frame. Of course that would not be practical. Rather negotiators will find that they repeatedly throughout the negotiation pause the content negotiation to revisit and seek agreement on the how frame.

The "who" frames

Do we interact as partners or adversaries (relationship frame)? Do we view the relationship as a by-product of doing business, or are we doing business as a by-product of having the relationship? Do we force our opinion or respectfully ask for permission (permission frame)? Do we expect a transactional relationship with equal trades of value, or will we look out for each other's interests where we can? Do we view our relationship as long term or short term? How will we ensure that if the relationship ends, it will do so in a way that protects each party's value and reputation? And if one party decides to leave or exit, how will that party ensure that the other party is better of than when the relationship began?

Within the relationship frame we may also create a specific behaviour frame. The purpose here would be to agree on the specific behaviours that we do and don't want to see from parties during the negotiation. This might include treating each other with respect, communicating face-to-face, agreeing to assume good intent behind all behaviours, and not disclosing information to the media.

Agreeing on these frames upfront can help align expectations. Specifically, agreement here will predictably reduce the likelihood that one party will experience frustration from not seeing their relationship-building efforts reciprocated.

One client brought me in to review a past negotiation where the client had not performed very well. One contributing factor was that the other party had changed negotiation teams halfway through the negotiation. Strategically, the first team was very cooperative and the second team was very competitive. The second team also reneged on several of the agreements that had been made with the first team. And of course, none of the rapport, trust and relationship created with the first negotiation team was transferred to the second negotiation team. Here negotiating the "relationship frame" upfront could have helped the client prepare for, manage, or even prevent the transition.

Note that we don't always face a long-term relationship. In some instances we are explicitly negotiating in preparation for going our separate ways. Even here it might help to agree on behaviours e.g.: "Perhaps at this point we can agree that trust has been irreparably broken, and that we do not wish to work together after this. With your permission I would still suggest that we agree to conclude our business in a respectful and ethical manner, with utmost care for each other's reputations (reputation frame)."

The constraints frames

Can we agree on the constraints that we have to consider for this negotiation? What is the benefit of agreeing on how much time (time frame) we have available for the negotiation? Perhaps we may align our deadlines so that neither party can use time as a tactic. Also we tend to use exactly the amount of time that is available; if insufficient time is allocated we will do a rushed job, and if too much time is allocated the negotiations may drag out unnecessarily.

What is the benefit of agreeing which systems we will consider (systems frame)? If we do not take specifics into account — an organisation's culture or a company's general ethos or a department's processes — then we may end up in a negotiation where the outcome is too creative/disruptive and with far too big a scope to be practical for our situation. If we neglect to discuss and agree on the constraints frames we might also end up with two parties getting frustrated with each other because one is perceived to be too creative/impractical and the other is perceived to be too narrow-minded.

There is a risk in discussing the constraints frame, and it is that we make the mistake of assuming we have to fit within a system that limits scope to such a degree that value creation becomes impossible. Specifically, a fundamental reason many negotiations don't result in better outcomes is because parties assume too restrictive a constraints frame. Thus much of value-generating negotiation is in fact aimed at loosening up (perceived) constraints frames.

These frames are not set in stone. These are merely suggestions for elements of the process that we wish to agree on early — the reader is encouraged to come up with his or her own. Also, note that it is neither appropriate nor feasible to negotiate all of these before every negotiation ("Hi, I'd like to negotiate the price on this electric razor, but first I want us to agree to these fifty rules for how we shall negotiate..."). Rather we stay consistent with our intentional, comprehensive, agile, precise and situational approach. This means we pick the frames that are most likely to be important for our specific negotiation. If during the negotiation we realise that we need to agree other frames, then by all means, pause the content negotiation and renegotiate the process. Remember, if we aren't getting our desired content outcomes, it is likely that we simply aren't following the right process for enabling those outcomes.

OPENING STATEMENT
AND OPENING BEHAVIOUR

First impressions last. We create opinions very quickly, and these opinions are all *sticky* to some degree or another. Negotiators therefore pay particular attention to getting the first impression right.

We dress intentionally. We control our body language intentionally. We consider what we say, how we say it, when we say it, where our eyes look, the firmness of our handshake, the other party's emotions, and anything else we believe might influence the other party's opinion.

The opening statement (or indeed, the opening *question*) is how we start the negotiation, or how we start a meeting, or how we start the conversation after we have had a break. One aspect that distinguishes the opening statement from all other statements is that we have had time to think about and prepare what to say! We may even have the opportunity to rehearse and role-play the opening statement to minimise the risk that what we intended to say a certain way comes across completely differently when we actually say it.

One recommendation is to build in elements of the frames in the opening statement. A completely made-up example, which isn't tailored for any specific negotiation you might have, is:

> With your permission [permission frame], I would like to offer to set
> the scene for today's meeting [why frame]. I wish to start with saying
> that I am glad that we are on this long journey together [relationship
> frame]. I also wish to acknowledge that we are here today because
> recently some specific things have not worked out as expected [history
> frame], and I hope we can continue our tradition [relationship
> frame] of finding a way to agree [agreement frame] on a solution
> that will be beneficial to both parties [mutual outcome frame].
> Given that we only have one hour today [time frame], I would like
> to suggest that we use that time to focus on trying to understand
> how each party views the recent events [how frame]. Can I begin
> by asking [permission frame] for your commitment [commitment
> frame] that no matter what direction the conversation takes, that we
> ensure that we always seek to end the meeting with the relationship
> and the current negotiation in an improved state compared to the
> start of the meeting [improvement frame]?

DESIRED END STATE

Skilled negotiators begin with the end in mind. We know what we want at the end of the process, we know why we want it, and we have one or multiple ideas for how to get it.

How about knowing the desired outcome of each interaction on the way? Is that also important? Yes and no. It helps us focus the meetings we have, and that is a good thing. But being too obsessed with achieving a particular outcome in an interaction can make us come across as inflexible and effectively imposes a deadline on us. As we have discussed, the drawbacks with negotiating towards a deadline often far outweigh the benefits.

However, the other party's emotional state at the end of the meeting is something we can much more easily influence if we pay adequate attention. What state do we want? Often the answer will be that we prefer a positive state where parties feel good about each other, are excited about moving forwards, are in agreement, and have a mindset of looking for solutions.

So as we near the end of the interaction (which we are aware of since the first thing we do is agree on the time frame, right?), our strategy might be to ensure the last topic of discussion will induce the desired emotional state. Specifically, we want to avoid raising disagreements, introducing constraints, signalling concerns, or doing anything that drains the energy in the meeting. If we suddenly lose rapport or create a misunderstanding at this point we may not have time to fix it before parting ways. The psychological effect of primacy and recency states that we remember the beginning and end of an interaction better than what happened in between.

I have observed many meetings where the parties end in an excellent state, only for one party to damage the state by raising a concern, disagreement or character flaw as parties engage in small talk on the way to the door.

THE MYTHICAL LINEAR PROCESS

Hopefully we have now convinced you of the limitations of a fixed-step-by-step model, and encouraged you of the advantages of *an agile and situational* approach to negotiation.

However, we also appreciate that total flexibility may be daunting before you have a chance to get a feel for when to use each of the insights. So here I provide one example of a linear negotiation process, with the explicit understanding that I don't recommend that anyone blindly follow a linear process for any specific negotiation.

- Negotiate the brief (if there is one) so that it enables (rather than hinders) maximum opportunity for getting parties to agree to the outcomes we want.

- Look at the system and verify that this is the right negotiation to have given the outcomes that we want. Maybe we don't want to engage in a negotiation, period.

- Start building rapport and a relationship with the other party or find someone who already has a good relationship and can negotiate on our behalf.

- Start influencing early, and start finding other people in the stakeholder diagram who can help us influence the other party.

- Agree with the other party on why we are negotiating, what we want to achieve, and how the process will look.

- Understand the needs of the parties.

- Agree on criteria for how a final decision will be made and how fairness will be measured, then invent options, and make a decision on which options(s) we can agree to.

- Document the agreement.

- Monitor the implementation of the agreement.

- As the negotiation moves to the implementation stage, details that were assumed will often need to be renegotiated.

- Review and learn from the process.

As you read through this list you probably notice another reason that we can't provide a fixed linear process, and that is that many of the insights are applied throughout the process. Building rapport, trust, relationship and agreement, or ensuring understanding and satisfaction of needs, are not events. Rather these activities take place continuously throughout the dynamic and parallel negotiation processes that make up "the negotiation".

ALTERNATIVES TO THE CURRENT NEGOTIATION

You cannot simultaneously prevent and prepare for war
ALBERT EINSTEIN

Develop alternatives

The term BATNA (Best Alternative To a Negotiated Agreement) was introduced in the book *Getting to Yes*, by Roger Fisher and William Ury, and has become an ubiquitous term in negotiation. It effectively describes our most desirable backup plan, i.e. what is our best alternative elsewhere if we can't find an outcome together with the other party.

It is considered proper due diligence to develop multiple alternatives to the current negotiation, where the most desirable one will be our BATNA. Having an attractive alternative elsewhere reduces our dependency on the other party in this negotiation, thus enabling us to walk away if we are not happy with the content, process or relationship of the current negotiation. If the other party does not have an attractive alternative at this point, he or she may feel forced to give into our demands. For this reason the BATNA is often referred to as the greatest source of power in the division game.

As the integration and maximisation games aren't driven by power, the BATNA is less relevant for these negotiations. However, despite our best intentions, any negotiation can deteriorate into division, and we don't want to end up in a division negotiation with someone who has a power advantage that allows them to dictate terms. So developing alternatives is a good insurance policy.

It is also possible that through the process of negotiation we realise that there simply is not an available option or deal that could work for both parties, and then we again have to resort to considering other alternatives elsewhere.

The term BATNA is a bit unfortunate because it implies that it is an alternative to having a negotiation. However, our BATNA can indeed be the result of another negotiation. Once we look at it this way we realise that the BATNA may simply be any negotiation in our stakeholder diagram (see chapter 10). And remember, early on in our preparation we ask ourselves: "Is the current negotiation the most appropriate negotiation to have given the outcomes we want to achieve?" The search for our BATNA may indeed reveal the right negotiation for us to have, and it may not be a negotiation with the party that is presently in front of us.

Note that when I negotiate with you, my BATNA may be with another party, or it may also be with you. Alternatives simply mean that I don't need your agreement or permission to pursue them. For instance, if we can't agree on how to divide the house after our divorce, I may simply resort to sticking with the status quo and doing nothing until we find a better option. Meanwhile my ex-partner desperately needs money and can't afford to wait. This would be a situation where me having a BATNA, and her not having one would give me a significant power advantage.

There is also a third option, and that is when my BATNA involves doing something without a counter party. If I am a distributor selling to a retailer I may negotiate with this retailer, other retailers, or I may expand my business to also perform retailing myself.

A final point is that we typically don't accurately evaluate the certainty of our BATNA. For example, you have a job you don't like and you might believe that you can easily get another job. That potential other job is not a BATNA: it's a potential BATNA. It is not a BATNA until you have that contract in your hand. And still, even at that point it might disappear.

Of course, while overestimating our BATNA can be dangerous, it can be equally detrimental to underestimate it. After being made redundant from a job she had held for thirty years, an acquaintance of mine was convinced she couldn't get another position. Six months later she finally built up the courage to apply for three jobs and was immediately offered two of them — one with a fifty per cent raise!

Consider reducing the attractiveness of the other party's alternatives

Particularly in hostile negotiations where the other party is trying to coerce us and for some reason we are unable to switch to integration or maximisation, then we may be forced to play division. Since the BATNA is the biggest source of power in the divisional game, then we may want to reduce the other party's perception of their BATNA.

- Reduce perceived certainty: e.g. we may openly ask the other party what they will do if they pursue their BATNA. Often they will not have thought it through in sufficient detail, and simply asking them to walk through the steps may cause them to realise that their BATNA is not certain and may even be improbable.

- Reduce perceived desirability. Sometimes a BATNA will be an exact replacement for our negotiation, e.g. another car dealership may offer the exact same model for a cheaper price. However, often our BATNA is a substitute that is difficult to compare. I may negotiate my salary for my current job, and my BATNA is a different job for a different company with a different culture, work hours, tasks, travel distance, etc. In this case my current manager might help me think through my decision, and emphasise how staying may do a better job of satisfying most of my important needs.

- One very competitive strategy is to deliberately ruin the other party's BATNA. An example could be in a suicide intervention, where a subject in financial trouble threatens to kill himself so that his family can qualify for his death benefits. Here the suicide has become the subject's alternative to dealing with his problems. If the subject was informed that his policy would be cancelled in the event of suicide, then his BATNA would instantly disappear, perhaps leaving no other option than to stick with the negotiation of getting his life in order.

When to talk about alternatives, and when not to

One of my MBA professors used a vivid example that effectively illustrates the impact of talking about alternatives in a negotiation. Imagine having an argument with your partner, and at some point you tell your partner, "You know, I really think you should agree with me, because if you don't I could always go down to the bar and pick up someone else."

What would *that* do to the relationship? And what is the likely reaction? One possibility is that the other party now starts developing their BATNA, and maybe at some point their BATNA becomes more attractive than *you*!

We need to acknowledge the risk of using a definition of negotiation such as, "You and I negotiate because we think we can get a better deal than our respective BATNAs." The risk is that we may come across as playing the division game even if we aren't.

I have still to find anyone who, when first hearing about the other party's BATNA responds: "Yay, it makes me very happy to hear that. Thanks for sharing. I truly enjoy understanding how replaceable I am." Bringing up one's BATNA will predictably have a negative effect on rapport, trust and the relationship.

So should we then *not* have a BATNA in certain negotiations? Well, we already have negotiations with no BATNA. No matter how our children treat us we will always love them. Not having a BATNA in that instance doesn't bother us. In fact, not having a BATNA means that we have to work harder at finding mutually beneficial outcomes… and we do…and we succeed.

The BATNA is certainly an important insurance in the event that our negotiation doesn't work out to our satisfaction. So yes, it is proper due diligence to create one, or even multiple. But while playing integration or maximisation we don't talk about alternatives, and don't focus on them. It will be more beneficial for us to focus our interaction on "What could we achieve together?", "How could we achieve that?", and "How can we achieve even more?", than to constantly ask ourselves "Is our deal better than my BATNA yet?"

Is there a WATNA?

When things turn really ugly, where at least one party is so upset that simply walking away is not enough because they really want to get back at you (or someone else), then we really need to be aware of the Worst Alternative to a Negotiated Agreement, or WATNA.

Whereas a BATNA essentially says: "If this negotiation doesn't work out for me I'll go elsewhere", an intentional WATNA says: "If I am not happy then something bad will happen [to you] as a result." One example of this is when one or both parties take actions towards mutual destruction, hoping that the other party will come to their senses and give in before it is too late. While there are indeed distinctions between threats, warnings and education on the likely consequences of certain behaviour, we usually have little control over how the recipient will interpret these. And while we may hope for compliance, all power moves are likely to result in undesirable by-products.

Because most of us aren't hostage or crisis negotiators, I would suggest that if our negotiations deteriorate to the point where an intentional WATNA by the other party becomes an issue, then we have not done a good job of managing that relationship. Remember one of our first points in this book: prevention is often easier and cheaper than fixing the mess that can otherwise occur.

We should add that the presence of a WATNA might also be generated by other parts of the system, e.g. a change in policy, political climate or state of the economy. In this case the WATNA is not the result of someone's intentional threat, but rather it is the presence of a considerable risk.

And we also want to raise the possibility that a WATNA beyond the control of negotiating parties *can* also have positive effects in aligning all parties' interests in avoiding the WATNA. This creates interdependence that can in turn motivate parties to come up with an outcome that they can agree on.

6

BUILD STRONG
RELATIONSHIPS

——— — ——

When working with clients I hear a range of views on the importance of the relationship. Some see it as important, others see it as a parameter to be manipulated, and collectively we don't do much to improve it.

Skilled negotiators work proactively on the relationship to make sure it supports our negotiated outcomes. If nothing else, we may at least want to ask ourselves these questions.

- ◆ What types of relationships are there?

- ◆ What type of relationship do we have now/want?

- ◆ What are the specific behaviours we need to adopt/avoid to create the relationship we want?

- ◆ What other parameters and events could affect the relationship?

- ◆ What would our desired relationship allow us to do?

TYPES OF RELATIONSHIPS

Weak | strong

How important is the relationship in negotiations? To figure this out, think of someone you trust completely. How do you negotiate with that person? It doesn't really feel like "negotiation", does it? We rather try to figure out what works for both parties, we don't worry about contracts, or dispute resolution clauses etc. We *do* worry about each other's wellbeing. And what happens when something goes wrong? We acknowledge the possibility of unintentional mistakes and things outside the other party's control.

Now consider someone you don't like or don't trust. Someone who lies a lot or who has turned on you in the past. How would you negotiate with this person? Perhaps your first answer is: "I wouldn't!" But let's assume that you must. My guess is that in that case you would try every available mechanism for ensuring compliance, e.g. a contract to specify responsibilities and punishment for non-compliance. We will give only what we need in order to get something back; we will trade, tit-for-tat. And what happens when something goes wrong? Well, we are likely to assume this was a result of intentional ill will from the other party.

We negotiate *very* differently with those with whom we have a strong relationship; the process will be easier, and both parties will seek to create more value over the long term. Based on this insight, I have introduced an exercise that effectively offers a shortcut to seminar participants (or readers) who don't have the patience for learning all the negotiation theory.

> Identify the most difficult person in your life, who dislikes you the most, or is the least cooperative. And make him or her like you. If you can achieve that, then you will be able to improve the strength of all your relationships, and that will ultimately result in more value.

We can view relationships on a scale from zero to ten, where zero is a non-existent relationship, and ten is a very strong relationship. The stronger the relationship, the more potential we will have to engage in a negotiation that maximises value for all. Of course that scale is not complete, because we can have destructive relationships as well. On our scale this would be represented on the negative axis. Our insight still holds: moving towards a positive relationship is likely to be positive for the negotiation, and vice versa.

Competitive | cooperative

Are parties looking to work with each other or against each other? Competitive relationships are, as we've said before, very likely to result in the division game. However, as negotiators we have options for influencing people to cooperate with us whether they want to or not.

Cooperative relationships, on the other hand, often lead to the intent to play integration or maximisation. However, whether this intent translates to actual cooperation is often determined by the parties' skill in changing the process. Sadly, despite good intent, most of these negotiations still end up played as the division game.

Competitive and cooperative relationships do not determine how the negotiation pans out, but they significantly influence how easy it will be for negotiators to influence the process to enable integration or maximisation.

Communal | exchange based

In a communal relationship we look out for the other party; we focus on satisfying their needs irrespective of whether we also satisfy our own. The extreme example of a communal relationship would be the one with our loved ones, where we look out for them just as much as (and sometimes more than) for ourselves. It is conceivable that a parent, if presented with the need to choose, could be prepared to sacrifice his or her own life in order to save the life of a child.

In contrast, exchange-based relationships involve equal trades of value. We only give something because we have to in order to get something in return. And if a relationship with a different party will give us more value then we'll move to that one. No hard feelings. A typical example of an exchange relationship is going to your dentist; you may prefer to keep seeing the same dentist, but the relationship only involves a service in exchange for the exact value of that service.

Both of these types of relationships have their place, but behaviours that are appropriate in one may be seen as unacceptable in the other. Equal trades increase attraction between parties in exchange relationships, but reduce attraction in communal relationships. Just imagine if your best friend wants to borrow $100 dollars, and you respond with "And what will you do for me?" or "OK, but sign this contract to ensure I get the money back." How well will that go down?

Is there a link between communal relationships and negotiating to satisfy each other's needs, and a corresponding link between exchange-based relationships and negotiating by trading? The answer is yes; if we want parties to negotiate in a manner where we focus on satisfying each other's needs (even if that results in unequal value creation and appropriation), then one of our first steps is to try to establish a *communal* relationship.

Which comes first, the way we negotiate or the relationship? As with many insights in this book, the relationship is circular. The more value we create for each other, the stronger the relationship will become. The stronger the relationship, the more easily we can pursue value creation.

Short term | long term

I have come across negotiation training that advocates different negotiation approaches depending on how long we expect the relationship to last. The recommendation is usually the competitive division approach for short-term relationships and the integration game for long-term relationships.

However, we have already discussed that we don't know if the person we negotiate with today will directly or indirectly affect any of our future negotiations. We assume that they will. Also, since integration has more value-creation potential than division, why not try to use it in "quick" negotiations as well? Integration does not necessarily take longer than division.

Of course the other party has probably not read this book, and people on autopilot tend to automatically adjust their negotiation approach based on the expected duration of the relationship. Unfortunately, the incentive to lie, manipulate and take advantage of other people seems to increase if we think we'll never see the other party again.

I once applied for a very nice role as a manager of strategy and market segmentation at a large telecommunications company. The interview process was very pleasant, the interviewers were friendly, and eventually they called me with an offer of employment. I was told to expect the contract by mail the next few days. Guess if I was excited!

A week passed and no contract arrived. I called up and was reassured it was on its way. Another week passed and I was again reassured it was on its way. Then two months passed, during which time none of my calls were returned. At the end of two months I received the following SMS to my mobile phone: *Role on hold, sorry.*

I later learned that an internal company restructure began in the days after I was offered the job. As it became clear to my future manager that she would no longer need me, the incentive to build a relationship was (apparently) instantly removed.

Luckily the reverse also tends to hold true as well, i.e. if we can demonstrate to an adversarial negotiator that he or she can derive more value from having a long-term relationship with us, he or she will be more likely to work on the relationship to protect the investment.

Independent | dependent | interdependent

The link between two parties can be described as independent, dependent or interdependent. If there is independence then the parties don't need each other and there is no reason why they *have to* negotiate. Parties may of course still choose to negotiate.

The link can be where one party is dependent on the other. This would increase the power of the party that is not dependent.

The link can be one of interdependence, where both parties (perceive that they) need each other. This can thus encourage, or even force parties to cooperate and seek mutually beneficial outcomes. However, it can just as well become an incentive to try to break the interdependence.

For instance, there are countless examples in the world of groups of people who are interdependent by virtue of sharing the same block of land, town, apartment building, or office. When these groups don't want to share the territory, they try to either create dependence (e.g. by taking control and thus ruling the other groups) or independence (e.g. by physically sealing off other groups, or even forcing them to move away).

So which relationship do we want? As negotiators we specifically seek to avoid the power disadvantage of being dependent on the other party. But all the remaining options (interdependence, other party dependent on us, and complete independence) will each individually be the best option in selected situations. So again, we have increased our awareness of another insight, and we need to remain agile and adapt it to our situation.

HISTORY

Because negotiation is an ongoing process, we know that we rarely identify a clear starting point. By the time we realise that we are negotiating, the wheels are already in motion.

History among parties

We previously shared that one of the first things we need to understand as negotiators representing clients or stakeholders is what transpired before we entered the picture, so to achieve this we establish a timeline. One of the many things we want to capture on that timeline is what has happened between parties in the past, and how each party perceives that history. This will often give valuable insight into parties' motivations, and indicate what they might do next.

For instance, if we negotiated in the past and you used power to force me to accept a bad deal, you are now aware what by-products that might have produced. When we this time meet for a new negotiation, it is likely that I will bring all of that baggage with me. While I may not verbalise any of my intentions to get even, if you understand our history you will already know what to expect.

It is also possible that we tried things in the past and they didn't work. That means we might be more hesitant this time around, and perhaps evaluate options too early if we anticipate that there may be obstacles. Our history will hold lessons, and it will also fuel our fears and expectations for how the current negotiation will pan out.

Each party's history with others

It is also valuable to consider the parties' histories beyond their interactions each other. Each party (individual or organisation) may have had their current behaviours, beliefs, expectations, fears, motivations, or needs shaped by what has transpired in the past. Often we can get a more accurate reading on these things by looking at the other party's history from second position. In fact, looking at their history *helps us* adopt second position.

Anything that is part of the other party's history may affect our negotiation with him or her. Specifically, our independent histories may provide explanations for why and how we pollute our current interaction — e.g. transference. For example, if my last supplier broke my trust, then I may start by distrusting my present supplier. If my last girlfriend wanted me for my money, then I may fear that my present girlfriend has the same agenda. Thus our independent histories may still provide explanations for why and how we pollute our current interaction.

PLAN THE RELATIONSHIP

We plan the negotiation. We plan how to use time. We plan our questions. We plan our opening statement. We plan many, many aspects of the negotiation. But how many of us plan a relationship? Should we? What would be the benefit if we did?

Timing

When is it easiest to "make friends"? How easy is it to build a strong relationship with someone who is in an important position, or who is powerful or popular? It is comparatively difficult because many people are trying to befriend people in these positions. It may be difficult even to get access to these individuals, let alone build trust and a strong relationship with them. And when you finally meet, they may be guarded and on the lookout for how you might want to use them.

Conversely, how many people work hard to connect with non-influential, non-important, non-powerful, or non-popular people? Significantly fewer. In relative terms, how much easier might it be to build a relationship with them? And is it possible that people who are not in influential positions today might hold influential positions (with access to resources, relationships, information) that are key to our negotiation tomorrow? Absolutely.

Is it also possible that those who are in seemingly non-influential positions can already be instrumental in getting you introduced to, connected with, or even influence the person you want to deal with in the end? A healthy negotiation mindset is to assume that we do not know what connections people have, and to assume that every person we deal with may be in a position to open a door for us in the future.

Would that mindset change how you interact with the night-time cleaner you meet while working overtime, the barista who serves your coffee, or the cab driver who takes you to work? It should.

Plan the exit

A venture capitalist will not invest in a company unless he or she has a clear understanding of when and how to exit that investment. This is a terrible analogy for relationships, so please disregard it. Specifically, we now know that expecting a shared future makes people prioritise the relationship, and when that expectation ceases, so do the efforts put into building that relationship. And what do we think might happen if parties already on day one expect that the relationship is finite?

Rather than assuming that the relationship will end, skilled negotiators instead acknowledge that relationships sometimes do end. This awareness allows us to plan what to do in the event that this happens, without leading us down a path of negative negotiation behaviour that could in itself provoke the demise of the relationship.

On a timeline, when do you think parties will show their best side? Usually it is at the beginning, when both parties anticipate plenty of shared value and recognise how much they depend on the other party in order to realise that value. What happens when all that value has been delivered and/or the other party doesn't need us any more? Perhaps you are familiar with the following quote by Malcolm S. Forbes: "You can easily judge the character of others by how they treat those who can do nothing for them or to them." As negotiators, we anticipate the likelihood of this occurring and we prepare accordingly.

We also observe that parties regularly wait until the point where the relationship is damaged to try to fix it. Sadly this is sometimes the first point at which parties realise that the relationship is important to the negotiation! Fixing the relationship at this point tends to be difficult because:

- emotions may be high;
- resentment may already have been built up;
- trust may have been destroyed;
- damage may already have been done;

- parties may already have started looking for alternative parties to negotiate with; or

- parties no longer expect the relationship to continue, therefore see no additional value being created, and assume the only remaining task is to divide perceived value.

The key takeaway here is that it is usually much easier to agree on a constructive process for how to deal with the fall-out from a conflict while parties are still enjoying a strong relationship. This may include negotiating the appropriate relationship and behaviour frames. An elegant example of this was shared by a naturally skilled negotiator I was introduced to in Hawaii: "We live on an island so it becomes very clear that a businessman arriving on our shores will probably not stay forever. So my first question to such a businessman is always how he will ensure that I'm better off when he leaves."

Should disaster strike and parties no longer expect a future relationship, they tend to become self-serving in the way they negotiate. So we have a clear motivation early in the negotiation to prepare for how to deal with the possibility of the relationship souring. Keep in mind, however:

- talking too much about what might go wrong may put a damper on the relationship, unintentionally damage trust, and create negative self-fulfilling prophecies; and

- remember the discussion earlier in the book about prevention vs. problem solving. If we are putting effort into planning the relationship, we may as well plan for how to prevent relationship problems rather than merely how to fix them.

BUILD RAPPORT

So where do we start in building a relationship? We build *rapport*. And what is rapport exactly? Again, there are many definitions, but for our purposes it is the feeling or sensation that we are in sync with the other party, that we are operating on the same wavelength, that we are "similar", or that we have a connection.

I usually ask my participants: "If you were travelling in a foreign country on the other side of the world, and you walked into a bar, and you found one of your compatriots among a group of local people, who do you think you would build rapport with the fastest?" So far one hundred per cent of participants have said: "With the person from my country." This might not be a person we would have socialised with at home, but in this environment we expect this person to be "most similar", and therefore the person we will most easily build rapport with.

Next: you are going to the bathroom and can't take your suitcase with you — which person in the bar do you ask to mind your bag for you? So far, over ninety-nine per cent of participants have said: "The person from our own country." (The only exception was a Russian man who jokingly said: "You obviously don't know Russians!")

It appears that there may be a link between rapport and trust. We certainly want to build trust, so how can we intentionally build rapport?

Be sincere

Be sincere and genuine in wanting to build a relationship. We have had so much exposure to manipulative ploys that we can unconsciously tell whether the smile of a real-estate agent, politician, or secondhand-car salesperson is genuine or not. So people are likely to pick up incongruence in your manners if you try to fake building rapport. Being caught faking rapport, or being caught being disingenuous in any other way, can instantly destroy trust.

This is relevant for many other topics in this book. Be sincere and genuine when trying to build trust, when building credibility, when listening, and when communicating. It is not just what we say, but also how we say it (and how we do everything else) that influences people.

Care about the other party

We enjoy the attention of others. We want to tell our story and we want people to listen to us. We want people to understand us. We want people to agree with us. And we want people to look out for us. You can give another person these experiences by adopting the second perceptual position. Later we will introduce active listening skills, which we will use to *demonstrate* that we care, that we listen, that we understand and that we agree.

Be similar (match)

As discussed above, if we observe two people who have rapport, we are likely to see that several of their behaviours are similar or even mirrored. Does rapport make us copy each other's behaviours, or does copying each other's behaviours create rapport? The short answer to both questions is "yes". The relationship between the two is circular; rapport results in mirroring of each other's behaviour, and mirroring behaviour can create rapport.

Focus on agreement

Can you disagree with your friends and still remain friends? Most of the time the answer is "yes". In fact, we probably recognise that there are individuals we have a lot of respect for *because* we know they stand up for themselves and don't always agree with the majority. In some instances we call them leaders.

So, is the insight here that we should disagree with people to have them respect and look up to us? Not quite. Being allowed to disagree is a luxury that comes with strong relationships. But disagreement does not help us build the rapport required to create new relationships.

If you are unconvinced then I invite you to go to a public gathering and start talking to people. Agree one hundred per cent with half of the people, and pick just one major point of disagreement with the other half. You don't have to be argumentative or difficult, simply share that you disagree. My prediction is that people in the first group are much more likely to want to speak with you again.

We get permission to disagree by first earning credits through agreement. This suggests a useful adaptation of the emotional bank account that we could call the agreement bank account. The more agreement we put in, the more disagreement we can withdraw later.

Given the importance of agreement, we have dedicated an entire section to the topic (see chapter 12). As we will discover, agreement is always available and we just need to learn where to look for it.

Let the other party talk

Building rapport also involves avoiding breaking rapport. Specifically, one of the most common unintentional ways we break rapport is by interrupting someone mid-sentence. If interrupting once breaks rapport, then interrupting repeatedly ensures that rapport is obliterated.

If we skilfully apply active listening skills, then the other party will end up doing most of the talking. In addition to rapport building, there are several benefits to having the other party talk.

- S/he is likely to prefer the sound of his/her own voice.

- S/he will probably find his/her view most persuasive.

- S/he probably likes getting views across to others.

- Listening is difficult.

- If the other party talks then you have an opportunity to agree with him or her. We like people who agree with us.

- It is an opportunity to give him or her our attention.

- Physiologically s/he will have higher energy levels when talking than when listening.

- His or her brain has excess capacity that sits idle when listening (or worse, wanders off topic or prepares rebuttals), but talking will keep his or her brain occupied.

- We learn about the talker. This will help us identify what to match in order to build rapport, and what needs the other party wants satisfied.

A real world example I have of this was my interview for my first negotiation job. The CEO of a company and I had a ninety-minute coffee meeting, during which he spoke ninety-five per cent of the time. Here I wish to share three memorable quotes by the CEO that capture the entire conversation (negotiation!).

- Thirty minutes into the conversation: "Hey, I realise that I'm the one doing all the talking — am I interviewing you or are you interviewing me?"

- Thirty minutes later: "I don't know if I'm projecting, but you strike me as a younger version of myself."

- Thirty minutes later: "You are hired! Congratulations! Let's go introduce you to the team!"

Be likeable

We will go to greater lengths to accommodate people we like than people we dislike. Again, just think about what you will do for your best friend, or the person you love, compared to someone you dislike or even hate.

The example I use in my seminars is from an experience on Sydney buses. If a random person gets to the bus just as the doors are closing, the Sydney bus driver will quite often not reopen the doors, but will rather drive off. Even if part of the person's anatomy or clothing is wedged between the doors, the bus driver will still not accept a latecomer. Perhaps I exaggerate slightly.

Nevertheless, I have on eight separate occasions witnessed a beautiful girl walk up to a bus that is stuck in traffic nowhere near a bus stop. She will knock on the glass, show that beautiful smile, and voilà: Open Sesame!

The (male) bus driver probably realises on a logical level that this girl will never date him, nor become his friend, but he still feels such an urge to accommodate this attractive person, i.e. someone he likes.

So what makes us like people? A whole range of things. Note that some of these aspects are circular, e.g. we like people who have rapport with us and we more easily build rapport with someone we like.

- Similarity, Trust, Agreement, Listening, Liking, Attention — as above, these are all factors that build rapport and therefore liking.

- Recognition and familiarity. What we recognise feels familiar and we assume that someone who is familiar is also similar.

- Humour. We enjoy having a good time. We enjoy laughing. We like people who can give us that experience.

- Being interesting. We like people who are intriguing, mysterious, and knowledgeable. They make *our* lives more interesting.

- Attractiveness. Raw good looks, charm, charisma, power, or other things we are physically attracted to. Consistent with the halo effect, we typically rate attractive people as more competent, intelligent and sociable than unattractive people. However the reverse effect may occur in instances where we see the attractive person as competition, or if the attractive person has rejected us.

- Association. Consistent with transference, when we like someone or something, we are likely to increase our liking for those who are associated with what we like.

There is an interesting relationship between liking and exposure over time. The more time we spend with people we dislike, the more we dislike them. The more time we spend with people we like, the more we like them. But for every person we like there is a unique point of "too much exposure", and once we pass that point we start to dislike that person too.

Maximise interactivity

Many clients these days have an affinity for communicating via email. And yes, there are several advantages, but there are also limitations. One is the difficulty of building rapport. In contrast, a phone conversation makes it easier to build rapport, and face-to-face even easier again. This is because having the other party in front of us gives us access to the maximum number of signals as to how he or she thinks, feels, perceives, behaves, and prefers to communicate. Each of these signals can be matched (or mismatched).

Seeing the other party's reactions also gives instant us feedback on what we are doing. If something we do starts breaking rapport we may immediately spot a change in their facial expressions, gestures, posture, etc. This feedback gives us a chance to correct (or recalibrate) our behaviour to strengthen rather than weaken rapport.

Breaking rapport

So far it may seem that we've worked on the assumption that rapport is desirable. If all behaviours are appropriate in some situations, then we can infer that we may sometimes also want to break rapport.

What might be examples of situations in which we may wish to break rapport? Perhaps we do not wish to engage with a particularly pushy salesperson. Perhaps we are coaching someone and we wish to interrupt his or her negative behavioural pattern by doing something unexpected. Perhaps we find ourselves on a five-hour inter-city train next to a person who is committed to telling us all the ways in which she treats her pet better than her ex-husband. Breaking rapport does not mean I have to be rude or cause disagreement. I can simply signal with my intonation, posture and gestures that I wish to cut the conversation short.

One of the reasons we build rapport is that by being similar we remove noise and friction in the interaction. But another insight states that we better recall those experiences that are out of the ordinary. So a quite creative reason to break rapport (very temporarily) would be to help the other party better recall what we want them to recall.

MODEL DESIRED BEHAVIOUR

In negotiations we may want both parties to agree to adopt certain behaviours, and to avoid others. We may discuss some of these explicitly with the other party, and try to get agreement and commitment to them. A complementary approach is to model all behaviour that we wish to see reciprocated, and influence by demonstrating rather than telling. If we have rapport, then we stand a good chance of influencing the process covertly without explicitly talking about it.

One example is from a course I held for mining-industry professionals. On the first day of the four-day course one of the participants approached me and introduced himself by saying: "Hi, my name is John (not his real name), and I negotiate by punching people in the face!"

During the course John fell into autopilot in many of the simulations and discussions. His autopilot was very much as he had described. In response, I:

- listened actively without ever interrupting;

- agreed with his feelings, agreed that his reasoning had merit, agreed that the points were interesting, but I didn't disagree a single time;

- always responded with a question such as "How can we make that relevant to what we just discussed?" or "How could you have applied one of the discussed insights instead of what you did?";

- never raised my voice, reacted or dismissed his contribution;

- gave him my full attention in the breaks where I allowed him to speak completely uninterrupted; and

- on the few occasions when I broke rapport, I did so in a

humorous way to interrupt his pattern and insert a learning point for the group.

Towards the end of the course John had achieved a remarkable transition in behaviour and attitude. And this was achieved without me at any point telling him specifically to change anything! He turned from a die-hard competitor to quite the collaborator.

The benefit was not only for John. After the course I received a very nice message from one of the other participants, who shared that his biggest learning point in the course was how I had handled the "difficult" negotiator. I responded with a thank-you letter of my own, and admitted that this had been my biggest learning point too.

Agree on behaviours

While modelling desired behaviours allows us to model *all* desired behaviours, it doesn't necessarily result in the other party adopting them. This could be because we don't have rapport, or because the party doesn't have the situational awareness to notice what is going on around him or her. Also, sometimes we don't have time (or even the opportunity) to educate the other party in this fairly slow and indirect fashion. So going back to our relationship frame, we may explicitly agree on what we should and should not do in this relationship.

For instance, in a commercial relationship parties may want to agree that:

- parties will not use threats, coercion, power tactics or lies against each other;

- parties will not try to impose changes unilaterally, but will rather engage the other party to discuss how changes may work for both parties; and

- parties will do their utmost to protect each other's reputations.

Or in a romantic relationship parties may want to agree that:

- parties will be loyal;

- parties are or are not allowed to flirt with other people; and

- parties will share or divide housework in a certain way.

Don't reward bad behaviours

If the other party behaves badly (e.g. gets angry whenever s/he doesn't get what s/he wants) then we want to ensure that this behaviour does not unintentionally result in a reward. Otherwise we set a bad precedent that encourages the other party to continue with the bad behaviour. This suggests that we should avoid "giving in" to tactics such as emotional outbursts, threats, coercion, or manipulation.

TRUST

What is trust?

In negotiation we treat trust as the strength of my belief that you are looking out for me. If we were to unpack this definition further we can say that trust is the measurement of my expectations of your positive behaviour or actions towards me.

What does this mean? Well, if I don't know you, but I want to trust you (perhaps because you are very likeable), then I am likely to create expectations of you behaving positively. This will translate to some level of trust. As you start acting consistently with these expectations, my trust in you will increase. As I look back at your excellent track record of acting consistently with my expectations, I will expect this to continue into the future. I trust you.

Note that you have to act consistently with my expectations of *positive* behaviour. If I expect your behaviour to be negative, then you are in a difficult spot.

- If you act consistently with my negative expectations of you, then you are certainly predictable, but predictably bad. I know what you will do, but because your behaviour is negative I won't trust you.

- If you act inconsistently with my negative expectations of you, then I may get positively surprised, but this in itself makes you seem unpredictable and therefore not trustworthy. I will demand to see a repeated pattern of you acting positively before I will expect you to act positively.

Thus my having negative expectations of you (or expecting that I should distrust you) creates circumstances where it will be difficult for you to gain my trust. I have created a self-fulfilling prophecy.

Also note that I base my trust on *my* expectations of *your* positive behaviour. So if I have unreasonable, ill-informed, or unfounded expectations of you, then it doesn't matter if you act consistently with *your* expectations of *yourself*. Often I will fail to realise this distinction, and I will perceive that you are acting inconsistently with some form of objective expectations, when in fact I'm guilty of having expectations that you may not even be aware of, let alone agree with. This then emphasises the importance of sharing and getting agreement on all forms of expectations in negotiations.

Is trust good?

Imagine that you are currently deeply entrenched in a divisional negotiation with the other party. After reading this book you will probably be eager to try to change the game to integration or maximisation. Imagine that there is no trust and you propose: "I have a suggestion for how we can negotiate differently and therefore get more value. For it to work we will need to be open and start sharing information."

What do you think will be the likely response? One thought that may go through the other party's head may be: "Hey, what kind of tactic is s/he trying to apply this time?"

Imagine instead that there was complete trust. How much easier would it be to get the other party to follow your lead in changing the game?

It is hardly a surprise that we prefer to negotiate with people that we trust. And for good reason — the process will be easier and we are more likely to get what we want. In a trusting environment we are more likely to give the other party the benefit of the doubt, and acknowledge external influences beyond their control. Our relationship is more likely to be communal, and we are more likely to engage in integration or maximisation. Finally, we are less likely to pollute the process with misinformation, unwarranted accusations, or processes to enforce compliance.

While we prefer trusting interactions, it is important to ensure that the level of trust is appropriate and warranted. If we trust someone more than they deserve, we leave ourselves open to being conned, tricked, manipulated or exploited.

Does that mean we should start by not trusting the other party until they have demonstrated they are trustworthy? Well, that doesn't work either. One of the surest ways to destroy trust is by being distrusting. In the previous section we shared how this creates self-fulfilling prophecies. And in the section on perception we said that we see the world the way we are. So when we distrust others, this may be interpreted as us not being trustworthy ourselves.

Actually, it's even worse than that — we don't have to show distrust to damage trust. Simply talking about trust makes people suspicious! "You do trust me, don't you?" Again, we subconsciously pick up on the pattern that we expect to be trusted when we are honest, and we expect not to be trusted when we lie.

So where does that leave us? We wish to trust no more and no less than warranted. At the same time we also want the other party to trust us as much as possible. Finally, we often wish to build a relationship where a high level of trust *is* warranted. One approach is neatly captured in the Russian proverb: *Trust, but verify.* In other words, we want to appear trusting to the other party in order to build trust, and at the same time we carefully protect ourselves in case the other party turns out to be untrustworthy.

How to build trust

So how do we build trust? There are many ways. If we start with our definition that I see trust as my belief that you are looking out for me, then I will be looking for signals of that. That means for me to trust you I want to see that you care about me, and that you have your attention on me. So my trust in you may increase if I perceive you are:

- doing things for me, e.g. giving me concessions, helping me create value, or satisfying any of my other needs;

- trusting me with (perceived) privileged information and value;

- making me feel that I get preferential treatment; and

- signalling a shared and mutually beneficial future.

There are more insights to share on building trust. A useful analogy is view trust as a house of cards: difficult to build, but *very* easy to destroy. This is partially due to how differently we process positive and negative experiences. We typically need to observe a repeated pattern of positive experiences before we start trusting. In contrast, trust can get obliterated after just one bad experience.

Trust is generally built with baby steps; and by that I mean very slowly and in small increments. Typically we observe that the other party is consistently acting in accordance with what we expect of him or her. This makes the other party seem reliable. A reliable person's behaviour becomes predictable. And we feel we can trust someone if their positive behaviour is predictably consistent with our expectations.

This also makes trust building a slow exercise; we have to both be expected to do things and deliver on those expectations. Thus negotiators understand the opportunity and value in both making and keeping promises. And the time needed to build trust is yet another reason why negotiators capture the pre-negotiation time, avoid having deadlines, and instead seek to negotiate for more time.

These are good guidelines, but there are also many shortcuts available to us. One is to demonstrate trust. For instance, imagine that you are sitting in a café. A person walks up to you, says that he is going to the bathroom and wonders if you would be so kind as to mind his laptop until he comes back. Also imagine that an hour later, having returned the computer, you realise you need to go to the bathroom. Who will you most likely trust with *your* possessions? Chances are that you will pick the person who already has demonstrated that he trusts you!

We can demonstrate trust in several ways. One way (which unfortunately is also an established tactic by those who only develop trust for the purpose of manipulation in the division game) is to share information that we probably shouldn't, or that could hurt us. We may for instance share a secret, perhaps drawbacks of the product we are trying to sell, or weaknesses in our personality.

Another shortcut relies on bringing with us a reputation for being trustworthy. We tend to assume that a reputation conveyed by seemingly independent sources is an objective representation of a person's past behaviour. This is good news for ethical negotiators who practise maximisation, because by creating value for everyone we interact with, we will automatically enjoy a great reputation. We will therefore often find ourselves in front of new people who already trust us and are ready to explore mutually beneficial options!

After building a reputation as someone who is trustworthy, the next opportunity to build trust is often by building rapport. So the insights on building rapport will help us to build trust.

Let us also re-emphasise the importance of consistency for trust building. Consider your view of politicians who are consistent in their message, compared with politicians who have a history of changing their position on various issues. Whether or not changing position was actually the right thing to do (e.g. acknowledging a previous mistake as more information becomes available), the politician who changes his/her view can come across as less reliable, less predictable, and therefore less trustworthy.

And we have also discussed fairness. What is the impact on trust of feelings regarding fairness? Recall that in communal relationships we tend to include the other party's needs in our own; i.e. by satisfying the other party's needs *we* feel better. In other words, we look out for the other party. Thus communal relationships are more likely to be high-trusting relationships. In contrast, if I seek to distribute value unfairly among parties, then I signal that I don't actually include the other party's needs in mine, I don't look out for the other party, therefore I am not in a communal relationship. Thus how fairly I intend to distribute value signals what type of relationship I perceive us to have, and therefore what level of trust you can expect.

How to damage trust

Negotiators are not only concerned with how to build and improve trust. We are also concerned with not damaging trust. In addition to the strategies above, negotiators who want to avoid damaging trust may wish to ensure that they:

- avoid lying;

- avoid reneging on promises;

- avoid using threats or coercion;

- are not perceived to be two-faced;

- are not perceived to be inflexible; and

- do not take unilateral action that affect others.

Managing negotiations with low levels of trust

As negotiators we will sometimes find ourselves in circumstances where we fail to or simply don't have time to build trust. After we make a mental note of reflecting on how we ended up here in order to avoid it in the future, we'll have to consider other options.

One option can be derived from our understanding that the need for trust increases when uncertainty increases. The need for trust increases when our control over outcomes decreases. Thus one approach for dealing with low-trust negotiations is to reduce the need for trust. For example if the US government was worried that BP would go under or renege on their commitment to compensate those affected by the Deepwater Horizon oil spill in the Gulf of Mexico, then having BP allocate a larger than expected amount of funds in an escrow account could have alleviated some of the need for trust.

Another option is to instead strengthen the interdependence among parties. While interdependence is not a substitute for trust, it can in some situations make parties realise that they are better off cooperating.

An alternative approach for dealing with low-trust relationships is to analyse why people defect or transgress. Typically, it is either because:

- the offending party thinks the transgression will not be noticed; or

- the offending party thinks the transgression will not be punished.

To deal with this we can set up mechanisms for increasing the visibility of transgressions. We can also attach incentives to discourage cheating before it occurs, or punish cheating after it occurs.

While this book has a Western bias, it is important to acknowledge that some insights are very contextual and based on culture. Trust is one of these. For instance, if negotiating with a party in Mainland China, it serves us well to realise that trust will typically not be built during the business relationship. In fact, trust is often a pre-requisite to negotiating business in the first place. To this end, trust tends to be conveyed through personal connections — by someone who can vouch for us.

Can there be too much trust?

Yes and no. The problem is not with trust itself. If I trust you completely, and if it is warranted that I trust you completely, then this is very desirable and can enable the processes for value creation.

Rather, what we want to look out for is the risk that I don't just trust that you have my best in mind, but that I also trust that you *understand me*. If I assume understanding, and as a result I become complacent in my communication with you, then we are going to have misunderstandings. These will lead to diverging expectations, which can cause surprises. And as we'll see in the next section, this can damage trust.

MANAGE EXPECTATIONS

Don't create surprises

Expectations are related to the topic of perception, but we have chosen to cover it here after the issue of trust.

So where do my expectations come from? Well, I expect that you will do something based on a number of things:

- what you said you would do;

- what I have observed you do in the past;

- what I would do in your shoes;

- my beliefs regarding what would be the appropriate thing to do;

- what I fear you might do; and/or

- anything else!

Let's for now just note that our expectations may be shaped by pretty much anything, and that they are not necessarily accurate. So what happens when our expectations are not met — when something unexpected happens? We are surprised. Is this good or bad? Do you like surprises? I imagine you like the positive ones, and not so much the negative!

We have seen that if a surprise is caused by the other person acting inconsistently with what he or she promised, trust will be damaged. While the other party may have had a good reason for acting inconsistently (e.g. due to circumstances outside of his or her control) and there is no reason for trust to be damaged, it nevertheless will be.

In fact, no matter how we formed our expectations of the other party, if reality doesn't pan out in accordance with *our* expectations, there is a risk that we will still feel less trust towards the other party. Remember how we said meeting expectations leads to reliability, which leads to predictability, which can lead to trust (if the behaviour towards us is predictably positive)? Well, any surprise means that expectations weren't met and we can therefore perceive reduced reliability, reduced predictability, and therefore also reduced trust.

Also remember how we in early sections of the book discussed that we often assume intent based on the impact on us. Specifically, every undesirable surprise presents the receiving party with a choice: should I assume good intent, or should I assume bad intent?

Given the potentially volatile outcomes of surprises, negotiators are therefore well advised to minimise them. We achieve this by managing expectations through redundantly explicit communication. As skilled negotiators we will constantly be on the lookout for any point where either party's expectations might diverge. At that point we clarify expectations by disclosing ours and asking the other party to reciprocate.

We can also move away from intervention and towards prevention, and realise that our behaviour can be the source of others' expectations of us. Therefore we need be very deliberate in what we say and how we act as negotiators, to ensure that we do not cause unintended expectations in the minds of others.

This insight will propagate through everything we do in negotiation. Imagine that we just left our first meeting with the other party. At the end of the meeting we agreed to meet again next week and continue where we left off. But instead of pressing the pause button for a week, our team eagerly starts thinking about options. Miraculously we come up with a fantastic option that we just *know* the other party will love. To be extra prepared we invest time in finding numbers and figures to support our case.

We begin our next meeting with the other party by announcing this great mutually beneficial outcome! How will they react? Well, perhaps they love the idea and just say "yes". However, there is also a real risk that they will feel surprised that all this work was done without their involvement. They may focus more on the fact that we didn't do what we agreed, and may perceive that we made a unilateral decision to go down a certain path. The surprise provided the other party with a choice, and they chose to assume bad intent.

In this scenario we would be well advised to consider ways to reduce the surprise.

- Inform the other party of what we're doing.

- Consult with the other party to let them share their view.

- Involve the other party in the process, e.g. by scheduling an earlier meeting, or inviting at least one of their team members to join us.

- Still do the preparation, but rather than dumping all of this on the other party, use a more indirect strategy for building commitment. E.g. we could in the meeting guide the other party to come up with the option that we already have in mind.

Investigate surprises

The other party is not the only one who experiences surprises in a negotiation. We will time and time again feel that reality does not pan out the way we expected. So what do we do? The first thing we need to do is remember to strictly observe, and avoid adding pollution from interpretation, adding meaning, assuming intent, transference, hallucination, assumptions, beliefs, opinions, judgements or emotions. We then need to consider where our expectations come from. Is the other party acting inconsistently with what he or she promised, or inconsistently with our assumptions?

We may also want to verify that we understand the other party's expectations. Diverging expectations may simply be the symptom of another deeper difference in understanding. For instance, say we negotiate with a business owner who has told us what he wants. We work diligently to come up with a solution that provides what he asked for, but we get surprised when he *still* doesn't accept the solution. There may be several reasons for this, and we need to *investigate* further before we can make *any judgement whatsoever*.

- He may genuinely have poor awareness of what his needs are, and he is developing his understanding of what he wants based on what we offer.

- He may have deliberately withheld information or given misinformation on what he really wants, and if we create a solution in response it will not be of interest to him.

- He may be trying to use tactics from the divisional game to manipulate us into giving him concessions, e.g. by appearing uninterested in our proposed solution.

Expectations and anticipation

Do you know anyone in your life who you would describe as a pessimist? Someone who always manages to look at the glass half-empty? Or even three-quarters empty?

Why are some people like this? One explanation has to do with expectations. If we set really high expectations, e.g. that we will ace the exam or get that large end-of-year bonus, then we might get disappointed! We are disappointed when reality pans out worse than our expectations.

Some of us attach so much pain to the feeling of disappointment that we manipulate our expectations. We reason that if our expectations are low enough then we won't feel disappointment in the future. Hey, if expectations are sufficiently low enough then maybe we'll even get positively surprised (and we do like *positive* surprises).

So what does this have to do with negotiation? We have already mentioned that if we look for something (e.g. value) then we are more likely to find it. This is partially because we will ask ourselves more constructive questions (e.g. "*How* can we create more value together?") that lead to ideas and actions for finding what we look for. Along the same line, if we set high expectations for what we want to achieve, then we are more likely to ask ourselves *how* can we achieve that, and our brain (or the other party's brain) is more likely to come up with an answer.

Yes, reality may pan out somewhere below our expectations, but our positive and proactive outlook is likely to ensure that we find, create and capitalise on more opportunities to create a better outcome than if we had set low expectations.

The fear of being negatively surprised also helps us understand why some people we negotiate with seem to be too focused on finding problems, and raising obstacles. Often this merely signals that they can't yet see a clear path to our desired outcome, and prefer to exit the process early rather than experiencing failure, disappointment and regret down the line. This also helps explain why we prematurely evaluate options and proposed solutions.

As indicated in the durability bias we can *now* anticipate the feelings associated with the outcomes we expect in the future. This means that simply setting expectations of a great future outcome can immediately make us feel better! This then ties nicely back to why we would want to discuss long-term, mutually beneficial outcomes with the other party early on in the negotiation: it can make both parties excited about working towards those outcomes.

As with any decision in negotiation, we need to consider risks and rewards. In this case, we would compare the benefit of aligning two parties to cooperate and play integration or maximisation throughout the negotiation to create more value, versus the risk of in the end not getting everything we envisioned and therefore potentially damaging trust, commitment and satisfaction.

Self-fulfilling prophecies

We have discussed how our (and the other party's) behaviour shapes expectations. This also works in reverse, where we may intentionally or inadvertently create behaviour in the other party through our expectations.

Introducing a person to a group as funny will influence people to treat this person as funny. Conversely, introducing another person as boring will influence people to treat that person as boring. This will in turn make it very easy for the first person to be funny, and very difficult for the second person to get any rapport going.

If this sounds far-fetched…

A: Why are you angry?

B: I'm not angry.

A: Yes you are, I can tell when you're angry.

B: I'm not angry.

A: Stop pretending and be honest with me.

B: I'M NOT ANGRY!

Unbeknownst to ourselves, we often set things up so that it becomes difficult for the other person to react in any other way than we expect. The way we treat the other person creates a predictable reaction that does not represent how they normally respond, but we of course extrapolate and feel that our worst expectations of have been confirmed.

Interestingly, people have a strong need to act consistently with our positive expectations of them, and act contrary to any negative expectations. Try this next time you have dinner out in a group. Describe one of your friends as a generous tipper, and see if that person feels an urge to tip more than he or she usually does. Then describe another person as a stingy tipper, and see if that person *also* feels an urge to tip more than usual.

Realising that people feel a need to live up to positive expectations of them, we may very well want to begin our negotiations with sharing some positive expectations of the other party, e.g.: "I have heard great things about you, particularly that you are one of those pleasant-to-work-with collaborators who is really good at finding value-creation opportunities."

The fact that people feel a need to disprove negative expectations of them means we could also try the reverse. However, sharing negative expectations tends to not go down too well, and may damage the relationship, and is likely to introduce the other party's ego as part of the negotiation.

The key lesson here is that our expectations of others shape their behaviour. Positive expectations of others create the most conducive circumstances for others to act consistently with those expectations. Conversely, walking into a negotiation expecting or fearing the worst of the other party is likely to make those expectations and fears a reality.

Expect expectations to diverge

Expectations are not static. While we may go to great lengths to align them, our behaviour in the next minute can cause the other party to adjust their expectations. Skilled negotiators appreciate the importance of checking and aligning expectations repeatedly throughout the negotiation process. This is part of being redundantly explicit.

7

COMMUNICATE LIKE A NEGOTIATOR

——— —

Communication is a cornerstone of the negotiation process. Communication is the main tool through which we apply all the insights in this book. We use communication to show empathy, build rapport, build relationships, ensure understanding, clarify perceptions and expectations, discover needs, discuss options, and more.

We also acknowledge that on autopilot, we don't communicate as clearly or effectively as we would like to believe. In fact, the majority of difficulties that we experience in interactions with others, and that we subsequently blame the other party for, will be related to how we communicate.

There are many excellent books on communication, so we will here focus on a handful of aspects that we feel are most critical to negotiation.

WITH WHOM?

Our effort is often focused on the communication (negotiation) with the other party. In the process we can neglect the necessary internal communication. Asking our stakeholders for input, involving them in our thinking, informing them of our strategy and the roles we expect them to take are all part of ensuring negotiation success.

It is interesting to note that police hostage negotiators, sometimes tasked with dealing with the least pleasant members of society, state that internal negotiations with supervisors, teams and stakeholders are more challenging than external negotiations with terrorists, armed perpetrators and hostage takers.

Commercial negotiators frequently observe the corresponding phenomenon in business.

OUR PREFERENCES FOR HOW TO THINK, ACT AND COMMUNICATE

How do we think? What does this have to do with communication? Well, how we think, how we perceive, how we communicate and how we behave are all connected. Specifically, the way we organise and process information in our minds tends to show up in the way we communicate. This insight then allows us to tailor our message to better fit with how the other party thinks. It also helps us match even more behaviours for improved rapport.

Single dimensions of how we think

We have shared that it is terribly complex to figure out "who a person is" and quite unreliable to try and extrapolate how a person with that profile would negotiate. In contrast, it is fairly easy to figure out the single dimension of whether a person e.g. prefers abstract to concrete communication, or prefers choice to direction. And we can immediately use such insights to close the gap between how people prefer to communicate, think and interact.

The following list[3] contains a number of attributes that we may wish to control | track | match | shift during our negotiations. Note that each pair are endpoints on a spectrum, and each party to the negotiation will have a preference of where on that spectrum they feel most comfortable.

- problem (undesired state) focus — outcome (desired state) focus
- avoid challenges — approach challenges
- diverge — converge
- compete — cooperate
- short term — long term
- concise — verbose
- slow — fast
- random — sequential
- static — dynamic
- reactive — proactive
- either/or — both/and
- analogue (continuum) — digital (binary)
- visual — auditory — kinaesthetic
- past — present — future
- logic — non logic
- things — people
- similarities — differences
- internal locus of control — external locus of control
- recall — construct
- whole — parts
- concrete — abstract
- why — what — how — who

- choice — direction

- risk of failure — probability of success

- fast/short path to conclusions — slow/long path to conclusions

Negotiators who have educated their autopilot to match all these dimensions with the other party can control | track | match | shift with little conscious effort. However, until we reach unconscious competence, negotiators are well advised to focus on the one or two dimensions that most significantly contribute to pollution and friction in the current interaction. These dimensions will be the ones where there is the biggest gap between our preferences and those of the other party.

Specifically, a common challenge for skilled negotiators is that we recognise patterns in negotiations that can allow us to identify mutually beneficial outcomes much earlier than the other party does. This has nothing to do with intelligence, but everything to do with insight about the process. Nevertheless, the skilled negotiator will often choose to hold back and match the speed with which the other party is moving towards an outcome. If we move too quickly we may be met with resistance instead of cooperation.

We can pick up indicators of how people think simply through observation. I recently sat on a bus, which took a surprising turn down a wrong street. The driver corrected the action, but within five minutes took another wrong turn. Now stuck on small winding roads, it would take him twenty-five minutes to get back to the location where the wrong turn was made. During this entire episode I observed the passengers' behaviours and took notes for my book (after calling and rescheduling my meeting). What I observed were two distinct groups forming on the bus. In the group next to me, every single sentence uttered during the half an hour was problem focused.

- "Hmpf, I'm going to miss my appointment!"

- "Pfft, this is what happens when you have foreigners drive the bus!"

- "Hmpf…"

- "Mutter…mutter… mutter…"

- "Jesus, this is not the right way!"

- "Sigh!"

- "Where…is…he…going?!"

This group of people immediately built great rapport with each other. And that is completely understandable: they subconsciously realised that their thinking style with its focus on problems was matching. Soon they also started matching each other's tonality, length of sentences, posture, head movements, eye contact and gestures.

Another group formed in the front of the bus. Individuals in this group also built great rapport with each other by trying to solve the problem. For the entire twenty-five minutes this group guided the bus driver back on track. And once back on the main route, this group kept advising the driver for another thirty minutes to prevent the problem from happening again!

People in both groups really seemed to like their group members, but there was no communication between the groups. I could even detect that at least one of the groups (the solution-oriented one) found the other group (the problem-focused one) increasingly annoying and unconstructive.

In summary, the way we think is reflected in aspects of how we communicate and how we behave. Individual traits are often readily observable and we can match them for increased rapport and understanding. Should the negotiation require it, once we are in rapport we can influence the other party to shift how they think, communicate and behave.

Our communication needs

I had been interacting with two experts in the venture capital field. Each time I met up with either one of them individually, that person would quite forcefully dictate how he wanted the conversation to look. Specifically, they both habitually interrupted me while I was sharing my view, and threw me very specific instructions regarding what they wanted to hear. These conversations felt very unpleasant.

+ Rapport was repeatedly broken.

+ I was repeatedly interrupted.

+ I didn't feel that I got a chance to share what I wanted to share.

+ I didn't feel that I had a say in how the conversation should look.

+ I felt there was an underlying assumption that they were more senior, or smarter, or more important than me.

+ I did not feel acknowledged.

But in both cases it was clear to me what was happening: both individuals organised information in a certain way in their brains, and they wanted to get the information in a format that could easily fit within their existing representation. They were also time conscious, and wanted to have the dialogue take as little time as possible. Because of the way their minds worked, they were also constantly thinking three steps ahead, guessing or assuming what I would say next. Aspects of communication such as eye contact, respectful language, acknowledgement, or humour were of less importance to them — it was all about reaching outcomes efficiently and effectively.

How do I know this? I applied the insights in the previous sections. It was particularly easy because my autopilot was programmed similarly to theirs before I became a negotiator. I could completely relate to what they wanted. So as a negotiator I adjusted my communication style to fit with what they preferred, and rapport immediately picked up. At this point in the interaction, having rapport was more important for me than having information delivered in the way that was easiest for me to process.

A few weeks later all three of us met for the first time, and communication completely broke down again. Specifically, communication between the two of them broke down. Each ended up visibly angry with the other, because they were both so used to dictating to other people how they wanted information to be presented. The entire conversation was filled with variations on the following dialogue.

A: *So can you tell me the three things that you tried?*

B: *Actually, for you to understand better, I think it is better if I start with the background.*

A: *No, I'm not interested in that, just tell me if any of the options will work!*

B: *It is not that simple! I need to give you the entire picture!*

Did this communication breakdown have anything to do with the content of the negotiation? No. It was all in the process, and specifically the inability of parties to adapt their preferred communication process to the current situation.

We all have communication needs. Some of us use short sentences, others long. Some of us vary our tonality, use gestures, keep eye contact, touch the other party, and nod our heads to demonstrate that we're listening. Other people are rather undemonstrative. Some of us need to start with the big picture, others feel uncomfortable if they don't know the detail. The technique of control | track | match | shift applies as much to communication as to the other concepts in this book.

And these communication needs will change based on the situation. For instance, some of us may find it very easy to be accommodating, and have total focus on the other person in our relationship when we experience no external stress. But once we feel overloaded, or are up against a deadline, our inner task-completion-robot (or autopilot) kicks in and our conversation might become more harsh, firm, concise and dispassionate.

If people around us don't understand the cause for that change in our behaviour, they might assume that this is who we are all the time, or that something they did caused this change in us. And if other people can jump to conclusions and make incorrect assumptions about us, then it is likely that we may be guilty of making the same incorrect assumption about others.

MEANS OF COMMUNICATION

We can unpack communication into several parts. A common breakdown identifies:

- words;

- voice variation — pitch, volume, pace, intonation, pauses, etc; and

- body language — gestures, posture, eye contact, pupil dilation, facial expressions, etc.

One of the most frequently quoted percentages in communication books and communication training suggests that communication is fifty-five per cent body language, thirty-eight per cent voice variation and seven per cent words. While I don't believe the original research by Albert Mehrabian is representative of real-world communication and negotiation, I do agree with the general insight that communication is much more complex than words themselves. And, I would like to suggest that we also communicate through:

- actions

- lack of action

- other people or the media

- affiliation

- use of props, drawing, music

- touch

- symbols such as emoticons

- use of time, e.g. time to respond, being on time, time of day

- appearance

- signalled importance, e.g. do we listen, do we bother to remember names or details

- proximity, angle, relative height of our bodies, seating arrangements, choice of venue

- movement, velocity, direction, acceleration

And, all of this is context dependent. Let me share an example. When my brother was growing up he collected Smurfs. Smurfs were tiny, blue fictional characters that spoke a language where many words had been replaced with "Smurf". An interesting exercise is to pick a context (e.g. a fight with your partner, or just after your partner gives you a nice present) and see if he or she can interpret a "Smurfed" sentence such as "You are the Smurfiest Smurf I have ever Smurfed!" It is surprising how often we can interpret that sentence as it was intended, despite the fact that all the key words are missing!

Each type of communication has advantages and disadvantages. Face to face makes it is easier to gauge responses to what we propose. We can get coaching without alerting the other party if communicating on the phone. It is easer to keep track of what is being communicated if everything is in writing. It is usually easier to say no or stall for time via non-real-time communication such as email. No channel is consistently the best one. Rather, the situational negotiator evaluates what is most appropriate given the current negotiation and current context.

Intentional | unintentional

If we are driving along the road and we see the car in front of us unexpectedly slow down and then swerve a bit, is that a form of communication? Yes! Is it an intentional message? Probably not. Does it still tell us that something may be going on in that car (e.g. the driver is on the phone, or reading the street directory, or suffering a heart attack)? Yes! Do we know what specifically is going on? No. Does it matter that we don't know? No, we can still take that communication to mean that we may want to keep our distance from that vehicle until we know more!

We communicate all the time. Regardless of whether or not that communication is intentional, it still influences.

Conscious | unconscious

When we communicate *consciously*, we tend to be in control of what to communicate, how to communicate, what to include and what to leave out. In contrast, we have little-to-no control over (and often no awareness of) what we communicate unconsciously. A very powerful exercise that will help you build self-awareness is to have someone film you while negotiating. I am confident that you will immediately identify at least ten behaviours that you weren't aware of, and would prefer to change. And that was my experience too. I believe the first words I uttered after seeing a recording of myself in the first negotiation course I ever attended were "Oh dear…"

As skilled negotiators we use our observation skills to pick up on *both* conscious and unconscious communication. When these are inconsistent (or incongruent), it serves us well to investigate why that is the case. It may for instance signal that the conscious communication we get is not complete and/or not truthful. And even if there is no intent behind some of a party's unconscious communication, it can still pollute the interaction by having an undesirable *impact* on the other party. E.g. our habit of fidgeting may suggest we are nervous or uncomfortable.

Constructive | unconstructive

Problems become easier to solve the better we understand them. And the more information we have, the better we understand the problem, right? Not necessarily. Some information will be helpful in shedding light on what is going on (cause, problem, symptoms, actions, reactions, consequences). But irrelevant and inaccurate information would pollute the process and obscure the real problem. Similarly, in negotiations, some communication will help us work towards an outcome, and other communication will detract from our objectives.

For instance, trying to establish oneself as being smarter, better or more experienced than the other party is rarely constructive. Likewise blame, accusations, threats, personal attacks, judgements, and divisive opinions only serve to pollute the process. As skilled negotiators we communicate well, we communicate a lot, and we also filter our communication to remove the pollution. Our guiding criterion for any communication is "Is what I'm about to do likely to help me get me what I want?"

Direct | indirect

When planning negotiations we are usually more skilled at identifying the direct communication required than we are the indirect. By *direct* we specifically mean that our communication is clearly directed towards a party we are trying to influence.

Indirect communication involves sending a message to an intermediate party with the intention that this message will reach another party. We may for instance communicate with a third party, who will in turn communicate with the other party ("target"). We may be explicit about asking this third party to forward the message. We may also elect to communicate with the third party with the expectation that the "gossip" will still reach the target. This can often be a useful channel of communication because we are not perceived to be pushing our agenda to the target.

Indirect communication may also be directed to a third party with the full expectation that the target will overhear the communication. This approach has been used in countless hostage negotiations, where messages have been seemingly sent to the public via media, with the full expectation that the perpetrators would be watching the news on TV. Again, this information is likely to come across as more credible because the target perceives they have overheard something not intended for them, and is therefore less likely to assume that the communication is a ruse or manipulation.

Body language

There are plenty of sources on this topic. Even such a seemingly minor gesture as shaking hands when greeting others could fill an entire book. And if we expand the topic to consider the norms and expectations of the different cultures on the planet, we could fill a small library. Here though is a brief overview.

Many, but certainly not all, forms of non-verbal behaviour (gestures, postures, etc) are universal. A testament to this is the field of computer animation. By studying human behaviour, and attaching that behaviour to a cartoon of a sack of potatoes with eyes and eyebrows, an animator can fool (influence) a hundred per cent of the audience to perceive that the potato sack indeed comes to life. Even more astonishingly, the whole audience can often agree on what the character thinks or feels even if there is no speech. Yes, elements of body language can be that clear!

If I in a seminar demonstrate twenty different non-verbal behaviours, the participants can effortlessly interpret what they mean. Interestingly, despite already having the answers, clients consistently rate the insights on body language as one of the most important learning experiences. This is because, on autopilot during negotiations, we simply put our attention elsewhere, and what is right in front of our eyes suddenly becomes invisible. Remember that one of the first steps to becoming a negotiator is improving our awareness and attention.

The second insight on body language is that it contains a lot of noise. There are multiple reasons for why we would do a particular gesture or adopt a particular posture. We each also have our individual unique sets of non-verbal behaviours that we perform all the time. For instance, stroking our chin can be a sign of deliberation and deep thought…but recently I grew a beard and found myself stroking my chin all the time. Growing the beard didn't suddenly make me ponder life with any greater frequency, but it did change my default body language.

Negotiators are thus less concerned with specific behaviours, and more interested in groups or clusters of behaviours that all indicate the same emotion or thought process. We also look for surprises, specifically when a person's body language is different from what they normally do, and when a person's body language is different from what we would expect given the situation or what they just said.

For instance, if a person crosses her arms, then this is not a good signal for me to interpret — this might be a comfortable posture, or maybe she is feeling cold. But if she in response to what I said or did also crosses her legs, leans backwards, frowns, and faces side on, then I now have a group or cluster of indicators that each suggest that she probably didn't like what I said or did. Similarly, if someone says "No I'm not nervous" but keeps fidgeting with their pen, cufflinks, or touching their hands or legs, then what they say is incongruent with their body language, which could be read as anxiety.

In both of these scenarios the observed non-verbal behaviours are likely to provide negotiators with valuable information in addition to what is being said. Specifically, even though body language is filled with noise, it also has one striking benefit compared to verbal communication: it is notoriously difficult to credibly fake.

As professional poker players can attest, our pupils dilate significantly when we feel excited, no matter how much we try to conceal that fact. And if we fake one part of our body language (e.g. smiling), other parts will still be "honest" (e.g. the intensity of our gaze, the tension in our jaw, the rigidity of posture), and thus our resulting body language will be incongruent — and a giveaway for the careful observer.

INTENT | CONSTRUCTION | OBSERVATION | INTERPRETATION | IMPACT

In the section on intent | observation | impact we discussed how the sender only knows the intent, and the receiver only knows the impact of the communication. To get the entire picture the sender and receiver have to explicitly share the intent and the impact, respectively. We rarely do so. And as if this wasn't complex enough, we have also introduced the concept of conscious | unconscious communication. How do we marry the two concepts? If we were to visualise communication as a flow from the sender to the receiver, we would need to acknowledge that there are two communications in parallel. Let's break these two parallel communications into five steps, from sender to receiver.

First is the intended message. There is one message we intend consciously. There will also be separate messages that originate from our subconscious, e.g. if we lie, we may consciously want to craft a message that says: "I'm innocent!" Meanwhile our subconscious may send another message: "I am guilty", "I am uncomfortable with lying" or "There is something on my mind that I'm not sharing."

The second step is the construction of the message. We may consciously construct the words — "No, I did not have sexual relations with that woman" — and try to sound honest and confident. Meanwhile our subconscious may construct its own message, and this might surface as a trembling voice, our hands touching or holding onto our body, taking a step back, moving on the spot, or avoiding eye contact. Our subconscious may also alter the delivery of our conscious message by changing our tonality, making us try too hard to be perceived as credible, and so on ("I do like your new dress. I really do.").

The third step is where the receiver observes the message. The receiver will observe *both* the conscious and unconscious messages, but will not necessarily distinguish between the two.

In the fourth step the receiver will interpret the (combined conscious and unconscious) message(s), and add meaning. This process involves adding information, sometimes through logic, but also through assumptions, guesses, transference, hallucination, and so on. Often the receiver will not realise that this process is taking place, and will believe that he or she observed the interpreted message. This is a contributing factor to why even agreeing on what was actually said is often very hard.

In the fifth step there will be some form of emotional and cognitive impact on the receiver. Much of this may be completely unconscious. For example, few of us are trained interrogators, but we have been exposed to so many truths and lies that we have developed unconscious skill in recognising changes and patterns in people's behaviour when they lie. Specifically, when we spot incongruent messages we will often feel a loss of trust and rapport.

However, it is crucial that we realise that we do not have access to the facts about the sender's intent. Whether we guess consciously or unconsciously, we are likely to get it wrong.

In response to the impact on the receiver, there is usually some form of response or reaction. This is a reaction to the impact, and not a reaction to what was intended. If we are at the receiving end of communication then it serves us well to verify that the impact on us is consistent with what the sender intended before we react. Similarly, if the receiver's reactions surprise us given what we intended, then we do well to investigate what the other party understood and the impact on them.

If there is a disconnect — and it is very likely that there will be — then we may wish to walk through all five steps above together with the other party to identify where the message was first distorted and why. The appreciation we are building for how imprecise communication is should reinforce one of the key messages in this book — *it is not the other party's fault.*

QUESTIONS

The main insight about questions is that we learn more about the other party when we ask questions than when we make statements. Asking questions also make the other party talk, and we have shared why that is generally a good thing. Questions can also be used to stimulate thought and get the other party's brain to work towards solutions, options and possibilities — a process that is also likely to maximise commitment. And while statements provide the receiver with both the option to agree or disagree, carefully phrased questions can significantly limit the risk of disagreement.

Usually we don't disclose the reason behind asking a question, but that doesn't stop the listener from assuming. For instance, if during a job interview I ask the applicant "What do you want out of life?" this could be interpreted as:

- a sincere question aimed to see if the role will be right for the applicant;

- an accusation aimed at demonstrating that I think the applicant is not clear about his or her goals; or

- a sneaky way to uncover plans that don't suit me as an employer, such as travel or pregnancy.

If the listener doesn't ask me to clarify the purpose of the question, he or she will have to assume my intent. And we now know that as soon as someone assumes the wrong intent the conversation risks deteriorating and going off track. For instance, if my intention was the first one, and the applicant inferred the second one, then I will probably be negatively surprised by the applicant's defensiveness in answering the question. At this point our perceptions have diverged from reality and we may both experience a bad interview from this point on.

Changing our behaviour to using "good" questions and ceasing use of "bad" questions can be difficult. We have practised using our own style of questions for decades and now I'm asking you to re-wire the fundamentals of how you construct sentences — a skill that you use completely unconsciously most of the time. Don't worry if this takes a lot of practice, because it will.

Also take comfort in knowing that immediate benefits are available to negotiators by simply:

- using more questions and fewer statements;

- using more questions that lead to long and narrative answers, and fewer questions that lead to short answers such as "yes", "no", "five", or "blue";

- using more questions that have a low probability of disagreement, and fewer questions that cause disagreement;

- using more questions that are unambiguous and fewer questions that have multiple interpretations; and then …

- being quiet! Don't forget to give the other party a chance to answer the question. Specifically avoid the temptation to answer the question on behalf of the other party!

So how do we ask questions? There are many theories and approaches for this. We will here cover an approach inspired by Allan Parker, as it is the most precise that I have come across.

Broad WH questions

These are questions that start with "What" or "How". These questions typically give the other party maximum choice in how to answer, and the answers tend to be long, narrative in nature, and high in information. In general, the shorter our question the more choice and the longer the answer. The "What" question tends to lead to more abstract answers, and we use these to influence the other party's thinking. Conversely, asking "How" tends to lead to more concrete answers and we use these questions to influence the other party's behaviour. Broad WH questions are typically safer than other questions and have a low likelihood of resulting in disagreement. Note that neither question type is foolproof, and even Broad WH questions can lead to short answers and disagreement, e.g. "What are your plans?" may be met with "None of your business!"

Narrow WH questions

These include questions that start with "When", "Where", and "Who". This group also includes "How" followed by an adjective, e.g. "How specifically" or "How often". These questions tend to lead to shorter and more concrete answers. They have a slightly higher likelihood of resulting in disagreement. And they can be particularly useful in making very verbose communicators give shorter answers.

Alternative questions

Here we give the other party multiple options, e.g. "Do you prefer to be compensated with cash or shares?" The risk of disagreement increases as the other party may respond with, "Neither." The choice in how to answer these questions is reduced compared to the above questions. Specifically, this question assumes that trade-off has to be made, and parties may neglect the option of "Both". Note that asymmetry in the intonation or gestures we use when asking alternative questions may unintentionally disclose our preference for one of the alternatives.

Grammatical questions

These questions require a Yes or No answer. They typically begin with "Do you", "Shall we", "Can I", "Should you", "Must we", "Is it", "Have they", and so on. Because one of two expected answers is "No", which is the most competitive word in the English language, we have now dramatically increased the likelihood of disagreement and loss of rapport. In everyday conversations we often help each other out, so the question "Can you tell me about your holiday?" is likely to be met with a narrative response rather than "Yes". But as negotiators we wish to sharpen our skills so that they also work with those people who try to make our interactions difficult.

Negative grammatical questions

"Didn't you", "Haven't we", "Shouldn't you", "Can't I", "Don't you", "Isn't it". While these sound like questions, they are typically not. Rather they communicate an opinion, instruction or an accusation. These questions can also make it difficult to work out whether to answer Yes or No, particularly as the number of negations increase, e.g. "Didn't I tell you not to do that?" The meaning of a Yes or No answer is also culture dependent. E.g. answering "Yes" to the question "Don't you like mushrooms?" can, depending on culture, mean:

- "Yes, I do like mushrooms"; or

- "Yes, you are correct in that I don't like mushrooms."

Negative grammatical questions do not serve many useful functions in negotiation, and we tend to use these questions far too often. All we have to do is listen to a parent talking to their child ("Haven't we been over this before? Don't you know better than that?"), or listen to an antagonistic participant in a class or audience ("Isn't that incorrect? Couldn't that be done a different way?"), or listen to a prosecutor in court ("Isn't it true that you were at the scene of the crime?").

Tag questions

This is where a party shares a mix of statements and questions, and ends with one catchall question such as: "Do you agree?", "Don't you think?" or "Does that make sense?" Unless we agree (or disagree) with every single component question we don't want to answer that catchall question. An alternative response may be: "Which of those three questions do you prefer that I answer first?"

Complex questions

These come in many forms and are usually a mix of statements and questions. Often they are the symptom of hearing someone think out loud, and the last question may often be the question that the other party is interested in hearing an answer to. Again, a safe measure is to clarify specifically which question the other party wants answered: "That was too many questions for me to handle at once. Which one do you want me to answer first?"

Hypothetical questions

These take many forms. One is: "If the merger goes ahead, then what [could, might, do you suspect would] happen?" However, even Broad WH questions may become hypothetical, e.g.: "What could getting a redundancy package allow you to do?" Hypothetical questions trigger speculation and creativity, and are very powerful questions to use where we want divergent thinking in the negotiation. One such place is for developing options (whether options for content, any part of the process, or the relationship). Hypothetical questions can also be used to keep the conversation about potential and possibilities without the risk of suggestions being interpreted as firm commitments, e.g. "If we were able to give you everything you ask for, then what would you be able to do for us?" or "If you had a magic wand, then what would you change?"

Pre-framed questions

These are used to set the stage before asking a question. An example might be "Can I ask your permission to give you some feedback that you probably won't like?" Having permission can unlock many questions that would otherwise be too confrontational or risky.

Prosaic questions

These are actually statements, but they have the inflection of a question, e.g. "You don't like it?" These can be used to deliberately confuse the other party, as he or she can't be completely sure whether you've asked a question or made a statement. Again, there are cultural differences and in some languages these are more likely to be considered questions than in other languages.

Statements

Yes, some of us ask questions using statements: "I have a question: I don't understand your last point." Statements aren't necessarily bad, as long as they are focused on getting the other person to talk, e.g.: "Tell me more" or "Please help me understand how that could work."

Why questions

Why did we leave this one until last? Isn't "Why" a so-called open-ended question just like the Broad WH questions? Yes and no. The intention of asking why can be the same as asking "How come?" or "What would that give you?" However, the intention could also be: "Do you have a good reason or justification for asking that?" This can feel like an accusation or interrogation and may result in defensiveness. Because the listener doesn't know the intent of our question, it is possible that he or she will experience the unintended impact. This makes the "Why" question very risky.

The time focus of our questions

Are they focused on:

- the future, solutions, options, desired states; or

- the past, problems, constraints, undesired states?

Using past-oriented questions may unintentionally encourage the other party to come up with reasons, justifications and problems (confirmation bias) that all support why a proposal is not possible. By instead changing to future-oriented questions we can influence the other party to think of how it might be possible. For instance, after getting the response "I'm afraid I don't think that will be possible" to your request, do you follow up with:

- "Why not?"

- "What makes you say that?"

Or do you try:

- "What would have to change for you to believe it could possible?"

- "If you had to make it work, how would you go about it?"

- "What else could we try?"

- "If I told you we have already done it, how would that change your thinking?"

- "If it were possible, what would it allow you to do? If it were possible, how would you feel about it?"

What if they don't want to answer

Asking questions is no guarantee that the other party will answer, just as you may for strategic reasons decide not to answer one of theirs.

Of course, there are *many* reasons for asking questions, of which *one* is to get information. Let's say this is our sticking point — we want to find out about the other party's needs and they refuse to answer. An alternative option here is to simply tell them what we assume they think or want. People have a strong urge to not be misrepresented or misunderstood, so if we get it wrong they are likely to correct us.

And if we get it right then usually one of two things happen. Either the other party appreciates that we really understand them, or they may continue their stonewalling. However, usually their body language will give away how they feel about our guess.

If you are not yet convinced of the richness and value of non-verbal communication, then I recommend that you to try the following exercise with another person.

Ask them to close their eyes, and think of the saddest moment in their life. Ask them to explain that emotion to you, exactly where in their body it is located, how they would describe it, and so on. Try to have them relive that emotion. Note what happens to their posture, facial expressions, gestures, tonality, pace, volume, breathing pattern etc.

Then take a short break, do something else, then try the exercise again, this time asking the other party to think of the happiest moment in their life. Again, observe all the non-verbals which will be nothing like the non-verbals you observed the first time around.

LISTENING

We have shared that we communicate in multiple ways, not just in words. It follows from this that in order to listen we may wish to pay attention to all these modes of communication, not just words. The reader might struggle to believe this, but in our workshops, listening is often one of the major lessons for our participants. How can this be? It turns out that listening is surprisingly difficult. If you are unconvinced, then please try the following exercise with someone:

Pick a topic that you and another person strongly disagree on.

Let the other party state their view.

Let them talk uninterrupted for three minutes.

Then repeat back to them what they just said.

If they think you captured less than ninety-five per cent of what they said the restart the exercise from the beginning.

Once you can paraphrase back what you heard with ninety-

five per cent accuracy, switch roles so that you can state your
view uninterrupted for three minutes.

And continue the debate as per above...

When we run this exercise in our workshops we typically introduce it as a
debate, and it is not until after step three above that we inform the listener
that, rather than getting them to share their own view, they actually have
to repeat back what they heard. This turns out to be very difficult, because
while the other person is talking, we often get preoccupied with other
things.

- We evaluate whether we agree or disagree with what is being said.

- If we disagree we typically stop listening and start preparing our
  response instead.

Does this sound familiar? There are numerous other barriers to listening.
For instance, as previously mentioned we have a lot of spare mental
capacity while listening — this is because we can process words five times
faster than the average person speaks. We may use that capacity to start
our own internal dialogue. Add to this that many of us fear that if we listen
and understand we might get persuaded! And if we dislike the other party
then we may not want to hear what they have to say. We may also have
expectations of what we will (or want to) hear, and miss what doesn't fit
with those expectations. Sometimes we are too emotional. And sometimes
we aren't listening because we are busy guessing what will be said next. If
the speaker's style is too different from ours we may find it frustrating to
listen. These are all indicators of us being in first perceptual position.

Rather what we want to do is to step into second perceptual position.
Here we give our undivided attention to the other party: we hear what they
say, we try to understand what they mean, we try to feel what they feel, and
we notice the conscious and unconscious elements of the message. Crisis
negotiators rely heavily on active listening skills for this, and these skills

are just as useful for division, integration and maximisation.

Active listening skills (ALS)

When the other person speaks there are several things we can do to demonstrate that we are listening, and thereby improve the chances that we actually understand, and later remember, what the other party is trying to say. However, it is not sufficient to just understand. We also want to *demonstrate* that we listened, heard, understood, and that we at least partially agree — these are ways in which we help satisfy the other party's communication needs. And when interactions become contentious, the other party will typically not be prepared to listen to us until they are satisfied that we have listened to them.

Questions

The first component of active listening is the use of questions to get the other party to talk. In the process they vent emotions and disclose information. Here broad WH questions are good as we give minimal direction and expect long answers. Even narrow WH questions can be useful to demonstrate that we are listening attentively for details as well.

Minimal encouragers

We can utter small words to show that we are paying attention, e.g. "mm-hmm", "yes", "ah", "uh-huh". However, minimal encouragers need not be words; they also include eye contact, nodding of the head, raising of the eyebrows, hand gestures or changes of posture. Minimal encouragers allow us to demonstrate that we are listening without interrupting the flow of what the other party is telling us.

Mirroring/reflecting

Here we repeat the last word or last few words the other party said before stopping. So if the last spoken words were: "…and I'm basically fed up with people blaming me," then we might respond with: "Blaming you?" This technique encourages the other party to continue talking and give us more information, without us guiding the conversation. Note that our voice variation (e.g. change in tonality) can very subtly manipulate the direction of the next part of the conversation. We could repeat those few words with intonation that communicates surprise, disbelief, humour, etc.

Paraphrasing

Here we check that we understood what the other party just said. If we were just told: "They fired me for no reason! It's probably my manager's fault. She hates me. I'm sure this is all her doing!" then we might check our understanding by saying: "So your boss invented a reason to fire you because she doesn't like you?" We demonstrate that we listened, and we demonstrate that we are keen to ensure that we understood. A valuable by-product of paraphrasing is that the next words uttered by the other party will be agreement; we know they will agree with our message since it is actually *their* message.

Summarising

This is a similar concept to paraphrasing, but here we demonstrate that we have understood the key points of the entire conversation up to this point, not just the last thing that the other party said. Again, if we summarise correctly, we will be met with agreement.

Ask for correction

After summarising or paraphrasing, adding "Did I get that right?" or "Am I understanding so far?" demonstrates to the other party that we are not set in our view, and are very interested in ensuring that we have complete understanding.

Emotion labelling

This technique is used to show that we are really listening from the other party's perspective. "You sound quite sad..." or "I can see that you are upset and it is becoming clear to me why." We rarely share the spectrum of emotions that we are feeling, and if someone nevertheless understands how we are feeling then we perceive that they have really listened to us.

Note that if we as listeners make the emotions sound like a negative trait, this technique may backfire as the other party becomes defensive.

Effective pauses

Particularly in western cultures we tend to feel uncomfortable with silence. So simply being silent after the other party has finished speaking will encourage him or her to fill the silence and continue with conversation. And if the other party gives us a very short answer to one of our questions, we can use the pause to signal that we are waiting for more words. This can be used to encourage a two-way dialogue without explicitly stating it. Silence can also be used for effect just before or after we say something to make it appear more important.

This of course only works if the other party is uncomfortable with silence. If we find ourselves at the receiving end of dead silence we may simply call the tactic ("You seem very quiet", "I'm waiting for you to say something") or use the silence to direct our next question ("What are you thinking?").

I-words

When we give feedback to the other party we can reduce the risk of him or her feeling accused by phrasing the comment to be about us. Instead of saying, "You stress me out" an alternative is to use the XYZ technique: "When you do X (action), Y happens (effect), and as a result I feel Z (impact/reaction)." For example: "When you take longer than planned to get ready, we have less time to get to the destination, and as a result I'm starting to feel quite stressed."

As we are now aware of the concept of transference, we will realise that the link between the other person's action (X) and our impact/reaction (Z) may not be rational. If so then we may simply explain the transference instead (XZW): "When you do X (action), I react with Z (impact/reaction) because of W (explanation)". For example: "When you look at me that way (X), I feel uncomfortable (Z), because my last partner used that look when he/she accused me of something (W)."

Linking

Here we demonstrate that we are making an effort to gain more clarity about what the other party is saying. We do this by taking the last thing that was said and link that to something the other party said earlier. Not only did we listen, we are also actively trying to see how everything interrelates. Note that we are not linking to something that *we* said earlier, as that would be an indication of us being in first perceptual position. Rather the focus is squarely on the other party and his or her message from second perceptual position.

Reframing

This technique is often used if the other party is very emotional or for any other reason uses inflammatory, emotionally charged or otherwise unconstructive language. When we reframe we essentially paraphrase without the inflammatory language. If we hear "That guys is a @!#$%^, and his work is @#$@#", we may reframe that as: "So you really don't like him and you are not happy with the quality of his work?"

Taking notes

Writing down what is being said allows us to sit in complete silence without the risk of verbally directing the flow of conversation. Taking notes signals that we are taking in what is being said and that it is important enough to be documented. It also helps our own recollection as we are using all our perception channels (we listen to the words, use muscle motion to write them on paper, and we see what we wrote).

Note that we want to pay attention to the manner in which we take notes. The inferred message may be positive ("What you are saying is important and I don't want to forget.") or negative ("I'm going to document every point you say so that I can report you to the boss, or use it against you somehow."). Interestingly, if the other party sees our note taking as negative, it may have either positive or negative effects. A negative effect could be when the other party censors important information out of fear that it is being documented. A positive effect could be an emotional negotiator censoring his or her inflamed language (and thus making the process more constructive) out of fear that it is being documented.

Acknowledge merit in the other party's argument
This is an extremely powerful technique for building agreement without agreeing to something we don't agree with (phew!). "I see how that could work in some situations…", "I can see how that could make sense…", "I agree that I would be tempted to do the same if I were in your shoes…" or "That is a valid point…".

Precision listening skills
The section on perception equipped us with an appreciation for how the words we use can be, and often are, responsible for polluting the communication. The immediate result is often misunderstanding. Flow-on effects can include diverging expectation, damaged trust, disagreement, conflict, negative emotion, damaged relationship, and more.

So perhaps the way we communicate should then help us manage or even prevent that pollution. We can clean up our language when we speak, and as listeners we can help the other party improve the precision of his or hers.

Let us consider a situation where we are told: "Employee performance is poor; we need to fix things urgently!" This one sentence is figuratively a minefield that can trigger the need for us to ask a range of clarifying questions.

- Which employees specifically?

- What would be the three concrete things that make up the word "performance"?

- What specifically do you see, hear or feel to draw the conclusion "poor", and poor compared to what?

- Specifically who does the word "we" refer to?

- What options do you have in mind when you say "fix things"? What other options might there be? How will we know when things are fixed?

- What concrete numbers and units of time can we replace "urgently" with?

While it is clearly impractical for us to go to this level of precision listening for extended periods of time, we do want to get used to clearing up confusion when we spot it in order to prevent larger problems. There is certainly a trade-off between the benefit of ensuring understanding and the friction that the process adds. Specifically, where there has been an argument, misunderstanding, if we are taking instructions, or working under time pressure, the cost of *not* ensuring complete understanding may be prohibitive.

Help the other party use active listening skills

We have no way of automatically knowing what the other party understood from our message or what the resulting impact was on him or her. What we *can* do is to explicitly ask the other party to share their understanding, i.e. to use paraphrasing from active listening skills, as illustrated in the following example. I had ordered a replacement copy of my citizen certificate, and I called up the Department of Immigration to check the status on this. The following conversation took place.

OFFICER: *What is the reference number?*

FILIP: *I was not provided with one. However, I called the other day and your office said they could check the status of my request using just my personal details.*

OFFICER: *OK, what is your name?*

FILIP: *[aware that the spelling is unusual] F for Foxtrot, I for India, L for Lima, I for India, P for Papa.*

OFFICER: *I can't find you on the system. What is the reference number?*

FILIP: *I still don't have one, but since we found my request using my details last week, can we first verify that you got my name right?*

OFFICER: *I typed in your name. It didn't work so I need your reference number but you refuse to give it to me.*

Note the distortion of "need your reference number", and the accusation and attribution of intent by the word "refuse". Still, I continued trying to ensure she had my name right.

FILIP: *I would be very happy to provide a reference number, but unfortunately I was not given one when I lodged my request. Since the spelling of my name is unusual, can we please just verify that you got it right?*

OFFICER: *I got it right; it didn't work; and I need your reference number.*

FILIP: *We won't know that until you share with me what you typed into the system. Can you please repeat it back to me, just to double check?*

OFFICER: *The line isn't very good. Can you speak clearer?*

This was an even stronger indication that the message might be lost in translation. It also gave me an opportunity to avoid the defensiveness I was picking up on.

FILIP: *I am sorry the line is bad and I'm afraid I can't make up for this by speaking any clearer than I do now. However, a bad line makes it even more likely that my name didn't come across clearly. Can we please try one more time?*

OFFICER: *Fine, what is your name?*

FILIP: *[repeats spelling] …and can you please confirm what you heard?*

OFFICER: *[repeats spelling correctly]*

FILIP: *Yes that is correct. How did you go?*

OFFICER: *It worked. I see here that we have processed your request and sent the certificate to you by registered mail.*

FILIP: *Excellent. Thank you for your help and have a nice day.*

Negotiation often requires us to be patient, thorough and avoid reacting to unnecessary accusations and inflammatory language. Fortunately negotiation also improves our ability to reach our outcomes. So being patient, thorough and non-defensive is a small price to pay.

Role of the listener

What do you assume your role is when you listen to your boss? To your partner? To your children? What role do they assume when they listen to you? Here are just a few roles that people assume:

- to understand
- to interpret
- to advise
- to probe
- to disagree
- to agree
- to coach
- to be the victim
- to talk!

It turns out that as listeners we are often on autopilot here. We tend to predominantly use two or maybe three of these styles. We typically change our role based on who we are speaking to or other situational factors.

And while we as speakers actually have expectations of the role we want the listener to take on, we rarely share these expectations. The result is that the listener isn't listening the way we want them to, which creates friction and frustration — i.e. pollution.

Just imagine, what if you really want the listener to understand you but they insist on giving advice? Or imagine you were just fired and want the listener to be supportive, but instead they insist on explaining why such a decision might rationally make sense for the firing manager in the current economic climate.

These roles are very easy to get right as long as we make a conscious effort to clarify the roles. But we don't because we are on autopilot and it doesn't even cross our mind that this is important.

What are we listening for?

Where to begin? We may listen for:

- agreement

- needs

- signals of divergent or convergent thinking

- abstract or concrete language

- focus on past, present or future

- indicators that the other party is ready to look at options

- consistency and inconsistencies

- type of questions used

- congruence

- hidden agendas

- and more…

Particularly, when we listen we may wish to actively distinguish between "facts" and everything else. Now, after the section on perception, perhaps we could argue that there are no facts. Nevertheless, there is still value in identifying what is highly unlikely to be fact, e.g.:

- feelings
- assumptions
- expectations
- guesses
- perceptions
- opinions
- judgements

When any of these are introduced but remain unchallenged during the interaction, there is a risk that they will be perceived as facts. While we have emphasised the point of agreeing as much as we can, and particularly early on in the negotiation, we need to weigh up the risk of disagreeing with the risk of unchallenged perceptions turning into facts.

Of course, to challenge a statement does not necessarily need to come across as disagreement, but instead as a signal that we are genuinely listening and trying to understand. E.g. compare "That is incorrect" with "You mentioned that you pick up the kids from school every day. I'm trying to figure out what number I could put on that. Is it five times per week and fifty-two times per year? Or would there be any weeks during the year where this does not happen? School holidays? And are there days where your wife picks up the kids?"

NEGOTIATING FEEDBACK

We have included this topic because people rarely realise that giving feedback is just another negotiation. Specifically, when we receive feedback we may experience negative feelings that prevent us from taking the feedback on board. Usually our reaction is related to *how* feedback is given, rather than the underlying message. Thus we may wish to negotiate with people who give us feedback so that it is given in a manner that has the highest likelihood of leading to improvement. The insights in this section are of course equally valuable for giving and receiving feedback.

First things first.

- Do we have permission to give feedback?

- The right?

- Is it our responsibility?

- Are we qualified?

- Have we consciously assessed whether this is likely to result in the desired outcome?

- Have we consciously assessed the potential risks of going ahead?

After changing the words "give feedback" to "negotiate", we may wish to take a minute and let it dawn on us that these are important questions to ask ourselves before entering *any* negotiation!

The following recommendations for giving feedback will help to make it more effective in leading to our desired outcomes for improvement, and reduce the risk of defensiveness.

- Be specific and descriptive. As we discussed in the XYZ technique, describe what we observe, and the consequences (which may include the impact on us). Avoid polluting the feedback by trying to add meaning to what we observed.

- Acknowledge that the person receiving the feedback probably had positive intent. And if we don't understand the intent, then we can use broad WH questions to find out before giving our feedback.

- Negotiate the feedback. Give the other party the opportunity to explain their view. They may very well experience a crisis as a result of the feedback, so we need to let them feel understood.

◆ Note that the purpose of the feedback is for the other party to agree to take it on board and see a change in behaviour. If we don't care whether the other party accepts the feedback then we aren't giving feedback — we are just polluting the process with our opinions.

◆ Focus on desirable behaviours and states rather than undesirable behaviours and states.

◆ Demonstrate how easy it is to take feedback by asking for it yourself.

INCLUSIVE LANGUAGE

We have highlighted that it is important to consider not just our own point of view and our own needs. Rather we also wish to consider the other party, and ideally we want to consider all parties together.

Thus we recommend limiting the use of "I, me, mine" and instead replace that with "we, us, our" whenever we can. This is not just semantics. Changing from talking about my needs to our needs forces me to actually change into third perceptual position and think of what needs we have in common.

REDUNDANTLY EXPLICIT

Having read the section on perception, and read up to this point in the section on communication, I hope that the reader appreciates just how likely it is for the process to be polluted by misunderstandings and perceptions.

This is one reason why negotiators are typically excessively explicit in our communication in an effort to maximise clarity and understanding. We often say what we do, what we plan to do, what we have done, and what we have refrained from doing, even if it is obvious. Remember, prevention is often easier and cheaper than intervention, and we want to prevent pollution.

As a result of this approach, the other party is more likely to:

- understand our intent at all times, even if the impact on them is different — this will limit unnecessary pollution from accusations and judgements;

- understand our perspective, how we see the world, and what we want to achieve — this will help the other party help us get what we want; and

- agree on our shared history, the level of agreement, trust, the number of concessions, the relationship, etc. This will limit negative surprises and divergent expectations.

And as we mentioned in the section on past | present | future, reiterating and emphasising the good things we do increases the likelihood that they get noticed and remembered, which increases the likelihood of reciprocation.

CROSS-CULTURAL CONSIDERATIONS

So far we have assumed that the negotiators are at least speaking the same language as we are. But this is of course not always the case. Even people who have learned to speak other languages may still think in their native language. Thus our careful attention to specific words and the structure of sentences may get completely lost as the other party translates what we just said into another language before processing it. Essentially we have an interpreter involved in the negotiation, and we have little to no insight into what this interpreter does!

Negotiators who only speak one language often make the assumption that languages match perfectly, and that if we translate word for word from one language into another then the meaning is kept intact. Those of us who speak several languages know otherwise. Rather we may have to use completely different words and syntax in the other language to convey the same meaning, if conveying the same meaning is even possible!

We already know that a word in one language can have multiple and different meanings depending on the context. A different language suggests a different culture and therefore a different context. While both a Norwegian and an Italian may realise that their current context is one of *disagreement*, each party will live by very different cultural norms of how to communicate and behave in such a case.

To illustrate just what a minefield cross-cultural communication (and therefore cross-cultural negotiation) can be, let me share one negotiation I had with a Danish company.

One aspect of the content in this negotiation was related to the figure "86". During a two-month negotiation I spoke on the phone with four representatives of the company. With each person I verified that we were still in agreement on the critical figure "86". A month later I flew to Denmark to conclude the negotiation face to face. We were still in full agreement and I flew home. To my surprise the company sent me a draft agreement a few days later, and the agreement referred to the figure "68". I called the company, but no one on the Danish team seemed to understand the problem. They genuinely believed we had always discussed the figure "68".

So what had happened? As it turns out, in Danish you reverse the last two digits of numbers in speech, so one-thousand-two-hundred-and-thirty-four becomes one thousand-two-hundred-four-and-thirty. So when we had discussed "eighty-six" in English, each of the Danish negotiators had internally, and quite unintentionally, translated this to mean "eight-and-sixty", and written down "68" in their notes.

Cross-cultural considerations are not limited to how we communicate, but also affect other aspects such as beliefs and values, the process and the relationship. We will not attempt to summarise all those insights here. Needless to say, what is already a very complex topic becomes many times more complex once we account for cross-cultural aspects.

8

THERE ARE FOUR
WAYS TO NEGOTIATE

DIVISION

Finders keepers — losers weepers

This is the game that has the least potential to generate desired outcomes, and highest risk of generating a polluted negotiation process and undesirable outcomes. It is the game with the easiest rules and the most predictable outcomes, which also makes it the most common game. In fact, almost all commercial negotiations I have advised on followed the dynamics of this game at the stage when I was asked to join the process.

In division parties negotiate to reconcile two incompatible positions (claims, demands, opinions) by trying to get the other party to move. Negotiation books frequently use the expression "splitting the pie" to refer to the goal of the division game, i.e. to claim the largest slice for oneself. Thus division is a zero-sum game where one party's gain is the other party's loss. This game therefore predictably translates into competition among parties.

While economists may argue that competition leads to efficient markets, some negotiators would argue that competition incurs costs and creates waste in the system by allocating resources to fight each other rather than for the mutual benefit of parties. Thus competition often shrinks the available pie, resulting in less value being available to be divided among parties. Sometimes competition goes so far that the figurative pie disappears and becomes negative. At this point parties negotiate to minimise losses. Unfortunately this game often perpetuates the continued loss of value rather than putting an end to it.

For example, the competitive negotiation may drag out (and time sometimes equals money), it may damage relationships, and the posturing and demonstration of power may literally cost money. Just take again the example of a union on strike — the total amount of money available to share between the company and the workers will be smaller after the strike than before the strike. Similarly, a price war that erodes margins may lead to a situation where parties experience negative profit margins (i.e. every product or service sold costs more money than it sells for).

That doesn't sound very appealing, so why do we play this game? We play this game primarily because it's the one we've had the most experience with. We are victims of habit and may simply be on autopilot. We might also be driven by our sensitive egos and tell ourselves that we will win if we play. Our mindset and assumptions about what negotiation is and what it can do might be flawed. We might be aware of the other games but aren't convinced that they work. Or we lack the tools to play them. Or we have the desire and the tools to play the other games, but don't know how to change games if the other party insists on competing. Sadly we are also often (unintentionally) instructed by the organisations we work for to play this game. And often we are the instigators of the game by selfishly insisting on outcomes that won't work for the other party.

I would recommend minimising the number of occasions we play the division game. However, we still need to know the rules as the majority of negotiations start out this way. And if the other party insists on competing at all cost, then we may have to play division, and then we probably want to win. So what does the division game look like when played by skilled competitive negotiators?

Define issues

Single-issue negotiations frequently turn into the division game. Older texts on negotiation suggest having multiple issues as this increases the likelihood of a cooperative process.

A large number of issues is not a bad thing as it improves the liquidity of the process and allows mutually beneficial approaches such as chunking (described in the options toolbox). However, the value does not come from the number of issues, but rather from the portion of the negotiation that can be framed as shared and unique needs (see the game of integration). Fortunately, the process of identifying more issues, or breaking big issues into small ones, also tends to uncover shared and unique needs.

In the division process issues are usually traded for either money (e.g. we buy a product or service), or for another issue (e.g. we trade more flexible payment terms for longer delivery times). This is the first point where a negotiator playing the division game is tempted to behave unethically; if issues can be traded for each other, then we want to give away things we don't care about, in exchange for things we do care about. Thus competitive negotiators often overplay the value (to self or to the other party) of issues they give away. It is not uncommon for these negotiators to even invent fake issues and obstacles, simply so that they can be traded for something valuable in return.

Starting positions, on your marks, get set...go!

The way most of us negotiate is to first sit down and fairly superficially look at what we want. Then we come up with what seems like the most obvious option for how we could get that. Interestingly, this process is unlikely to be driven by what we really want, but rather by what we perceive to be *the best available deal.* Because we only come up with one option, and we only consider our perspective, and we don't do a very thorough job in analysing what is really important to us, we will call this option an inflexible position. In commercial negotiations, this position will often be at what we later refer to as the material level, i.e. hard, quantitative parameters such as price, number of units, and so on. Note that we at this point haven't given any thought as how to get the other party what they want, or how to create *more* of what we want.

The other party is likely to go through exactly the same process, and then of course arrives at a position that is attractive from his or her perspective only. Because neither party considers the other's needs when developing its own position, we are likely to end up with two incompatible positions. That usually means competition.

Our self-focus is but one of many reasons for incompatible positions. Recall how relative valuation suggests that we make the other party's position our referent point, e.g. by wanting a twenty per cent discount compared to whatever the other party wants. Setting our outcomes this way predictably results in incompatible positions, and therefore in competition.

And now the division game begins. Each party's desired position (frequently centred on price) can be placed on a single line or dimension: one party wants the agreed price to be high; the other party wants it to be low. Thus parties are working against each other and, as in war, they each try to get the other party to back down. The game ends either when the two parties' positions meet, or when the parties give up and there is no deal. It is important to note that sometimes, e.g. in prolonged conflicts between countries or groups of people, the game never ends and costs continue to be incurred as a result of the competition.

Negotiation range

So how do the parties' positions meet? Well, either one or both will have to move their positions towards the other. Giving something up that we want in order to make progress is called giving *concessions*. Because both parties expect to need to move their position by giving concessions, both parties will, prior to the negotiation starting, have established a range of agreeable outcomes, from the best possible outcome to the worst acceptable outcome.

Let's assume a seller of a non-differentiated product prices it at $2 million, but has the flexibility to reduce the price to $1.5 million. This is the seller's negotiation range. The buyer may hope to be able to get the product for $1 million, but is prepared to pay $1.7 million. This is the buyer's negotiation range. Theory says that each party hopes to start with their best possible outcome, and give concessions until they reach agreement or pass their worst acceptable outcome, whichever comes first.

A deal is theoretically only possible where the two negotiation ranges overlap, and in our example that is between $1.5 and $1.7 million. The traditional negotiation term for this is Zone Of Possible Agreement, or ZOPA. Now, in reality many of the things we negotiate do not have a clear value, so we cannot clearly define our negotiation range. Also, in reality our ego and emotions often override our calculations and we either grow or shrink our negotiation range in response to how the other party negotiates with us.

Few negotiators would disclose their negotiation range. If one negotiator were to disclose theirs (e.g. "I can pay between $5000 and $7000 for the car"), the other party would immediately take the most attractive number as an offer ("Great, so you say you can afford to pay $7000 for the car!"). So there is a disincentive to share information in the division game. The lack of available information often means there is no way of working out the ZOPA, making the concept of limited practical use to negotiators.

We can find a terrifying exception to this in the world of kidnappings. A disturbing trend is for kidnappers to first do their homework about potential hostages' net worth, e.g. by getting access to bank statements, tax returns, or estimating the value of physical assets. Kidnappers subsequently use this information to estimate the ZOPA, and adjust their choice of hostage and negotiation strategy accordingly.

What determines our worst acceptable position? If we have no alternatives to this negotiation, then we (as buyers) should be prepared to pay the amount that corresponds to the value of the product to us. So if we value a product at $1.3 million, then we should be prepared to pay just below $1.3 million. If the seller values keeping ownership of the product at $1.5 million then he or she should be prepared to sell for any amount above that. If there is no ZOPA, then there should not actually be a deal. This is important: "no deal" is often a completely valid outcome in negotiation! Because we have no way of knowing the other party's true negotiation range, the absence of a ZOPA may not become clear to us until hours, weeks or years into the negotiation.

If parties have attractive alternatives then these may override the parties' negotiation ranges in the current negotiation. In our example, if the buyer can get the same product for $1.1 million elsewhere, then the buyer has no financial reason to pay more in this negotiation. Likewise, if the seller has another buyer lined up who is prepared to pay $1.8 million, then the seller has no financial reason to accept anything less than $1.8 million in this negotiation. And if either party has such alternatives then there is no ZOPA, and no deal will be the outcome in this negotiation. (As a side note, in relation to ZOPA, after having trained Russians in negotiation I would like to emphasise how important it is to understand what acronyms mean in other languages before establishing the acronym...)

Note that this is the rational (and thus theoretical) view of how to play division. In reality, our perceptions and emotions will play the larger role in determining our negotiation range. If we are confident we'll open more aggressively and insist on getting a better outcome. If we feel unfairly treated then we may exit the negotiation well before our worst acceptable outcome. If we lack confidence or are dependent then we may revise our demands downwards to reduce the risk of losing the deal.

Furthermore, if we change to a different game we may find agreement that doesn't even exist on the straight line between the opening positions.

Predictable patterns of the game

Where do the two parties meet? If parties have equal power (and we'll discuss power later on), then parties are likely to meet near the middle of the two starting positions.

You might now have had a brilliant idea: "If the result ends up in the middle of the starting positions, then I can improve my outcomes by having a more extreme opening position!" That is true. And the other party will come to the same realisation. When we now revisit the game the midpoint remains unchanged, but both parties now have more extreme, or even unreasonable starting positions.

This tactic of having extreme opening positions introduces a couple of risks.

- If my opening position is too extreme, then I run the risk of the other party not taking me seriously and breaking off negotiations.

- I don't expect to get the opening position. But for it to work I have to credibly say that: "It's the best I can do." This is of course a complete lie. So I start the negotiation with a lie. Is that a good way to build trust and a relationship? No. Unfortunately this is just the beginning: if we wish to win a competitive division game, then we are incentivised to lie, manipulate, misrepresent, coerce, threaten and use tactics. And this isn't actually that surprising, because the game is all about me trying to get you to give up what you want, i.e. to get you to do what you don't want to do.

The example of equal power may be a bit academic, so let's see what happens when the parties have unequal power. In this case the outcome typically ends up near the more powerful party's opening position. This suggests that division is a power game where the more powerful party wins at the expense of the other party. A predictable dynamic in this game is therefore that parties seek to build their power as a means of dictating outcomes.

Power and alternatives

So how do we build power? As it turns out we can derive power from a number of sources within the content, process and relationship. Let us first revisit a source we have previously introduced, the BATNA.

If we have a transactional relationship and I have an attractive deal elsewhere, then I will only negotiate with you if that deal can be made more attractive for me. This puts all the pressure on you to accommodate me — if you don't, then I have no reason to stick around. I'll simply exit our negotiation and pursue my BATNA instead.

Many competitors would argue that the BATNA is the single most significant source of power in negotiations. I would say this depends on how we define power. Having a BATNA certainly means we can protect ourselves from a worse deal than our BATNA. But having a BATNA doesn't motivate the other party to give us (nor help us create) anything *more* than the BATNA.

Of course, unethical negotiators realise that they can pressure the other party to give away even more value by lying and creating a fictitious BATNA that is more attractive than their real BATNA. So in the division game we will see many threats and tactics related to the BATNA, e.g. "I have several people who are ready to take this deal if you don't."

Power and WATNA

When disclosed in a competitive negotiation, the BATNA effectively becomes a threat: "Give me what I want, or there will be no deal." If the other party has no attractive alternatives, then our BATNA may actually be the other party's WATNA. As soon as the competitive, and arguably unethical negotiator realises that the WATNA is yet another tool, he or she may have an incentive to introduce one in order to force the other party to give in.

Power and information

In the division game information also translates into power. Negotiators withhold information, they lie (i.e. intentionally omit, distort or generalise), and they try to tactically outmanoeuvre each other in a largely zero-sum game. If we don't have sufficient information, then we are limited to making assumptions based on our interaction with the other party. This makes it much easier for the other party to get away with misrepresenting what they want, their negotiation range, their BATNA, their timeline, and anything else.

Power and hard | soft styles

We can explain some power dynamics in the division game by identifying two common forms of behaviour among unskilled negotiators. These behaviours can be explained by revisiting the content | process | relationship split. On autopilot, many people will place disproportionate focus on claiming the content of the negotiation. In the process they will ignore the relationship, or worse, use it as a tool to manipulate outcomes. This is traditionally considered the "hard" style of negotiation.

Similarly, on autopilot, another portion of the population will place disproportionate focus on the health and harmony of the relationship. In the process they give up content in order to avoid confrontation, conflict, disagreement and other perceived threats to the relationship. This is traditionally considered the "soft" style of negotiation.

So what happens when a hard negotiator meets a soft negotiator? Typically the hard negotiator will leave with all the spoils as the soft negotiator gives away all the content in an attempt to not upset the relationship.

But when a hard negotiator meets another hard negotiator, the resulting power play often results in value destruction — either due to the costs associated with fighting each other, or because of parties walking away from a potential deal.

Note that we don't advocate either style, because both of them are the result of uneducated autopilots. Still, they are very common autopilots and you will come across both of these dynamics in your negotiations.

Power and dependence

It is also important for us to flag another major source of power, and that is the balance of how much the parties depend on each other, which is related to the concept of dependence that we introduced earlier. You have a power advantage if I need you more than you need me. Similarly, you may get a power advantage if I am bound by a contract, or if I owe you a debt. And if I don't have a BATNA but you do, then I might also depend on you.

One example is where I sell a product and you are the only potential buyer. If this example sounds unreasonable, just think of any product or service that would only be sold to the government in your country. Or perhaps we are discussing a romantic relationship and I perceive that you are the only person I want.

To enhance power parties have an incentive to lie and fake their level of power by pretending that they are not dependent on the other party. This may manifest as acting disinterestedly, or even threatening to walk away from the negotiation unless a concession can be made. These patterns are just as common in commercial negotiation as they are in international negotiations, political negotiations, hostage negotiations and even romantic relationship negotiations.

Also note that competitive negotiators may try to change the system to make you dependent on them. This is not a position we want to be in if the game is division. Thus one of the many risks that we want to consider as negotiators is the degree of dependence that might be created by any action or agreement.

Power and perception

In my seminars I usually link power and perception with the following scenario. Let's say that I'm the president of the United States, and I control the largest nuclear missile arsenal in the world with one big red button. Do I have power? It would certainly seem so.

Now, let's say that a rat has chewed the cable that connects the big red button to all the missiles, but I am unaware that this has happened. How much power do I have? The instinctive reaction might be that I must have less power now since I can't launch the missiles anymore. However, if I don't know this, and you don't know this, then we are not aware of any change to the previous scenario. Thus my power to affect your behaviour remains unchanged.

Let's take the example further. Now let's say that I as the president discover that the cable is broken, but I tell no one. How much power do I have? Since you are still not aware of any change, we could argue that you perceive that I have exactly the same amount of power as when the big red button was operational. And this is despite the fact that I know I can't use the power that you perceive.

This suggests that parties react to perceived power rather than actual power. It also suggests that one way of achieving power is through deception. There are several additional insights that make this even more interesting. The first is that the threat of using power can be *more* effective than actually using it. The other insight is that we are typically very flimsy in the manner in which we assess power. We will typically pick a few, very non-representative signals of the other party's power, and use that as the sole source for our assessment!

During the first lecture I ever gave at a university, I struggled to get the students to argue with me — and I thrive on healthy debates! When I asked the class why this was, I got the response: "Of course we are not going to argue with you. You are the lecturer and have all the answers." The debate I was looking for promptly started five seconds later, after I shared,

"What if I told you that two days ago I was *not* a lecturer?"

Note that the perception of power directly influences our expectations of outcomes. If I believe that you have a power advantage over me, then I will lower my expectations of getting what I want. Effectively I negotiate with myself before I negotiate with you! And if I perceive that I have a power advantage, then I may start negotiating very tough because I expect that you will give in. Of course, both parties may either overestimate or underestimate their relative power. One of many reasons why division games end up in deadlocks is because both parties overestimate their relative power.

Finally, we said that power is a perception. But what about real power? Surely being able to launch all those missiles is power? Or having a budget a hundred times larger than the other party in an IP lawsuit is power? Yes, that is true. And for that power to work it still has to be perceived. This was well captured in the film *Dr Strangelove*, in which the Soviet Union had developed a doomsday device that would automatically be triggered by any nuclear attack on their country. This is real power, but the doomsday device failed as a deterrent (i.e. failed to influence behaviour) because it was secret, and thus, in the movie, the Soviet Union's enemies did not perceive the power.

The temptation of power

Skilled negotiators understand the link between use of power and its negative by-products. Thus power-wielding negotiators typically signal a fundamental lack of understanding of the influencing process.

I recently caught up with my manager from a previous career a long time ago. He told me a story about getting in trouble at work because he had pulled rank in an argument, saying words to the effect of: "In the end I'm senior to you so we'll do it my way!"

When I raised the option of changing to one of the other negotiation games (neither of which are power based), he responded with: "What is the point of having power if I can't use it?" Well, I would suggest that if we have the power advantage, then at least we know that the other party is less likely to engage in a power battle with us. Hostage negotiators know this, and their way of summarising the concept is: "Don't give the bad guy a gun."

If we have a power advantage we could use it to win the division game, but typically we will get better outcomes by playing the other games. And I would suggest that getting a better outcome is more important than getting a chance to use power for the sake of it.

Also note that while perceived power can be used as a tool in the division game, sometimes it is simply a need that the other party (or we!) want satisfied. So in some situations we may even offer to help the other party build a perception of power as a means of satisfying his or her needs, particularly in the eyes of that party's stakeholders!

Concession strategies

Negotiators who specialise in the division game quickly realise that the pattern in which we give concessions signals how many more concessions we are prepared to give. Competitive negotiators therefore consciously manipulate their concessions pattern to give the illusion there won't be many more.

To illustrate this point, let's assume that you are placing a bid on the house that I'm selling. I have advertised it for $8 million (it's a nice house). You want to play the division game and decide that you want to get it for $7 million, so you start by giving me a low offer of $6.5 million. I immediately extend my hand to you and say: "Deal!"

What is the first thing that goes through your head? I'm going to guess either "What's wrong with the house?" or "I bet I could've got away with paying even less!"

A challenge in the division game is that the lack of credible information exchange means we don't know what the negotiation range of the other party is, so we're left having to guess. One signal we pick up on is how resistant the other party is to give the concession. The harder we have to work for a concession, and the longer it takes, the more we convince ourselves that we are approaching the other party's worst acceptable outcome. Obviously this can then be used as a deliberate tactic by dramatising our response when giving concessions.

Another signal we pick up on is the pattern of concessions. In the house example above, let's say my first concession was from $8 million to $7.5 million ($500,000 jump), and my second concession was from $7.5 million down to $7 million ($500,000 jump). What is your expectation? That I'll probably give you another few concessions!

But what if my first concession was from $8 million to $7.8 million ($200,000 jump), and my second concession was from $7.8 million to $7.75 million ($50,000 jump), and my next one was from $7.75 million down to $7.73 million ($20,000 jump). What is your expectation now? The successively smaller concessions probably signal to you that we are closing in on my walk-away point. Again, this pattern can be manipulated and used as a deliberate tactic.

When we discuss the other games we will suggest that the concessions game is not something we advise in negotiation. Think about it: how can you get what you want by giving it away? For the division game, we share the concept of concessions because it is a structural necessity. We need to stay aware of the various concession ploys that are used to manipulate us.

- The other party may use anger or emotional outbursts to elicit unilateral concessions from us (i.e. getting content in exchange for relationship).

- The other party may dig his or her heels in and wait for us to give a concession to get the negotiation moving (i.e. getting content in exchange for nothing, or in exchange for process).

- The other party may suggest other trades where he or she gets content in exchange for process, e.g. "We will only negotiate if we first get a particular concession."

- The other party may suggest trades where he or she gets something specific, but offers something vague that can be renegotiated at a later time.

- The other party may suggest trades where he or she gets something for certain, but we only get the possibility or promise of something.

- The other party may suggest trades where he or she gets something now with a promise to do something in return in the future.

- The other party may propose a false trade merely to get us to disclose what we are willing to give in return, and then withdraw the offer.

And when giving concessions there are a couple of things to keep in mind:

- We can take a page from the crisis negotiation game and ensure that we label and emphasise all the good deeds we do. This is to counter the risk that the other party will take our concession for granted as soon as it has been given (or later on even forget that we gave a concession).

- For a similar reason, avoid making concessions early. These will typically be taken for granted and usually don't count towards other demands later in the process.

- Offer resistance. We wish to discourage the other party from asking for more concessions. We thus make the process arduous, and request counter-concessions of equal or more value each time. Interestingly, this process will make the other party feel more responsibility for, more commitment to and more satisfaction with the outcome. Meanwhile we build up goodwill by demonstrating that we conceded from our initial demands — this can in turn create a need (desire or guilt) for the other party to reciprocate.

♦ Keep offers hypothetical as long as possible. E.g. rather than "I will give you this price if you offer me that delivery date?" we may say, "If I were to give you this price, then would you offer me this delivery date?"

In the division game both parties give concessions. Having a clear understanding of and strategy for how to give concessions reduces the likelihood that we on autopilot become victim to the other party's concessions strategy and tactics.

Power, manipulation and tactics

We've already started to see how the division game encourages the use of tricks and tactics. In competitive negotiation tactics are used to manipulate the game in either party's favour. Some tactics work by manipulating the perception of power, others hijack our autopilot by taking advantage of cognitive biases, mental traps and psychological needs. Such tactics are often examples of the unethical application of the fifth approach to influence: manipulation of perception and feelings.

Indiscriminate use of tactics makes the negotiation process less efficient. Parties use tactics to get an advantage in terms of claiming content from the other. However, as parties get more well versed in the use of tactics, and counter-tactics, the tactics cease to provide a benefit. The result is just a slower process, and extra verbose and detailed agreements to counter every possible tactic. Add to this that we don't like being manipulated, so the use of tactics can quite often damage rapport, trust and relationships.

But we need to be familiar with the tactics so that we can avoid being exploited by them. Here we introduce a few, and you are encouraged to familiarise yourself with the hundreds of common tactics that are discussed on the web. Often, simply being aware of the tactic is sufficient to neutralise its effect.

The hot potato

This is were we give the other party our problem and give the other party the responsibility of figuring out a solution, e.g. "I'm sorry, I know the price is $1200, but I only have $1000 with me and I'm only in town for a day. What can you do for me?"

Reopen previously agreed issues

This tactic can be applied a number of ways. Essentially it works by taking advantage of our psychological need to move things forwards. So when the other party threatens to go back and reopen all the work we put behind us, we may feel tempted to give away some content to avoid that ordeal. This is an example of exchanging process for content.

Withdraw offer

This is where the other party, after having made us an offer or after we have reached agreement, threatens to withdraw the offer unless we give some more content. The tactic works by first getting us to increase our attachment to the outcome (endowment effect, commitment bias) before suddenly changing our expectation from trying to get our best possible outcome to hoping to at least get our worst acceptable outcome: "Yes, we really tried to find a way to pay you your desired salary, but market conditions suddenly changed and now we don't even know if we can offer you a job at all."

Bait and switch

This powerful tactic involves the other party offering us something desirable, and later retracting this offer (with a credible excuse, e.g. due to "a miscalculation", to preserve the perception that intentions were good) and replacing it with a less desirable offer. The tactic works by getting us motivated for that initial deal. As we anticipate the deal, we will due to post-decision rationalisation come up with additional justifications for why we want the deal. Note that all of these justifications come from within ourselves, i.e. there's no opportunity for reactive devaluation to kick in. However, also note that we would not have come up with these justifications if it weren't for the initial fake offer!

This tactic often requires us first to invest considerable effort, which triggers our need to not leave empty handed (commitment bias, effort justification). So when a less desirable deal becomes available we are likely to tell ourselves that this deal is still good enough.

Secondhand-car dealers and retailers use this tactic frequently. Spot it the next time you travel to a store to buy an advertised product that "…just happens to be out of stock. But this other more expensive item is available!"

The nibble

Once we have negotiated everything and are ready to close the deal, the other party asks for just one last concession. For several reasons (including post-decision relief, and the contrast principle of the nibble being seemingly small in comparison to the entire deal) we agree and give a unilateral concession (content) for which we get nothing in return. Some negotiators use the nibble several times to make us move to their desired position in several mini-steps. See progressive entanglement for how a similar strategy can be used ethically.

The call girl principle

This tactic states that services are more valued before the service has been rendered, and suggests when we may want to have the price negotiation. Depending on whether we want a higher or lower price, if we buy services we may wish to discuss price afterwards, and if we sell services we may wish to agree price beforehand.

The add-on

This tactic can be used if we realise that our opening position was not ambitious enough, perhaps because the other party seems too eager to agree. Based on the insight that negotiations are never about price, but often about price for something in return we continue explaining our offer: "Of course, for that price you only get the bare bones of our services. The full suite will cost twice as much."

The takeaway

This is the opposite of the add-on. E.g. if we suggested way too high a price for our services, we can credibly reduce that price by saying: "Of course, that price includes all the bells and whistles that you probably don't need, so let's remove them from the offer. How much can you afford to pay?"

Defer to higher authority

This is a version of the classic good-cop/bad-cop tactic. In this instance the other party claims to want to help us out (good cop) but his hands are tied because of his boss or other stakeholder (bad cop), whom we'll of course never get to speak with.

Puppy dog close

Based on the endowment effect, this tactic exploits how we factor in our emotional attachment to things by getting us acquainted with the item we are considering to buy. For example, we may be able to take the cute puppy home for a few days, try the gym for a few weeks, or keep the luxury car for the weekend. Once we've experienced the pleasure of having the item or service we don't want to lose that feeling.

Artificial credibility

If we see something in writing we will find it more credible than if we're just told verbally. And if numbers are very exact, e.g. 81.37%, we find them more credible than nice even numbers, e.g. eighty per cent. The reason is that we assume the first number must be the result of a precise calculation, whereas the second looks estimated.

Confidence

One of the many shortcuts we take is to assume that confident people have a reason to be confident. Our thinking here is along the same lines: "The other party wouldn't sound this confident unless he or she knew what they were talking about." Similarly, when we are about to hear a supporting argument, we sometimes tune out and assume that the other person has done the thinking for us. This particularly applies to topics that we are uninterested in or unfamiliar with.

Door in the face

This tactic relies on the guilt indebtedness that is a result from cultural expectations of reciprocation. Here someone initially makes a big request they expect to have declined. When we do politely decline, that request is replaced with: "Oh, well can you at least agree to this much smaller request then." At this point we often (irrationally) feel that we owe the other party a request, and because the second request is smaller (but not necessarily small), we often go along.

Foot in the door

In this tactic the other party will first ask us for a small commitment that we are likely to agree to, and later ask us for a bigger commitment. Often we will feel a need to comply with this second request too. There are several reasons why this tends to work, including a feeling of guilt that we have set expectations that we have to live up to.

Making an offer

The main insight here is that the first party to make an offer (i.e. share their starting position) is likely to anchor the negotiation around a certain position or number. This is a reason to open first. The main drawback is that we typically don't know the other party's negotiation range, and therefore risk making an offer that is either too low (i.e. missing out on value) or too high (i.e. losing credibility or the effect of the anchor). Therefore the traditional recommendation is to open first if we are well informed about the content of the negotiation and the other party's willingness to pay.

Does this mean we let the other party open if we are not well informed? Unfortunately the answer is not that simple, and we need to consider more variables.

If the other party believes that they are in a very poor power position *and* they are unskilled negotiators, then chances are that they may pick an opening position close to their worst acceptable outcome. Under these circumstances we may want the other party to make the first offer.

But if the other party believes that they are in a strong power position, then they are likely to feel confident to open near their best possible outcome. Similarly, if they are skilled negotiators they will realise the importance of intentional anchoring, and are still likely to pick an aggressive opening position near their best possible outcome. If we suspect that the other party will open (and therefore anchor) aggressively, then we may prefer to make the first offer and at least anchor the negotiation in our favour.

This will of course involve the risk of opening too high or too low. To mitigate this risk we may wish to use the add-on/takeaway tactics.

Deadlock breaking

Because division offers few tools to resolve perceived conflicting issues, many of the deadlock-breaking techniques in the game are typically focused on avoiding talking about the deadlock and hoping that it will go away by changing the process, e.g. by:

- taking a break, going for a walk, changing the venue, changing the negotiators, etc;

- reiterating the amount of agreement to date, emphasising the momentum, and building momentum by moving to other issues;

- emphasising the stakes and the costs of not reaching agreement;

- developing own power, and reducing the other party's power in order to be able to dictate the outcome rather than negotiating; or

- using tactics, e.g. the hot potato where the other party is given the responsibility of resolving the deadlock.

Once we gain an appreciation of the other games we will discuss more effective forms of deadlock breaking. In fact, one of the most powerful tools for breaking deadlocks is to change the game! The term "deadlock" is unfortunate as it suggests there may be no way forwards. In the other games (integration, systems maximisation, crisis negotiation) we avoid the term and rather dispassionately view a deadlock (or disagreement) as a natural step in the process of finding mutually beneficial outcomes.

The first thing we need to acknowledge when encountering a deadlock in the competitive division game is the possibility that the deadlock could be an intentional tactic. Such a tactic would put pressure on us, as we may now fear losing the deal and may be tempted to give concessions in order to move the negotiation forwards. If this is the case then we deal with the deadlock like any tactic. For example, we may simply name the tactic, or note it but don't mention it, or call the bluff, or use another tactic in return.

It is also important to acknowledge that a deadlock may occur because there simply is no way for parties to agree, i.e. no ZOPA. If this is the case then parties may as well go their separate ways.

Expected outcomes

We said this game is predictable. So how does it end? Well, there are a number of options.

- Compromise. This is where the point of agreement lies somewhere between the two opening positions.

- Power win. This is where one party exerted enough power to force the other party to give in, either partially or completely.

- No deal. Parties may realise that there is no ZOPA. Or one party may be so unhappy with the relationship or process that they exit the negotiation due to this.

- Uncommitted agreement. This is where one party resents the process or relationship so much that they want to exit the negotiation, but have to accept due to lack of alternatives. But as soon as an alternative pops up, this party will abandon the current agreement.

- Escalation. This is where the negotiation stalls, and parties either escalate the power used, or move the negotiation up the chain to different negotiators and/or parties.

- Perpetual battle. Either parties refuse to move their positions or there is no ZOPA *but* parties don't have the option of walking away.

- Mutual destruction. This is where parties threaten with mutual destruction as a means of acquiring power. The hope is that the other party will give in first, which doesn't always happen.

It is important to reiterate that the incentive in the competitive division game is to use power, deceive the other party, withhold information, make a point of making the other party feel replaceable, and use (sometimes unethical) tricks and tactics to make the other party give us more of the pie.

None of these activities are good ways to build rapport, trust, understanding, agreement, commitment, relationships, value or satisfaction. Even in the most fair outcome, the compromise, both parties may resent having had to give away some of what they want.

Changing the game

If you and I are stuck in a competitive division game, then I may be able to change the game by demonstrating to you that we (or you) will be better off if we:

- first get agreement that what we are doing is not working — "Is this working for you? Are you getting what you want? Are you making money? Me neither!"; then

- open up the possibility of trying something else — "What would you suggest if you had a magic wand to change the process?" Or, "If I were to tell you that I have an idea for how both of us can get what we want (or more), would you be prepared to let me show you how?"

For example, if I'm running any type of membership organisation with fees (e.g. a gym, club or association), then rather than you and me haggling over the $80/month fee, what if *I* give *you* a $20/month commission on every new member you find me? The variations on this are endless.

Another approach is to demonstrate that you will be worse off if we don't change the game. This is an example of using power, not in order to win the division game, but instead to demonstrate that I would win (or the other party would lose) if we played it. Hostage negotiators use this approach by setting up their tactical team in parallel with the negotiation. This makes it increasingly undesirable to engage in a competitive division game with law enforcement, and in comparison dialogue seems rather attractive.

Though we don't have a tactical team to back us up in commercial negotiations, we can still draw on power from outlining consequences. If the other party is in a position to dictate the terms of the negotiation, we may choose to acknowledge that, *and* acknowledge the risks of coercing us. "I guess it is obvious that I have no choice but to agree to your terms in this negotiation, and I probably will. But I'm sharing this with you because I know what happens when I feel coerced. At some point I'll resent the deal, and I might renege what I agreed, or I might walk away all together. So for this deal to last in the long term, we probably have to review how to make the agreement feel fair for both of us."

When division can result in win/win

In its most basic form win/win is when parties get what they wanted out of the negotiation. Typically we don't see such outcomes from the division game. Rather we see compromises, where some or all parties feel that they missed out on something they wanted.

Because parties are typically self-focused and self-serving when they pick their desired outcomes, the game typically ends up looking like a tug of war. In some cases, as a result of luck, parties still feel that they got a win/win. In the division game, win/win outcomes thus occur despite the process, rather than because of the process.

One such circumstance is when a deal structurally has sufficient value for all. For example, two co-founders selling a company for $50,000 after ten years of operation may feel that going halves is a compromise because they each wanted much more. However, if the company sold for $2 billion, then half the pie amounting to $1 billion for each party may feel like win/win because of the enormous value in absolute terms. But finding ourselves in negotiations where excessive value is already visible on the table is the exception rather than the rule. Parties in the division game usually feel that an equal share of the available value is insufficient (either in absolute or relative terms), and therefore focus on claiming a greater-than-equal share.

Another circumstance where division can lead to win/win is where parties prefer completely unique parts of the pie. Let's say that my brother and I collectively inherit a house and a car, and I just want the car and my brother just wants the house. If we are honest about our preferences then agreement can be reached very quickly and we will both be very happy with the outcome. Win/win. But if we try to hide our true preferences as a competitive tactic, or we become greedy and try to claim all the value, then we risk polluting the process and we might not find the win/win outcome.

Finally, occasionally circumstances are such that a natural win/win appears, and we can't miss it regardless of how we negotiate. For example, let's say that you have a car for sale. The engine is broken but the chassis looks immaculate. You have a quote from a repair shop prepared to pay $2000 for the car to use it for spare parts. Thus the car is currently worth $2000 to you. Let's also say that the same car is worth $12,000 to me, because I need that exact model of car for a photo shoot today, and no one anywhere has one for hire. My challenge is that the only other cars of that model that have a new-looking chassis also have a working engine, and the cheapest advertised car costs $12,000. Thus a deal with any price that we agree on in the $2001 to $11,999 range would actually create more value than is available to either party today.

But these are all exceptions because parties (due to luck or circumstance) immediately identify that their desired outcomes are compatible. In contrast, the vast majority of situations where we observe parties in a division game, they perceive their desired outcomes to be incompatible, and therefore pollute the process with everything we've seen so far in the division game.

Fortunately, the games of integration and maximisation lend themselves more naturally to finding win/win outcomes, and beyond!

Blog entry: "Stubbornness, pride, and general pettiness in our negotiations"

Let me close the section on division with a blog entry that I wrote to illustrate that no matter how educated we are about negotiation, we risk falling back into bad habits and the unproductive divisional approach to negotiation on autopilot.

Let me first clarify two points.

- Yes, I am, in fact, a professional negotiator. Really.

- While I introduce four separate approaches to negotiation in my book, we all revert to the least productive approach from time to time; the one where parties seek to develop power in order to make the other give in.

Girlfriend: Can you please hold my bag for a second?

Negotiator: Sure.

Girlfriend: Ha! Now you have to carry it!

Negotiator: No, honey. You insist on bringing all this unnecessary stuff with you on our walks, so you carry the bag.

Girlfriend: Well I'm not going to carry it.

Negotiator: OK, I'll just leave it here on the ground then.

Girlfriend: Fine. Go ahead. I know you will break before I do.

This is ten pm at night. In the bag my girlfriend has her phone, money, keys, ID, (and probably two bricks, a tent, scuba diving gear, a coffee machine...). We start walking away. About fifty metres away I look over my shoulder to make sure the bag is still there. My girlfriend smiles. She smells victory: I'm too uncomfortable with the risk of someone stealing her bag. One hundred metres away. One hundred and fifty metres away. The bag is now a small dot in the distance. As we pass a man walking in the opposite direction, I seize my chance to influence my girlfriend.

Negotiator: Honey, doesn't he look a bit shady? I reckon he might steal your bag.

Girlfriend: I guess you better go get it then.

Damn. She countered my tactic. Very uncomfortable with the risk and stakes in this negotiation, and not being able to take my eyes off the bag, I stop walking.

Negotiator: OK, well I'm too uncomfortable with this. I'm not going to get your bag, but I will stay right here and watch out for anyone stealing it. You better hurry up and go get it before anyone else does.

Girlfriend: I'm not going to get it.

Negotiator: Hey, that car just made a U-turn and is pulling up next to your bag. They most definitely saw it.

No reaction from my girlfriend as she stands her ground. I start running towards the bag. Halfway there, red and blue lights start flashing from the dashboard, indicating that this is in fact an undercover police car. While running, I wave with both hands, signalling that it is my (girlfriend's) bag.

Police: [sternly] Is this your bag?

Negotiator: It's my girlfriend's bag.

Police: Why did she leave it here?

Negotiator: Because she is a stubborn, stubborn girl and she has to win.

Police: So why don't you carry it?

Negotiator: I can't give in. If I do this for her then she'll start making all the rules in the relationship.

At this point the two undercover police officers smile and give each other a knowing look. I tell myself that this is because they understand what I'm going through.

And then she arrives, walking slowly towards us. I recognise that smug grin. It now extends from ear to ear.

Girlfriend: I won!

Negotiator: No you didn't. I'm still not going to carry your bag. I was just not prepared to lose it to make a point. We both know that you will do anything to win. So I'm just going to sit here, next to the bag, until you pick it up.

Girlfriend: We'll be here for a while then.

The cops drive away. I feel good about giving them something to talk about on their otherwise uneventful night shift.

Negotiator: Just…pick…the…bag…up! I've had a long day and I'm tired.

At this point the negotiation changed from division to integration, where we seek to understand and satisfy the needs of both parties.

Girlfriend: Awww, yes you look very tired. Here, give me the bag and let's go.

On the walk home, it took all my willpower to not resort to telling her: "I won…"

INTEGRATION

The glass is neither half empty nor half full — it is always full because we need both air and water.

If division describes the process whereby I try to get you to give up what you want and instead agree with what I want, then integration describes how we seek to ensure that both of us get what we want. In integration parties will typically seek creative ways to agree on one mutually desired outcome.

Using our pie analogy, integration changes the game from focusing on the relative size of our slice, to focusing on getting each party the size and type of slice they want. Sticking with the analogy, this approach often involves rearranging the toppings (i.e. ensuring a more effective split of value according to parties' preferences) and making the pie bigger (expanding the scope of the negotiation to satisfy more needs and satisfying them better). Using negotiation terms, integration is a process of identifying and satisfying parties' needs.

Note that while it is easier to achieve integration if parties voluntarily collaborate, we can still play integration with parties who insist on competing with us. However, the latter approach requires more skill on our part, and fewer options for value creation will be available.

Discover needs

Participants in classes often ask for complex real-world examples. But when real examples are used I find that eager students of negotiation quickly lose track of the process and instead get drawn into discussing the content. So even with my Executive MBA participants, I introduce the process of integration with the simplest example I can think of.

Two people are sitting at opposite ends of a classroom. Jack sits in the back corner by the window, and Jill sits at the front of the room. Jill asks Jack to open the window. Jack wants it closed so he refuses. If they were to play the division game then the issue would be about the window; Jack's position would be *window closed*, Jill's position would be *window open*, and the likely compromise might be *window half open*. This outcome is not ideal for either party, and the other available outcomes are less desirable for at least one of the parties. But we want to play integration. So let us start by unpacking each party's needs.

What needs is Jack trying to satisfy by insisting on having the window closed?

- He wants the climate in the room to be comfortable.

- Because he recently had a chest infection he definitely does not want to sit in the draught.

- He does not want to miss out on anything covered in the lecture by wasting time arguing.

What needs is Jill trying to satisfy by insisting on having the window open?

- She also wants to focus on the class, but she can't because she is too warm.

- She is indifferent to sitting in the draught.

Let us also continue the car example from the closing section on *division*. Here the seller may want at least $2000 dollars for his car, but is happy to get more. But perhaps I, the photographer, have more needs.

- I want to pay less than $2000 dollars.

- I *only* want the car for the photo shoot.

- I do *not* want the hassle of getting the car to the photo shoot.

- I do *not* want the hassle of getting rid of the car after the photo shoot, and especially not the hassle of placing an ad to sell the car and spending weeks meeting tyre-kickers.

In the section on *needs* we will introduce a number of tools that help us to identify the large range of needs that we typically want satisfied. Many of these needs are universal and they only become important when they are *unsatisfied*. E.g. both Jack and Jill probably want to be treated with respect, feel good about themselves, feel included, feel acknowledged, come across well in the eyes of others, and feel that their opinions matter. But because none of those needs are presently unsatisfied, neither Jack nor Jill would consider them as relevant for this negotiation. But if any of these needs become unsatisfied as a result of the process or relationship, then they instantly become part of the desired outcome for the affected party or parties.

Categorise needs

To help us identify options later on, it is useful to categorise all the needs we have discovered into three different groups:

- shared

- unique

- perceived conflicting

Shared needs represent what both parties can agree on, and what both parties can get. Options that satisfy shared needs generate value for both parties, although parties might value those needs differently. In the case of Jack and Jill, both parties want a comfortable climate in the classroom so that they can focus on the lecture. That is instant agreement! In fact, shared needs are a great source of agreement and for mutually beneficial options, and are therefore a powerful way to build common ground.

Unique needs represent what a party wants that is irrelevant to the other party. Thus there is no competition and we should still be able to satisfy these needs. In the case of Jack and Jill, Jack specifically does not want to sit in the draught.

Unique needs are a great source of value creation in negotiation. They can be satisfied in a variety of ways, and we'll explore more in the options toolbox. We wish to emphasise that while your unique needs are irrelevant to me, there may be a cost or benefit for me associated with satisfying them for you. I may satisfy a unique need of yours that:

- brings greater benefit to me than you;

- brings me the same benefit;

- brings me some benefit;

- brings me no benefit but costs me nothing;

- costs me something;

- costs me the same as the benefit to you; or

- costs me more than the benefit to you.

Negotiators who use the trade strategy typically stop trading once parties can no longer identify additional trades that bring value to him- or herself. In contrast, negotiators who use the satisfy strategy attempt to find options for satisfying at least the first four types of unique needs, and all types if we can somehow get compensated for our incurred cost.

Perceived conflicting needs represent what can only be satisfied for one party at the expense of the other party. For instance, unless the negotiators in the division game immediately stumble upon agreement, their positions will be perceived conflicting. We intentionally use the word *perceived* to emphasise that in the majority of cases, conflicting needs can actually be reframed as either shared or unique. And if that can be done, then we also enable more options for satisfying these needs.

The remaining perceived conflicting needs that have not been reframed as shared or unique tend to be split among parties. Note that all the value created at this point can be accounted for in five groups.

- the value I get from having my unique needs satisfied

- the value I get from satisfying shared needs

- the perceived conflicting parts

- the value you get from satisfying shared needs

- the value you get from having your unique needs satisfied

In the division game the majority of the pie is typically perceived conflicting, and parties fight to get the largest share. In the integration or maximisation games the vast majority of value can be reframed as shared or unique, and the total value will be significantly more than the sum of the original conflicting value. This reduces both the *absolute* and *relative* size of the remaining conflicting value. It also reduces the *importance* of the remaining conflicting needs, and makes the task of dividing the conflicting value of less importance to the parties. Since the satisfy strategy usually results in one party getting disproportionally more value from unique needs, it is often seen as a fair argument for why the other party should get compensated with a bigger slice of the conflicting value. Both parties should be happy with this as they each get more value than was available by merely splitting the conflicting value. The value was created, and the size of the pie is now larger.

So how do we satisfy these needs once they are identified? We create options.

Invent options to satisfy needs

After I share Jack and Jill's negotiation with my students, I give the group forty-five seconds to shout out options that would satisfy both parties' needs. Usually I get about ten in that time.

- Jack and Jill could open the window and swap places.

- Jack could open the window and then move to a seat away from the window.

- Jill could take off her jumper or borrow a thinner jumper from someone else.

- They could ask for the air conditioning to be switched on.

- We could all move to a different lecture theatre with a more comfortable climate.

- We might be able to open another window that is further away from Jack.

- Perhaps we could open the door instead.

- Maybe we can get a portable fan and place it near Jill.

- Perhaps we could reschedule the lectures to the evenings when it is cooler.

- We could let Jack go home and rest, record the lecture, and email it to him.

Now, how many of these are better for both parties than the compromise of leaving the window half-open? And was it more difficult to follow this process? No, just different.

Let's also revisit the car example. What are some options for the two parties?

- The seller could lend the car to the photo shoot for a fee, and then sell the car to a repair shop for $2000.

- The seller could first sell the car to the photo shoot, and then offer to pick it up after the photo shoot to save the buyer from having to get rid of it, and then sell it again for $2000 to someone else.

- The seller could first sell the car to the photo shoot, and after the photo shoot offer his services to take care of the car and manage the sales process in exchange for a commission.

- The seller could offer to deliver the car to the photo shoot in exchange for a better price.

- The buyer may anticipate having to re-shoot the car so may offer to pay the owner $5000 to *keep* the car for another two years, but lend it to photo shoots as required. And afterwards the seller could still sell it to a repairer for $2000.

- The seller could first rent the car to the photo shoot, and then use the information from the buyer to realise that many other second-hand cars on the market have damaged chassis. He could then suggest to the owners of one of *them* that they use his chassis in exchange for a portion (if more than $2000) of the appreciated value of *their* cars when sold with a working engine *and* an immaculate chassis.

Options generation is the key to value creation. If we have performed the needs analysis well, then plenty of options will pop up with very little effort. Note that we list all options without evaluating them. But don't stop there! This is an exercise in creative thinking, thus we want to run with ideas and see where they may take us. If the biggest danger in needs analysis is not fully understanding needs, then the biggest danger in options generation is converging on a solution or an option too quickly.

Questions that help us stay in options generation mode are:

- "What if we tried _____?"

- "If we want the outcome to look like _____, how could we achieve that?"

- "If _____ happened, what would that allow us to do?"

- "What else could we try?"

Throughout the options generation process, keep the following points in mind.

- Emphasise agreement. And even when discussing points of disagreement, reiterate the parts we can agree on.

- Verify our understanding of needs. Throughout the process we will get clarity on assumptions we have made earlier. As we propose options that get rejected, we ask: "How come? What would make that option more attractive? What needs are not satisfied? What might happen if we accept this option?" Keep track of the unmet needs and modify the options to include and satisfy those needs.

- Create multiple options. And if the options are not satisfactory, then modify them.

- Accept all options. Do not evaluate at this point.

The options have a tendency to become more creative once we get going. This is a good thing. Many successful negotiations work because negotiators stick with this process until they identify options that both create value and are practical. And then negotiators will continue a bit further to see if the options can become even better.

Categorise options

In the options generation phase we consistently observe negotiators struggling with the instruction "Do not evaluate options yet!" Many of us fall victim to the temptation of stopping a particular train of thought before we waste too much time on something that we think will never give any results.

However, time and time again the most valuable options materialise from ideas that were not satisfactory in their first five, ten or even one hundred iterations. In every iteration negotiators think of new options, or build on, refine or combine existing options. This is not what we are used to doing, but if we think the way we've always done then we'll arrive at the same conclusions we've always reached.

When inventing options we also categorise them. For some reason people seem more comfortable coming up with crazy ideas if there is a box called *crazy ideas* on the table in front of them. Likewise, I find people more likely to come up with ideas that are too costly to be practical if there is a box for that too. And people feel more comfortable putting things in those boxes if they have already put a few backup options in the *realistic ideas* box. Now, the beautiful thing is that we can later ask ourselves, "How can we make that idea less costly?" or "What would have to change for that crazy idea to become more practical?" If we don't capture these ideas in the first place, then we effectively kill the proverbial seed before we know what the tree would have looked like.

The boxes I tend to use in options generation are:

- options for mutual gain (typically includes options that satisfy shared needs, or complementary sets of unique needs);

- options that can be satisfied for one party at no cost to the other party (unique needs);

- options that can be satisfied for one party at a small cost to the other party (unique needs);

- options that can be satisfied for one party at a prohibitive cost to the other party (unique needs); and

- options that are (presently) too crazy, too creative, or too impractical.

I repeatedly find that a major source of value creation can be traced back to options that were once placed in that last box.

Evaluate and select options

This is the best bad idea we have, sir
— *From the film Argo*

Ideally we find an option that satisfies all the needs of all parties. Let's emphasise that point; if there is one option that allows all parties to get everything they want then there is no need to enter the process of choosing from options. This is what we strive for.

However, sometimes we are not completely successful, and we might end up with some options that are better for one party, and some options that are better for the other party. Unskilled negotiators at this point run the risk of reverting to the division game by self-servingly pushing their desired option.

There is of course much more nuance to this insight. We may not like an option because:

- it is the best option we could find, but it still doesn't satisfy the needs we have shared that we want satisfied;

- we created an option to satisfy what we believe were our needs, but once we saw the option (and checked our gut reaction) we realised that we had additional needs were not being met by this option; or

- the option does satisfy our needs, but we are trying tactics from the division game, and are pretending that we don't like it in order to elicit more concessions from the other party as compensation for, what we argue, is an unfair outcome.

If we end up in the first scenario, then there is usually an indication that we either aren't playing the integration game sufficiently well, or that no perfect outcome is available. At this point we may wish to consider the maximisation game instead, or exit the negotiation

If we end up in the second scenario then we know what the problem is — we don't have a sufficient understanding of needs. So explore more needs and generate new options that satisfy all of them.

If we end up in the third scenario because the other party is using intentional tactics, then we may not realise it, and our process may become polluted by the deceiving party's lies and misinformation. The important point for us is not to revert to playing the division game by giving away arbitrary concessions to get a deal. Rather we keep probing for needs: "What could make this option more attractive for you? How come? If you get that, what will that give you or allow you to do?"

The temptation to compete and claim most value for oneself increases once all of that value is clearly visible on the table (remember, on autopilot we want *the best available deal*). To circumvent disagreement on options once they have been generated, we may wish to agree on the criteria for selecting the final option *before* we have generated the options. The criteria can be anything that parties agree defines success in the negotiation. We could for example agree upfront to select the option that meets one or more of the following criteria.

- It creates most total value, i.e. that does the best job of satisfying needs.

- It is the one that most parties can agree on.

- It is the one that is best for the relationship.

- It would cost the least to implement.

- It would require the least time to implement.

- It would require the least resources to implement.

- It would be quickest to agree on.

- It is the most considerate to the party that happens to get the smallest share.

◆ It gets the largest amount of points if all parties were to allocate a hundred points and vote among the available options.

◆ It would ensure that all stakeholders were rested, fed, healthy, felt appreciated, felt valued, felt included and felt respected.

A simple example from my childhood that I know will resonate with a couple of readers is negotiating how to split value with siblings. If my parents got us sweets or dessert and asked us to split them fairly we would negotiate in the most self-serving way possible. However, by asking one of us to split the loot into two piles and letting the other choose which pile to take, our parents ensured that we would come up with the fairest possible split.

So there seems to be a benefit in agreeing *how* to split value before we know how much value will be created. There also seems to be benefit in ensuring that this split caters to parties' shared needs.

MAXIMISATION

If division could be started by asking ourselves, "How do I win over the other party?" and integration could be started by asking ourselves, "How can both parties get what they want?" then maximisation could be started by asking ourselves, "How can we maximise value for everyone?" Note that by "everyone" we don't just mean ourselves and the other party, but we also aim to include all those parties who might affect or be affected by the negotiation.

In maximisation we step back from the presently identified negotiation, and instead consider the system. What motivates people in the system? When they act, what are the results on other people? And how do those changes propagate through the system? How will the system change in reaction to what we do? How do those effects propagate back to us over the longer term? Where is value created and destroyed, and for whom? What are the leverage points that may require a small intervention, but will have a big impact on value in the system? What would we need to change in this system to maximise the value available to all parties?

In changing from integration to maximisation, we may need to change one or several of the following:

- the scope

- the strategy

- the structure

- the stakeholders and/or parties and/or people

- the system

- the stakes

- our mindset

- our emotional state

- our role

- time

- the context

- the mode of interaction and/or communication

Set up the right negotiation

It probably feels like this should have been one of the first topics in the book. And yes, when it comes to preparing and starting the negotiation, this is the first step a skilled negotiator considers. However, to do this well we need to understand the factors you've read about up till now.

Most people skip this step. Rather we simply find ourselves in a negotiation, and we negotiate. Rarely do we stop and ask the really, really fundamental questions.

- Do I even want to negotiate?

- Am I clear about what I want?

- Is the current negotiation the best way to get what I want?

- Am I really the best-positioned person to influence the parties?

- Have I picked the right parties? Should I be one of the parties?

- Given what I want to achieve, is the formal topic of the negotiation going to make it easier or more difficult for me to get what I want?

- What would be the ideal set-up for getting me what I want?

For a while I tried to get a negotiation subject introduced at one university. Perhaps the most straightforward negotiation would have been for me to negotiate with the decision maker (i.e. the dean). But would this have been the most effective way to get my desired outcome? What if I instead offered free guest lectures to 1000 students, and then let a large group of full-fee-paying students on their own initiative request to get a negotiation subject to be taught by me...? Which of these two approaches would be more likely to influence the decision maker, and his or her stakeholders?

Sustainability

In 2012 I went to Hawaii to present on an initiative for a new International Centre On Negotiation. In the years leading up to that I connected with over fifty negotiators and academics with an interest in negotiation. Many of us share a view that the world would be a much nicer place for everyone if more people practiced a sustainable approach to negotiation.

While in Hawaii I attended an excellent presentation on sustainability. One example that was shared was the current United States approach to acquiring resources: "If we don't have enough, we venture farther away from our shores until we find more of the resources we need. But what happens once you venture sufficiently far away on our planet? That's right, you come back to where you started, and now the option of importing or claiming resources is no longer available."

In contrast, I was told the Hawaiian culture had a strong emphasis on sustainability. On an island, just like on a boat or submarine, the need for sustainability quickly becomes a high priority, as there are usually few alternatives.

Maximisation is to negotiation what sustainability is to the planet. Imagine if people negotiated in a manner that catered to shared needs by:

- considering all affected people, the environment and future generations as stakeholders;

- aiming to create value for everyone;

- avoiding destroying value for anyone;

- considering all future and long-term flow-on consequences of the current agreement and negotiation process;

- ensuring that relationships were always better at the end of a negotiation than at the start; and

- helping ensure that people were rested, fed, healthy, felt appreciated, felt valued, felt included, felt respected, and so on.

Many of us have a bias towards considering the value of options in the short term. Sometimes this is because that is how we are rewarded (e.g. annual bonus), but often it's because we simply neglect to properly consider the long-term effects of that option. And rarely do we consider the long-term effects of *how* we achieved that option, i.e. the effects of the process we followed. For instance, there are multiple examples where dictators, governments and companies have exerted excessive force or power in order to win. In the process of achieving their desired short-term outcome they also produce losers. Eventually these losers organise themselves and overthrow their oppressors, or get back at them in other ways.

A sustainable approach to negotiation is not necessarily always available, but it *is* available more often than you think. Considerably more often.

Systems thinking

We can look at many parts of nature and society as systems. The planet as a whole could be viewed as a system where animals, plant life, wind, water and sunshine are all elements. Likewise our bodies are systems, a company is a system, and the economy is a system.

Many systems are self-balancing through what are termed negative feedback loops. For example, if our body gets cold, it will balance itself by increasing the amount of energy that is spent staying warm. Likewise, if we get too warm, our body will balance itself and make us sweat in an effort to keep our temperature stable.

Systems can also have positive feedback loops, and these serve to drive change in the system. For instance, by introducing a species of animal with no natural enemies into a new ecosystem, e.g. introducing rabbits into Australia, the animal may multiply exponentially. The more rabbits we have at any point in time, the more rabbits we will have the day after. This is a positive feedback loop. If this were the only loop in the system, the rabbit population would eventually spiral out of control.

Systems are typically extremely complex, and there will be both positive and negative feedback loops in action. For example, if the rabbit population becomes too big, then the lack of food supply will halt the population growth. Also, as the population grows it increases the speed with which any diseases will spread, and this would also serve as a negative feedback loop to balance the system. Additionally, animals that eat rabbits (if they too are introduced) would experience an excess of food and would multiply over time, eventually also serving as a negative feedback loop to control the rabbit population.

How is all of this related to negotiation? As we shared earlier in this book, negotiators will often attempt to fix a perceived problem by some kind of one-off intervention, analogous to introducing one species of animal to deal with a specific pest. The mindset is similar to the way we hope that pharmaceutical drugs work; i.e. one drug for one illness.

But with this mindset negotiators fail to acknowledge the negative feedback loops in place, and therefore fail to understand that the system will work to balance itself after the intervention. We over and over again come up with oversimplified solutions to complex problems. One example is the supplier and giant retailer mentioned earlier. The stable state of the system was for the retailer to buy cheaper goods from overseas, and unless that negative feedback loop was broken things would continue as they were.

Negotiators can also benefit from the understanding of positive feedback loops. In particular, as we will see in the example below, systems can be set up to create value by themselves.

Dynamics of needs

Whereas in the integration game we identify and satisfy needs, we in the maximisation game realise that each need comes from somewhere within us or from within the system. Let us take one of many borders between two countries where we see a flow of illegal immigration almost exclusively in one direction.

We might simply accept that people in one country wish to flee to the other, and we deal with each of those negotiations, e.g. by building a wall or protecting the waterways. Alternatively we may take a step back and investigate how the system fuels the needs of the different parties. Perhaps we find that the policies of the originating country are creating the need to flee. Perhaps we find that the foreign policy of the destination country is exploiting the originating country and thus contributing to the contrast in attractiveness between the two countries.

A simple buyer/seller example converted to maximisation

An example I use to illustrate the relationship between the first three games is a simple one: buying a wristwatch as a graduation present to myself in Singapore after completing my MBA at INSEAD.

If playing the division game, I would walk into a shop, ask how much the watch costs, then make an offer of say fifty per cent of the price asked.

Then we would play a game of posturing, tactics, lies, and concessions, until at some point we agree on a price, or one of us breaks off negotiations. Who is most likely to "win"? The salesperson. He or she has an information advantage, knowing the true cost of the products. The salesperson also has the experience of having played this game with potentially thousands of customers.

If playing the integration game, I would try to understand the needs of both parties. My needs included:

- to get a watch at as low cost as possible because I was poor;

- to have one nice graduation gift that I could keep for the rest of my life;

- to get a good mark in my negotiation subject in the hope that my negotiation professor would one day hire me as a negotiator (one of our tasks in class was to negotiate something we deemed impossible to negotiate);

- to win: I wanted the bragging rights of being able to tell my classmates that I'm a great negotiator; and

- learn more about negotiation.

The salesperson's needs included:

- to make a sale;

- to not set a bad precedent, e.g. by having me get a discount and then see me telling everyone else that this salesperson gives in to pressure;

- as his end-of-year bonus was calculated on the average sales margin throughout the year, he would not want to make low-margin sales that might ruin his bonus;

- to not give in to a young, male foreigner in a game that the salesperson is more experienced in;

- to be perceived as a luxury retailer (he would therefore insist on jumping in a cab to deliver the watch in person);

- to allocate some cost (or rent) to the watch, which had taken up display space for the last six months;

- to look like a good negotiator to his boss; and

- to not get caught by an undercover mystery shopper, who would report back to the luxury brand if watches were sold cheaper than the permitted discount. A single offence could be sufficient to break the contract with the luxury brand, and result in a loss of the store's authorised reseller status.

Playing integration, we may come up with options that would improve the deal beyond what we could do with the division game:

- me providing sufficient documentation or evidence to prove that I was not a mystery shopper, but indeed an international student at a business school;

- me signing a document saying that I would not disclose the discount to any other person or potential future customer;

- selecting a watch that was not in stock and therefore did not accrue any rent;

- selecting a watch that was not in stock and could therefore (perhaps) bypass the system that calculated average sales margin for the year, and would therefore not affect the salesperson's bonus;

- having the salesperson buy a watch using his or her staff discount, and then sell that to me for a personal profit;

- picking up the watch myself and thus saving the cab fare;

- having the negotiation when the salesperson's boss was not around;

- giving the salesperson an excuse for a dramatic discount by say getting a classmate from my MBA to also buy a watch, but at full price;

- agreeing on the price now, but agreeing to finish negotiations next month when prices are scheduled to increase by twenty per cent, thus increasing the apparent discount to aid my bragging rights;

- finding a local, young and attractive female to negotiate on my behalf to deal with the constraint of there being three price levels in Singapore, one for locals, one for expats and one for tourists;

- finding a mutual friend or relative of the salesperson to negotiate on my behalf; and/or

- finding a way to access the tax-free option available if the watch leaves the country on a passenger's arm within thirty days.

If playing the maximisation game I would start by forgetting about the watch for the time being and instead ask myself: "How can we maximise the amount of value for everyone?"

- A thousand MBAs graduate from my business school every year. They can find $100,000 to cover the tuition and many qualify for a greater than $20,000 sign-on bonus from their first employer. I suspect many of them wish to buy themselves graduation gifts, so what if I could recommend this watch retailer in the section of the MBA welcome book labelled *Exclusive deals for MBA students*; would the potential of 1000 extra customers per year be appealing to the watch retailer?

- Given a large volume of new customers, would that allow us to increase the discount? Would that in turn increase the appeal of the deal to students? Would that increase the number of students who make a purchase? Would that in turn allow us to increase the discount further? This is a positive feedback loop: we essentially set up the system to keep creating more value by itself.

- Let's not stop here; let's think about the watchmakers. I will assume that inventory management is a consideration for them. They certainly don't want to miss out on customers, but they also can't dump prices on excess stock without hurting their luxury brand, so I will assume that a watchmaker would find some value in knowing what demand looks like twelve months in advance. What if I could get the students to collectively order their watches at the beginning of their degree, and have them delivered on graduation? Might the watchmakers appreciate this? Would they be able to pass some of the savings to the watch retailer? Would the watch retailer be able to pass some of that to the students? Who would then be even more likely to buy? Again, another positive feedback loop.

- What else can we do (which is a great question for options generation!)? Well, the watch retailer currently takes each order individually, and delivers each watch in person; the associated cost includes the hourly rate of the salesperson, the taxi fare, and the opportunity cost of not speaking to new customers instead. What if all of that only had to be done once? Would that add up to real money? Absolutely.

- And what else? Well perhaps given a sufficient number of customers, the watchmaker could create an exclusive edition of the watches for *INSEAD MBA class of* ____; perhaps by having this emotional need met, students would now be willing to pay *more* for the watches rather than less, thereby generating more money for both the watch retailer and the watchmakers;

If I helped enable this then I would propose that it is fair for me to get a cut of the value created. Oh, I would also expect to get my own graduation watch for free…Maximisation is about setting up the system so that it creates the outcomes that we want. And…it…is…powerful!

A case in point: OzHarvest

Another example of maximisation is the OzHarvest charity. Here the founder, Ronni Kahn, had several personal needs that would be satisfied if she could help others who were less fortunate. Ms Kahn was not inspired by helping a handful of people — she wanted to help a million people. In order to achieve this she would need to negotiate the system so that it would:

- create the amount of value that she wanted to be distributed;

- satisfy people's deeper personal needs so that they would be motivated to contribute; and

- be self-sustaining, and not rely on her pushing or controlling the operation.

OzHarvest focuses on feeding people who have no way to obtain food for themselves. With her background as an event producer and after analysing the system Ms Kahn discovered that enormous amounts of food were wasted in her city every day. How good would it be if this food could be redirected to those in need? Disposing of food normally incurs a cost that she could help the providers eliminate. Disposing of food also creates methane, which is a significantly more potent greenhouse gas than CO_2. So OzHarvest is good for the food providers, good for the hungry, and good for the environment. And Ms Kahn managed to attract people from all walks of life to contribute to the charity.

One example she shared was of a very successful businessman who had all the money he wanted, and was skilled in all the areas he wanted to be skilled in, but he was seeking to satisfy much deeper needs: meaning, belonging, self-esteem, and a sense of contribution.

This doesn't mean that everyone at OzHarvest works for free. Specifically, Ms Kahn realised that some aspects of the charity relied on the kind of certainty that can't be guaranteed with volunteer staff; donated money would be used to ensure critical success factors such as reliability of delivery and hygiene.

She negotiated the system in many ways. One obstacle she faced was food providers' fears of being sued if a recipient of food got sick after eating any of the meals. So Ms Kahn lobbied the government to eliminate the risk of food providers being sued if food was given to charity, and thereby eliminated the main motivator to discard good food rather than give it to someone in need.

Another obstacle was getting those who had access to excess food to actually engage in this new venture. She addressed this by effectively enquiring about the obstacles the food providers perceived, and then she removed the obstacles one by one.

- Some providers were hesitant to engage in a new, unknown venture. So Ronnie Kahn pointed to the precedent of similar ventures that were operating successfully in the US.

- Some providers expected increased cost, effort or complexity would result from having to dispose of the food in this new manner. Ms Kahn kept her focus on the outcome and kept proposing options, and modifying options until they satisfied the needs of the providers: "OK, so if I show up with a refrigerated truck, in this location, with this equipment, at this time, then will it be just as easy for you to hand the food to us as it would be to put it into the garbage bin?"

At the time of writing OzHarvest has delivered over 15 million meals to people in need. I met up with Ms Kahn in February of 2012 to ask permission to include her story as an example in this book. And what I learned was that she hadn't consciously applied systems thinking and maximisation. Rather she was on autopilot, but her autopilot actually *does* maximisation. Of course the rest of us typically have autopilots that favour division, but we *all* have the option of educating and reconfiguring our autopilot.

When win-win is actually win-lose

A theme of this book is to increase scope and take a broader look at negotiations. The further away we get from a specific negotiation, the more potential we have for creating value.

I had a candid conversation with a person who had a strong belief that capitalism automatically created win/win outcomes, because in the end companies would only sell products and services if people wanted to buy them. For instance, as long as consumers demand bottled water we have a win/win negotiation; customers get their water bottles, companies get their profits. Win/win? No.

This appears as a win/win because we only consider the parties who derive value from the negotiation. The rest of the stakeholders weren't represented in this negotiation and many of them are not getting their needs satisfied. Thus the game was integration and not maximisation. In other words, it's a win/win among the parties at the table, but a win/lose between this group and other groups.

So let's look at the system and see what is happening.

+ Water companies often get free or cheap access to natural sources of drinking water. Clean drinking water is an increasingly scarce resource on the planet.

+ Removing the water from these regions means other stakeholders in that region are disadvantaged, e.g. local communities, farmers, future generations, wildlife and the environment. This affects the regions where the water is sourced, and downstream regions that now also have access to less water.

+ Creating plastic bottles uses up resources and pollutes the environment.

+ Transporting water bottles uses up resources and pollutes the environment.

- And if some of us argue that the environment is not a stakeholder, then remember that all future generations of people will have to live in the environment; so affecting the environment affects future generations.

- The system only recycles a portion of plastic bottles. The rest find their way into the environment, into the oceans, and plastic bottles tend to not be biodegradable.

- Plastic that reaches the ocean ends up on beaches, and in the stomachs of wildlife on land and at sea.

- Local water companies, councils or cities who often provide water of the same or higher quality straight out of the tap now face largely unnecessary competition.

- End consumers pay sometimes ten thousand times as much for bottled water as tap water, and are often under the illusion (as a result of misrepresentation in marketing and advertising) that the bottled water is a healthier option.

- Of course there are groups of stakeholders not invited to the table that do get value, and that includes all the people who get paid work as a result of the bottled-water industry, and customers who don't have alternatives to bottled water.

The effects on the system do not necessarily become apparent unless we consciously consider the system. Our good intentions of using integration to create win/win outcomes within a small group of parties may thus unintentionally create win/lose outcomes and value destruction in the system.

In contrast, pursuing maximisation means that we are trying to find ways to maximise value in the system, and maximise value to the stakeholders in the system. Just as many individuals struggle to change their mindset from division to believing that integration is possible, many may struggle in making the leap to maximisation. Thankfully we have great examples, such as OzHarvest, of how it works in real life.

Here's a summary of the message of this chapter so far.

- Division has the lowest potential for creating value or getting you what you want.

- Sometimes division is the appropriate game to play. But we play it way, way, way more often than we should.

- Integration and maximisation enable more valuable outcomes and are not necessarily more difficult, but they do require a very different way of thinking about negotiation, and they require different processes.

- Integration and maximisation are possible more often than we think. The main limiting factor is our belief in what is possible.

CRISIS NEGOTIATION

Crisis negotiation is fundamentally different from the other games. However, insights from any of the other three games can be applied to this one too. And as we've already seen, insights from crisis negotiation can be applied to the other three games. In fact, our everyday commercial and romantic negotiations consistently end up in crisis at various points. If we don't understand crisis negotiation we effectively become victims of the process at those points.

In brief, we have learned that division is concerned with competing for value, and integration and maximisation are concerned with increasing value. Crisis negotiation is often concerned with preventing significant value destruction.

Definition of a crisis

One definition of a crisis is a situation that is beyond the coping mechanisms of the people involved. A crisis may only apply to one person (e.g. thoughts of suicide, sudden health problems, redundancy) or it could apply to a large group of people (e.g. a threat by terrorists to pollute a city's water, an uncontrollable oil spill in the Gulf of Mexico, or any dramatic change in business circumstances). A key trait of a crisis is that, if unmanaged, it may transform into disaster.

In crisis negotiations, some or several of the following parameters may be considered extreme compared to regular negotiations:

- stakes

- emotions

- face issues (see Needs in a crisis)

- time pressure

- complexity and/or confusion

- diverging perceptions

- power imbalances and/or need for power

- the presence or risk of destructive outcomes

- personality disorders

Outcomes

Crisis negotiations also change the way we set outcomes. For the other games we try to achieve the best possible outcome, which may include getting everything we want, an abundance of value, to win or to satisfy some other need.

In contrast, in a crisis negotiation we are primarily concerned with resolving the immediate crisis only, not of all the associated problems. A police officer negotiating with a suicidal individual who is ready to jump off the top of a bridge is primarily concerned with getting the person to safety. The outcome is not to resolve the individual's suicidal tendencies for all time.

Reaching desired outcomes in crisis negotiations will typically involve at least two activities.

♦ Continuously containing and de-escalating the crisis. This may involve physically isolating people involved in an argument or a demonstration, or psychologically de-escalating the situation by letting the person experiencing a crisis vent his or her emotions.

♦ Reducing the likelihood and impact of possible negative outcomes (WATNAs). This may involve removing the public from a barricaded incident so that if the perpetrator starts shooting he is less likely to hit anyone. Or it could involve a health supplement producer recalling all products of a certain batch after a threat that the some products have been poisoned.

Types of crisis negotiations

Typical crisis negotiation scenarios include:

♦ domestic disputes

♦ workplace crisis

♦ suicide

♦ barricaded perpetrators, who sometimes take hostages

♦ kidnapping

♦ terrorism

One question we need answered as early as possible is: what is the purpose of the current negotiation? As we look at the categories above we start to see patterns.

For instance, in domestic disputes the perpetrator typically doesn't want anything from law enforcement, apart from being left alone. Of course, the other party (the victim) in the relationship may very well want the assistance of the authorities.

Sometimes the same is true for attempted suicides: subjects may not want anyone to interfere. However, in many cases the suicide is *not* the goal, but rather the subject has an interest in getting attention, empathy or furthering another agenda. Sometimes suicide attempts may be camouflaged as, for example, a hostage situation. Here the perpetrator intentionally provokes the police to shoot him, also known as *suicide by cop*. Of course, the subject may not be crystal clear beforehand about his or her desired outcome, and may decide in the moment based on the interaction with the negotiator.

Barricaded situations often occur when a crime goes wrong and the perpetrators barricade themselves to try and avoid getting caught. In the process they may grab one or more hostages. Usually the perpetrator has no interest in killing the hostages, but rather sees them as a bargaining chip with police. These situations are rarely planned and usually occur when the perpetrator is in a state of panic, and the perpetrator's main goal is generally to escape.

Kidnappings are different from hostage takings in that they are usually premeditated, planned and have a clear purpose. Some kidnappers may have an intention to harm or flee with the hostage and thus have no interest in speaking with law enforcement. Other kidnappers view the process as a business transaction where the hostage is merely a bargaining chip to be traded for something else.

Negotiations with terrorists are different again. Often the purpose is to send a message to further a political or religious agenda. Here too there are nuances; the terrorists may wish to harm the hostages as part of their agenda, or use them as bargaining chips to achieve another agenda.

When there is a purpose, this will certainly inform a crisis negotiator's approach to the negotiation. Of course, we also end up in crisis negotiations where there is no perpetrator, and no agenda. We may be facing a natural disaster, an explosion in a factory, or a dramatic change in the political or economic landscape. These situations may also include high stakes, high emotions and an inability by parties to cope with the situation.

Emotions in a crisis

A crisis can be characterised by a high level of emotions. Emotions and rationality do not necessarily go hand in hand, although they are not opposites. The main tools for a crisis negotiator are rapport building, trust building, listening and stalling for time. If these are used skilfully, the person experiencing the crisis will be allowed to vent, feel heard, and slowly move away from an emotional state towards rationality.

For example, in a barricade situation[4] the perpetrator can be expected to go through roughly the following sequence of emotions as time passes:

- rage

- excitement

- frustration

- stress

- rationality

- fatigue

- exhaustion

Note that while exhaustion can cause a person to want to give in, it can also make a person unpredictable. And running out of time may make a person desperate. However, the general trend is that we become less emotional, more rational and give more concessions the more tired, bored, uncomfortable or hungry we get.

When we are in the crisis mindset we tend to experience tunnel vision: we fail to consider alternative actions that may seem obvious to non-emotionally involved bystanders. As a crisis negotiator we want to help the person in crisis reach rationality and discover for him/herself how to resolve the situation. As time passes, the person in crisis starts to become aware of more available options.

Another important insight into negative emotions during a crisis is what is referred to as permanence. This means that at the height of our crisis we are likely to temporarily assume that the crisis will last forever. As a crisis negotiator it is then important to highlight to the subject that he or she has experienced multiple crises before, and has overcome every single one of them.

The crisis negotiator will aid the process by reframing what is said and putting the focus on the future. The other party may very well experience the crisis as a result of feeling trapped and desperate. By steering the conversation towards desirable future options, the negotiator can help change the other party's frame of mind out of the crisis. The negotiator may:

- emphasise how easy it would be to move forwards;

- raise the connection with, and responsibility for friends, family, etc;

- de-emphasise the negative aspects of de-escalating the crisis, e.g. by sharing that no serious crime has actually been committed yet;

- emphasise how the other party has faced crises in the past, and always managed to figure out a way forwards; and/or

- get the subject to talk about and even plan for the future.

These strategies are particularly important in situations where there is a risk of suicide or murder, as they can dramatically reduce the risk of anyone dying.

Note that when in crisis we tend not to be open to solutions straight away. Often we first want to:

- talk about the problem and vent our emotions;

- feel that someone is listening, hearing, understanding and agreeing with us; and

- then we are ready to resolve the problem. Usually we prefer if *we* come up with the solution. Often the crisis will be over before this last step. (And for crisis negotiations in romantic relationships, this last step can often be complemented or replaced with a hug!)

Note that what we term a crisis negotiation does not necessarily require a *perpetrator* who is experiencing a crisis. It is quite possible for example that a kidnapping is carried out as a very systematic, rational, although unethical and illegal business transaction: one hostage for a lump sum of money. This would still be labelled as a crisis negotiation. It is quite possible that the hostage, the hostage's family, friends, employer and even the crisis negotiator are all experiencing a crisis even if the hostage taker isn't.

Managing emotions

Can you control other people's emotions? Typically most of the participants in my seminar will say no. Then I ask:

- Can you make someone angry?

- Can you make someone feel insulted?

- Left out?

- Ignored?

- Unappreciated?

- Sad?

- Can you make someone laugh?

- Cry?

The answer to all of these tends to be yes. However, that is not entirely correct. We can certainly influence the emotions of others, but we do not have complete control over them.

Our emotional state affects others' emotional states, so if we are not in control of our own emotions we will struggle to intentionally influence someone else's. Thus changing emotions in others begins by first controlling our own. One place to start is by identifying our own emotional triggers. These are things that, when they happen, tend to cause us to react emotionally whether or not the other person intended for that to happen.

> What are your triggers? What are things that other people do
> in interactions that just rub you the wrong way and make you
> angry, frustrated, irritated or annoyed?

Once we have identified such triggers, we can make a conscious decision to not react when someone unintentionally presses these buttons. This is easier said than done for some of us. In one negotiation I advised a client who was parting ways with his business partner after an unsuccessful venture. My client had covered a disproportionately large chunk of the joint expenses incurred, and wanted to see a more equitable split of the costs. We created a strategy, part of which involved improving the relationship.

One day I met with my client and he had just sent a long and angry email to his former business partner. Surprised and a bit disappointed I asked: "How come? We had a plan!" In the following conversation I learned that the former business partner had bruised my client's ego — and one of my client's hot buttons was a strong need to get even if anyone attacked his ego.

Manage the environment

I recall a time I was talking to a woman in a bar and a very aggressive man approached us. He wanted to talk to the woman alone and told me to leave. I soon learned that the man had in the past taken the woman on a date and she had rejected him. The hint came from the eloquent statement "I am in love with she", which he repeated three times.

At first I didn't acknowledge the man, hoping that he would feel unwelcomed and leave. But rather than leave he became a lot more aggressive. He walked up to me until our faces were only a couple of centimetres apart (remember the opening scenario of this book?). In all of the animal kingdom this set up means one thing — get ready to fight.

So the first thing I did before I responded was to turn my body and head so that I was facing the woman instead, and I had my shoulder facing the man. While he probably didn't realise why, his aggression towards me subsided in an instant. At this point I proposed an option: I would remain where I was standing, but the two of them could go somewhere else to talk, as long as the woman approved. Thus I removed myself as the perceived obstacle, while offering the woman a way out. And after she shared that she had no interest in talking to him, the man walked away.

Our negotiation had nothing to do with the content of what he wanted to achieve. I simply removed a process element of the set up (close proximity head-on with another male) that was aggravating the situation.

The ways in which we can alter the environment in a crisis negotiation are perhaps as numerous as there are crisis negotiations. Some examples.

- Add people (police, someone's boss, or someone's parents).

- Remove people (the suicide jumper's ex-wife, whom he blames for everything, bystanders, or the media).

- Separate group members from their leadership.

- Have people clearly identified or recorded to counter antisocial behaviour driven by anonymity.

- Break coordination ability e.g. by controlling lines of communication.

- Change the location.

- Change how people are placed.

- Change the number of people representing each party.

- Change the seniority of people involved in the negotiation.

- Change the available time or the time of day.

- Remove any deadlines or cost of time for the negotiation team.

Needs in a crisis

People experiencing a crisis are likely to make as many material demands as people do in non-crisis negotiations. However, the key to resolving a crisis is primarily concerned with satisfying perception and deep needs. A standard framework used by crisis negotiators is the SAFE model, which was originally developed by Dr Randall Rogan. It explains that in a crisis, the key needs to look for and satisfy are:

- [S]ubstantive needs. These are typically the material needs or demands. Of all the needs that are important to the person in a crisis, the instrumental portion may be as little as two per cent. However, the person may make excessive instrumental demands to test the resolve of the negotiator, try to demonstrate power (because a person in power can demand things to get done), stall for time, or simply because the person is unclear about what he or she wants.

- [A]ttunement needs. This is concerned with feelings of rapport and trust with people, including with the crisis negotiator.

- [F]ace needs. This relates to helping the subject save face, keep dignity, pride and so on. These are perception needs, i.e. how we want to be perceived by others and ourselves.

- [E]motional needs. These may very well take precedence over all the other needs when a person finds him- or herself in an emotional state.

The main tool for satisfying face needs, relationship needs and emotional needs will be active listening skills. A person in crisis may not necessarily structure his or her demands in the most organised and effective manner; a formerly powerless person suddenly feeling powerful (e.g. through having a weapon or a hostage) might get especially sidetracked by the euphoria engendered by this shift.

In such situations the negotiators will often pursue a strategy of active listening, trying to keep the conversation going (even if just one way). The process of active listening is usually effective in uncovering and helping to mentally organise the needs that are important to the person, and so moving the person towards rationality. With time the situation often favours the crisis negotiator, as time allows the negotiation to be rebalanced so that the perpetrator wants something from the negotiator. For instance the perpetrator may develop physical needs such as hunger. Or the arrival of the tactical team may make the perpetrator realise his need for survival. The crisis negotiator may help satisfy either of those needs.

Satisfy | trade

Earlier in this book we discussed the benefits of a strategy that focuses on satisfying needs rather than making equal trades. The main point was that more value can be achieved by satisfying than by trading. And at the beginning of the crisis negotiation section, we said that we are not necessarily interested in maximising value in a crisis — we are primarily concerned with simply resolving the immediate crisis itself.

Crisis negotiators will apply a mix of satisfy and trade strategies. The crisis negotiator will typically try to satisfy as many face, relationship and emotional needs (with the exception of power) as possible for the perpetrator. Leaving these unsatisfied risks polluting the negotiation with ego needs, emotional needs and distrust, so satisfying them is often of interest to both parties. This will be the bulk of the crisis negotiation.

When the other party is experiencing a crisis, he or she may spend quite some time here before genuine substantive needs start to surface.

For substantive needs, the crisis negotiator is likely to instead apply the trading strategy. In fact, the crisis negotiator may intentionally make the negotiation about substantive needs drawn out, difficult and competitive. Why? Well there are a few good reasons.

One reason is that this approach can severely drain the perpetrator's resolve, and reduce his expectations of what he can get. In Gary Noesner's excellent book *Stalling For Time*, he shares an example of a plane hijacker giving up after failing to negotiate for a coffee. The hijacker asked for coffee with cream and two sugars. Hours later he received a cold, black coffee with no sugars. Later when asked why he gave up, the hijacker responded, "I figured if I couldn't even get a decent cup of coffee, I certainly wasn't going to be able to fly to Cuba."

Note that making demands may give the other party the impression that they are in power, and thus increases his or her resolve. So we wish to avoid having substantive needs labelled as demands (i.e. don't ask: "What are your demands?").

Another reason for trading substantive needs is that law enforcement may find themselves in a situation where the perpetrator has many hostages, but law enforcement has very few bargaining chips. Thus law enforcement wants to condition the perpetrator to trade often, and release as many hostages as possible with each trade.

WATNA in a crisis

While a WATNA may be present in the other games, it is usually a cornerstone of the crisis game and essentially describes the worst thing that can happen if we can't resolve the situation. In a hostage negotiation this might involve the hostage(s) being killed by the perpetrator (or accidentally by law enforcement). In negotiating with a terrorist who has poisoned food in a supermarket the WATNA may involve customers eating the product and getting poisoned. Even if the threat is a false threat, the WATNA may still be that the supermarket has to discard all of the products on the shelves, get a tarnished brand, lose customers, and perhaps even go bankrupt. In a suicide attempt the WATNA may involve the subject killing him/herself, intentionally or accidentally killing innocent bystanders or attacking law enforcement in attempting suicide by cop.

As crisis negotiators we need to get clear on what the WATNAs are, and how to reduce both the likelihood of them occurring and the impact if they do occur. This process may require the input of the other party, or we may be able to achieve this irrespective of cooperation from the other party. We also need to manage how and to whom we communicate the WATNAs, as awareness of the WATNAs may cause stress or panic for various stakeholders.

Note that the likelihood and impact of the WATNAs are not necessarily static, but may very well involve a slippery slope. For instance, at the point where the first non-perpetrator dies in a hostage situation, the probability of additional deaths drastically increases. This partly relates to the fact that the perpetrator now *will* go to prison if he gives up, and suddenly violent options and even murder/suicide may start to look more feasible to the perpetrator.

Similarly, the crisis negotiator can pick up on cues in the subject's behaviour and communication. For instance, a subject who seeks attention or talks about the future signals needs that are better met alive. In contrast, a subject who demonstrates hopelessness, helplessness, and/ or has a detailed plan for his or her suicide is statistically more likely to follow through with the threat.

Time in a crisis

Steve York has developed the 'pyramid of critical factors' in crisis negotiation. Those factors are:

- time

- power

- perception

- preparation

Without going into the details of power, perception or preparation, the use of time is critical in crisis negotiations but it is overlooked in many of the negotiation models. Time is often the factor that turns a normal negotiation into a crisis negotiation. The test may be: was the issue critical yesterday? And will it be an issue in a week?

Crisis negotiation can come from nowhere and even appear during a regular negotiation. Not recognising the symptoms can drive parties apart and may irreparably damage relationships, alter perceptions and change power balances.

For instance, from observations of how board members deal with unexpected issues, a typical reaction is for parties to regress, set deadlines for themselves, and get upset. And when board members act in an unusual ways it influences others to also react in unusual ways. Without proper intervention, a difficult but not insurmountable situation or problem can propagate through the system and transform the situation into a crisis.

The use of time through setting deadlines, talking through deadlines, responding quickly or delaying an action or conversation can all be used as tactics depending on the situation. Earlier we shared how stalling for time and offering resistance can wear down a subject until they give up or surrender to law enforcement personnel. This holds true for competitive business negotiations as well.

For instance, if we take the competitive approach to buying a car, should we follow the timeline set by the salesperson, or is it better to talk through any deadline and not reveal your timeline? For a crisis negotiator the answer is obvious — we want to control time. Controlling time allows us to reflect, do research, get advice and ensure that the financial terms are optimal. At the same time the salespeople will still live by their own timeline and deadlines. As we discussed earlier, as those deadlines approach, pressure to close deals increases. With the understanding of time, a crisis negotiator will buy their car at the end of the month, the end of the financial year, or on Christmas Eve. And we may even wait until fifteen minutes after closing time to make our decision to buy.

How we control time can have dramatic affects on the outcome. Remember that a crisis in one person's eyes may not be a crisis in another's!

The parallel approach

In non-crisis negotiation we realise that significantly more value can be achieved using a collaborative and non-coercive approach. In crisis negotiation we still advocate this approach, where appropriate. By now the reader should understand why: a forceful approach is likely to be met with resistance, and can negatively affect unrelated future negotiations. Thus the negotiator's first steps often involve building rapport, listening, increasing trust, becoming liked, and positioning him- or herself as someone who can help.

However, in some situations a cooperative approach alone will not be appropriate because we are not in a position to satisfy the other party's needs. Law enforcement crisis negotiators understand this, and therefore apply the carrot and the stick approaches in parallel. While the crisis negotiator connects with the perpetrator early on to build rapport and listen, the tactical teams will set up and prepare in case the option of force is needed.

As the negotiation progresses, if the collaborative approach doesn't work, or if the perpetrator doesn't want to engage in the negotiation, the negotiator will gradually start to inform the perpetrator of the cost of non-compliance. This does not have to be done verbally. Simply placing a SWAT van or armoured vehicle within sight may convey the message.

Essentially what law enforcement does is to rig the game in their favour (and rightfully so) by ensuring they have a strong BATNA to fall back on, should it be needed. Note that whereas pursuing our BATNA in non-crisis negotiations often just means no deal for the other party, in law enforcement hostage negotiations our BATNA can be the other party's WATNA.

Thus the parallel negotiation process simultaneously makes the cooperative process attractive by demonstrating how integration can create value, and makes the competitive process unattractive by setting it up so that the perpetrator will lose if choosing this game. This is consistent with one option we mentioned for changing the game from division to integration. This is also consistent with the approach we recommended for low-trust negotiations of making rewards and the costs of collaboration favourable compared to competition (or defection).

Of course, this process needs to be coordinated. It is difficult for a negotiator to build trust and rapport with a perpetrator, if the perpetrator at the same time can see the build-up of force, or even acts of aggression. This is the same issue that negotiators playing the integration game will face if it is clear that they are concurrently pursuing a BATNA. Visibly pursuing a unilateral alternative does not do a good job of signalling trust, relationship and collaboration. Consistent and congruent communication is key.

Manage communication

Realising how much more difficult it becomes to resolve a situation when people react emotionally, a crisis negotiator wants to make sure that he or she controls the flow of information to the other party and to all stakeholders. Thus one of the first tasks in a crisis negotiation is to contain the crisis. As part of that process we want to identify all the stakeholders, and everyone who may control the flow of information to each of them.

Law enforcement will go one step further and ensure that they get the only line of communication to the perpetrator. This helps contain the risk of the perpetrator speaking to the media. It also limits the perpetrator's ability to coordinate with accomplices.

Consider personalities and personality disorders

People with personality disorders are involved in a larger chunk of crisis negotiations than of non-crisis negotiations. The explanation is that people with some personality disorders are more likely to put themselves into situations that result in a negotiation with law enforcement.

For non-crisis negotiations we discussed that personality traits may be overshadowed by our emotional state, the patterns of negotiation we run on autopilot, and the situational and social context we are in. While these are still relevant for crisis negotiations, our behaviour is comparatively more likely to be influenced by our personality in a crisis than in non-crisis negotiations. Specifically, personality disorders (whether diagnosed or not) may begin to play a large role. So it is no surprise then that law enforcement negotiation teams both get training in detecting personality disorders, and also have access to qualified psychologists.

In particular, when personality disorders are not present negotiators focus much of their attention on understanding how the other party thinks, feels and perceives the world or situation. But when personality disorders are present this may become difficult, because we are unlikely to fully achieve the second perceptual position and think the same way as someone with a personality disorder does.

A simplified framework for crisis negotiations

Crisis negotiation is an enormous topic on its own, and there is certainly no one-magic-list-of-bullet-points that will resolve every crisis negotiation. That being said, here is a Mickey Mouse framework that will take you from no crisis negotiation skills to some crisis negotiation skills.

- Build rapport. Build trust. This increases the likelihood of an open dialogue, which increases the likelihood of a successful resolution.

- Understand time. Understand deadlines. Understand the changes in emotions as time passes. Negotiate for more time; we don't want deadlines on ourselves.

- Don't add to the emotions. This means staying out of the first perceptual position, and spending the time in second and in third position.

- Encourage communication and listen actively from second position while allowing the other party to vent for the purpose of reducing emotion.

- Reframe. Stop talking about problems and instead talk about solutions. Stop talking about the past and start talking about the future. Change from "you vs. us" to "we". Repeat back to the other party what you understood, but first remove any inflammatory language that was used. Reframe perceived conflicting goals to shared goals. Stop talking about blame and rather acknowledge the impact on the other party. Focus on areas of agreement rather than areas of disagreement. If it helps our cause, focus on long-term effects and consequences.

- Satisfy the other party's needs. Resolve the immediate crisis only, not everything. Don't rush. Be part of the solution (ally rather than foe). Help the other party save face. Help the other party "come up with a victory speech" to make him/her seem like the winner of the negotiation. Assure him or her that the consequences of complying (e.g. surrendering) are probably not going to be all that bad.

- If required, educate the other party about the consequences of non-compliance. Share your BATNA. Show how the other party's BATNA may not be desirable for him or her. But at all times make it easy for the other party to save face should he or she wish to give up, give in, concede or agree.

I hope that, after seeing the framework summarised like this, the reader realises how much overlap this has with our recommended approach for non-crisis negotiations. However, while we have more leeway to make up for mistakes in non-crisis negotiations, that margin of error is usually significantly reduced in a crisis.

9

UNDERSTAND WHAT
PEOPLE WANT

——— ——

NEEDS, INTERESTS AND MOTIVATORS

What are needs and interests? They are different terms for the same thing: a collective name for what is important and valuable to us. Different books use different terms and we will use *needs* from now on.

All needs are *motivators*. That is, changing how well (or poorly) we satisfy a particular need can change how we think, feel, perceive or behave. Thus satisfying (or not) other people's needs allow us to influence other people. Let us emphasise this point — the primary reason for why parties negotiate is in order to satisfy their needs. However, major obstacles include that we don't have a good understanding of our real needs, and we fail to acknowledge that there are multiple ways (i.e. multiple options) to satisfy our needs.

Every need is a motivator, but not every motivator is a need. For instance, playing calm, happy or classical music at a train station may reduce the motivation for rage or aggression. But hearing calm, happy or classical music is not necessarily something that people waiting for a train need or want. Similarly, in certain situations body angle or eye contact between competing males may motivate (influence) fight or flight behaviour, but the eye contact itself is not necessarily something that the two parties wish to satisfy or dissatisfy in that situation. Thus to influence others we aren't restricted to satisfying needs. But satisfaction of needs is certainly at the very core of why we engage in negotiation, and what we want out of the negotiation.

If needs are so important, then as mentioned before we had better make sure we become good at identifying them. So how do we do that? Well, we can find out about your and my needs in a number of ways, for example:

- I may think about what is important to me.

- I may try to put myself into your shoes (second position) and imagine what would be important to me if I were you.

- I can tell you about your needs and let you correct me if I'm wrong.

- I can ask you.

- I can look at a proposed option and think of reasons why I do or don't like it.

- I can consult various insights from psychology that can tell me about needs that most of us have.

- I can infer your needs from your behaviour and reactions when discussing options.

- I can ask your friends and others who know you.

- I can infer your needs from what you say or from your behaviour.

We can categorise needs in a number of different ways. Earlier we introduced shared | unique | perceived conflicting needs. This categorisation was useful to help us find options for mutual gain. In this section we will expand on these, and introduce additional ways to categorise needs. The primary purpose of these frameworks is to increase our awareness of different types of needs to look out for so that we don't unintentionally miss or ignore them in our negotiations.

NEEDS VS. POSITIONS AND CLAIMS

We distinguish between needs and positions/claims. Needs are truly important to us. Positions and claims are what we ask for, either because we believe this is what we want, or because we are using a tactic (e.g. to introduce a fake issue, or to anchor the other party's expectations).

A key insight is that we typically have very poor understanding of our real needs. Yes, we do. A simple test:

> Write down everything you want.

Would you be happy if you got everything? Would you be happy if you got everything you asked for in a romantic partner?

And once you get everything that you asked for, then what will become important to you? And how much are the things on your list influenced by what you think is possible, e.g. by what other people have, as opposed to what you really want?

I regularly run a motivational seminar at one university, and I start the seminar by asking all participants to list the top three criteria for a successful career. I then ask how many put "money" as the top criteria. Usually about half say they did. When I ask how many put money as one of the three criteria, everyone did. Three hours later, at the end of the seminar, I repeat the same exercise. Not a single participant puts money as one of the top three criteria! Most of us have a seriously deficient understanding of what is really important to us. And if we don't understand our own needs, then we are not going to ask for the right things in our negotiations, we will artificially limit the options available to us, and we will certainly not understand what the needs of the other party.

INSTRUMENTAL | TERMINAL

We want instrumental needs satisfied because they will allow us to satisfy other needs. This could be another instrumental need, or the terminal need. As it turns out, most needs are actually instrumental, because they help us satisfy something else. This is why one of the most powerful questions for negotiators is: "If you get that, what (else) will that give you or allow you to do?"

For instance, money is always instrumental. We want money because we can use it for other things, or simply having it gives us other things (e.g. power or security). Incidentally, this is the primary insight into why no participant put "money" as a key criterion for a successful career after the three-hour motivational seminar. This insight is important, because if we are struggling to find an option to satisfy an instrumental need, we may still be able to find options to satisfy all the downstream needs, which are actually more important to us.

For example, I may take the GMAT test (instrumental need) to be able to get into the MBA program of my choice (terminal need). If I keep failing the GMAT I may still find another way to get into the MBA program. The GMAT test is not an end goal in itself.

Likewise, while the sense of accomplishment that comes from completing the MBA could be a terminal goal on one time horizon, it is likely that the MBA is also instrumental to helping me satisfy other needs in the longer term. So again, if for some reason I can't get my MBA, then I may still find other ways to get all the things that an MBA would enable me to have. For example, if status was important to me then I could instead start a company that would give me the title of CEO. If access to the MBA alumni network was important then I could find other ways to become invaluable to that network, perhaps as a lecturer.

If we focus too myopically on the current instrumental need, then it is possible that we are dealing with an inflexible position, not a need. The better we understand both parties' downstream instrumental or terminal needs, the more choice we have in finding options to satisfy those needs.

MATERIAL | PERCEPTION | DEEP[5]

Material needs are likely to be the first things listed if we ask someone what they want. As we dig further and ask, "If you get this material need, what (else) will that give you or allow you to do?" we will start to uncover more perception and deep needs.

Material needs are typically 'things' or commercial terms such as money, products, payment terms and so on. These are typically the most expensive needs to satisfy, yet they are the least important to the individual we are negotiating with. They are often instrumental in nature. Unskilled negotiators tend to place disproportionally much weight and attention on material needs, which usually results in an overall focus on content over process and relationship.

Perception needs relate to how we wish to be perceived by others and by ourselves. This includes needs such as image, power, status, recognition, respect, popularity, affiliation, seniority and fame. When we ask for that large starting salary, perception needs may be related to how our new peers will see us, or how our previous employer will see us, or perhaps how our friends, family and loved ones will see us. Note that we may have different perception needs depending on who the audience is. A gang member may have a strong need to seem powerful in the eyes of his "brothers", but less so in the eyes of his mother, girlfriend or religious leader. Our perception needs may also change depending on which frame of reference we adopt.

Deep needs include our values, beliefs, emotions, physiological needs and psychological needs. These are typically the most important needs to us, and often the cheapest to satisfy. Truly terminal needs are typically deep needs. Deep needs are also the needs that either party is least likely to be aware of or self-disclose. The good news is that many of the deep needs are predictable.

◆ I suspect that you want me to listen to you, understand you and ultimately agree with you.

- I suspect that you want me to appreciate the extraordinary pressures and constraints that you have to work within.

- I suspect that if you are sufficiently tired, hungry, cold or bored your motivation to continue the negotiation will drop.

- I suspect that if the other party in your relationship leaves you then you will want to understand why, and get closure.

Many of the deep needs are completely invisible to us — that is, until they are unsatisfied. Once we feel ignored we realise the need to be acknowledged. Once we feel excluded we recognise the need to be included. It is thus very possible (and very common) for a negotiator to be driven by a deeper need, while this is completely invisible to the other party.

If you are not yet convinced of how important deep needs are, consider the scenario where a potential business partner proposes a new venture that would significantly increase your company's revenue. However, in the negotiation process the business partner insults you or coerces you, and you know that in the new venture this person will be your boss. Will you say yes to the deal? If you say yes, will you be committed?

I have seen a deal stall for over a year after one party at the outset of a joint venture made one unintentional but clumsy remark that offended another negotiator in a meeting. Similarly, a client of mine shared a story of having presented an option to his stakeholders that would benefit all of them, and save them from a bad WATNA, only to see the main decision maker reject the option out of spite for not having been involved in the idea generation stage. And I today *still* observe an acquaintance feeling resentment towards, and polluting interactions with, one person that denied my acquaintance the opportunity to join a social club forty years ago.

Do not underestimate the importance of having our deeper needs satisfied.

Values and beliefs

These can be defined as anything we believe has the potential to affect our negotiations. The difference between values/beliefs and other needs is that values/beliefs are typically so deeply entrenched in who we (think we) are that we are unlikely to change them in the short term. Some values and beliefs will never change no matter what.

The effect on our negotiations may be dramatic. For instance, let's look at a few values/beliefs.

- "I'm with the good guys so the end justifies the means."

- "Attack is the best defence."

- "Things happen for a reason."

- "This land was promised to us by God."

- "My brother sold his company for $3 million and I have to sell my company for more to not look like a loser in his eyes."

- "It is my right to get or have _____."

Imagine that a fictitious person holds some of these beliefs. Can we already guess how this person might negotiate, even if we know nothing about the content of the negotiation? Would these values/beliefs exist prior to any specific negotiation this fictitious individual will be part of? This suggests that the outcome of a negotiation may be severely influenced by values/beliefs that have nothing to do with the specifics of that negotiation.

Let's look at another negotiation in which we are all stakeholders: climate change. Here are a few possible beliefs that different stakeholders might subscribe to.

- "We should live our life in a sustainable way that leaves the planet better off for our children."

- "It doesn't matter what happens to this planet: the next life is the one that matters."

- "We inherited the earth from our ancestors."

- "We are borrowing the earth from our children."

- "You can't help others until you help yourself, and I can't afford to pay more for electricity."

- "If you can do anything to help another person you should."

- "Companies exist to maximise profit for the shareholders at all cost."

- "Companies exist to provide a service to society and therefore should be responsible corporate citizens."

- "Industrialised countries already have a good standard of living, they can lead the way."

- "Economic competitiveness is more important than the environment, and we don't want to incur costs to save the environment unless everyone does the same."

- "Every single action we take to reduce emissions is a good thing."

- "It's all or nothing."

Let us pick just two of these beliefs to illustrate the challenge in the following negotiation.

- One party believes in a religion where life on earth is merely a stepping-stone to the next, much better life and/or heaven.

- One party is non-religious and believes that this life is the only one we get, and our children and grandchildren will also only get one chance at life, and they have to live in the environment that we leave them.

These two individuals may negotiate with completely different time horizons in mind. For the first one the negotiation may comparatively more influenced by short-term needs such as reduced personal freedom, or reduced economic competitiveness in this life. For the second person the negotiation may be about the survival of all future generations.

In the next section we will talk about emotions. I'd like to link these two topics by sharing what happens when negotiators discuss topics that are closely linked to our values. In particular, our two fictitious negotiators in the climate-change debate may get very emotionally involved, particularly the second person, who feels a huge responsibility for future generations. It is thus possible for this negotiation to become very heated, and potentially even irrational at times. When we negotiate issues tied to values/beliefs we have to realise that these issues risk becoming very personal and positional. If we took these two negotiators and instead had them negotiate the price of a car, we would observe much less (real) emotional involvement, since the issue is not as attached to the parties' core belief systems. Less emotional involvement enables a more constructive, powerful and valuable approach to negotiation. To quote Steve York: "I care, but not that much."

Emotions, pain and pleasure

It is not what we get that matters, it is how we feel about what we get and how we get it that matters. One could argue that the majority of needs are simply instrumental to in the end helping us to feel good (making a move towards pleasure and away from pain). Whether the instrumental need is our salary, title, winning the negotiation by getting a discount, or creating value for people so that they appreciate working with us, these outcomes can be linked with emotions that we want to feel, or avoid feeling.

> Pick anything that you want to get from a negotiation and ask yourself: "If I get that, what (else) will that give me or allow me to do?" Whatever your answer is, keep asking that same question, and see if you can continue this process until you come up with an answer that either allows you to have one or more positive emotions or helps you avoid experiencing one or more negative emotions.

While in the exercise above we may consciously have to identify quite a few intermediate steps between a material need and the final emotion that we are trying to satisfy, we can subconsciously perform that process very quickly during actual negotiations. For instance, if I propose an option to you that sounds good but "feels" wrong, this simply tells me that your subconscious has already identified (or perceived) how one of your deeper needs or emotions will be unsatisfied by this option. It is then of little value for me to continue throwing logical arguments your way. I would be better advised to start exploring what emotions you are feeling, and what triggers those emotions.

Note that I am not trying to change your emotions directly. I would avoid saying: "You shouldn't feel stressed about that." Rather I would try to explore the cause of those emotions and deal with the cause. "What are the things you focus on, how do you interpret them, and what are the resulting thoughts or feelings that are making you stressed?" This is consistent with our systems approach to deal with the cause rather than the effect.

The emotions that seemingly interfere with our rational negotiations can actually disclose important information about unmet needs. In other instances the emotions that surface may be irrelevant to the current negotiation (as in the case of transference). Negotiators investigate the emotions to learn whether they are relevant or not. They avoid labelling any emotions as irrational before they have investigated them.

A recurring scenario in negotiations is when we are trying to get the other party (or they are trying to get us) to take an action that is different from the status quo. The status quo bias and the omission bias explain that people prefer to avoid making decisions that might lead to regret in the future. And remember that anticipating a future feeling of regret can actually make us experience that same feeling in the present. This can be a very effective motivator. We start feeling good when we plan our holiday. We instantly feel bad when we someone credibly threatens to harm us.

Emotions and rationality are often treated as opposite ends of a spectrum; i.e. either we are emotional or we are rational. We are guilty of that assumption in this book as well. However, this is clumsy. Rather, the opposite of emotional is non-emotional, and the opposite of rational is irrational.

While negotiations may become more difficult when people are irrational, negotiations do not necessarily become difficult because people are emotional. One reason irrationality is difficult is that irrationality suggests unpredictability. On the contrary, the needs and actions fuelled by emotions are actually rather predictable. That being said, it is also true that it is often harder to have a rational conversation when emotions are high, and many negotiations will be therefore become more rational once we reduce the intensity of emotions.

SHORT TERM | LONG TERM

Are short-term needs automatically aligned with long-term needs? Or is it possible that by satisfying our short-term needs we may in fact be sacrificing our long-term needs? Is it possible that eating cake, pizza or ice cream will satisfy our short-term need for instant gratification, but work against our long-term need for a slim waistline and healthy arteries? Of course.

Likewise, is it possible for people in an organisation to be incentivised in the short term to adopt behaviours that are destructive for everyone in the long term? Does the Global Financial Crisis ring a bell? Here the positive short-term pay-offs of selling bad investments were de-coupled from the expected long-term returns (or losses) of the same investments.

When we focus too myopically on satisfying short-term needs we run the risk of reducing the likelihood of satisfying long-term needs. Also, short-term needs tend to be perceived as conflicting more frequently than long-term needs, particularly as they are more likely to be measured in dollars. The flip side is of course that long-term needs are often shared.

Thus one way to move a competitive negotiation towards cooperation is by discovering and emphasising long-term needs for both parties, and realising that these are more likely to offer common ground.

And we can expect that parties are likely to have different time horizons. What would be the time horizon for a company? Well, for a large multinational company the expectation may be that this is a concern that will continue forever. The value of any project will include a calculation of net present value (NPV), which is essentially answering the question: "If I select this project that will generate X amount of money over the long term, what is an equivalent lump sum of cash today?" For many companies, business decisions will primarily be made on the basis of what projects will yield the highest NPV value while being consistent with company values and risk profile.

Now let's look at individuals — how long are our time horizons with regards to our needs? If we have the same job our entire life perhaps we are talking about forty-five years. For future generations that figure may be significantly smaller. If we look at how much time we have left on this planet, then the figure is our expected lifespan minus our age today, which will vary among readers. This timeline can be expanded if we also take into consideration the needs of our children, and their children, and so on.

And as we saw above, interesting things happen if we consider the effect of religion. If an individual believes that life on earth is simply a stepping stone to something better later on, then how does that affect their time horizon with regards to their needs? It could shorten it dramatically, and in the case of some more extreme religious views, needs on earth may not be very important at all. This is not a book that argues for or against religion — it simply flags that a person's religious view can have a *major* impact on how they negotiate. And similar asymmetries in how we look at time will surface when we consider the impact of different cultures.

PERSONAL | ORGANISATIONAL

Do employees (negotiators!) and the organisations they represent always have the same needs? Do they ever have exactly the same needs? No, because humans are also motivated by emotions, physiological and psychological needs, and a wider range of values, beliefs and perception needs.

It is important to realise that in any commercial negotiation, each party will have several lists of needs: one list for each negotiator, one list for each stakeholder, and one list for the organisation (or for each department within the organisation).

I was brought in to give feedback to a client organisation that had been unsuccessful in a recent negotiation. When asking for the needs it wanted met, I was given a list that looked similar to the following.

- find opportunities to build value

- improve the relationship

- create long-lasting commitment

- create partners, not competitors

I then asked the lead negotiator to give me his list of personal needs.

- reduce contract cost by X per cent compared to last year's contract in order to qualify for my bonus

Were these lists compatible? If not, which list do you think took priority? That's right, the negotiator focused exclusively on trying to bargain for a reduction in price, and in the process ensured that *none* of the organisation's top four needs were met.

The difference between personal and organisational needs is a key reason why bribes work; personal needs predictably trump organisational needs. Because the bribing company only has to cater to a smaller set of stakeholders (bribees?), this unethical approach is also tempting by virtue of being cheaper and less complex.

To further illustrate how personal needs can take negotiations off course, let's consider a story that a manager in a management consulting firm shared with me. The manager had been asked to interview a new candidate who was exceptionally qualified for the job. The candidate presented himself well, and aced the classic case interview that is used by a majority of global consulting firms. However, during the interview the manager began to imagine what it would be like to have this candidate in the office — a smart, charming, good-looking, alpha male who would probably be desired by the women in the office. But this was a role that the manager enjoyed! Because he expected competition in the social hierarchy in the office, he evaluated the candidate as "unsuitable".

This insight into how organisational and individual needs differ is important for several reasons. We need to understand that when we negotiate with organisations, we are negotiating with individuals in those organisations. A change of negotiators, members or stakeholders on either team can have a dramatic impact on which needs will drive the outcome of the negotiation.

This becomes clear when looking at international negotiations between countries. In 2006 neither Australia nor the US had ratified the Kyoto Protocol. But these aren't persistent views of the nations. These were the views of administrations that may spend a very limited time in office. Thus one option for influencing such negotiations is to spend less effort influencing the inflexible views of the current administrations, and instead work to ensure that the next administration (or negotiator) has a more favourable mindset. In 2007, Kevin Rudd ratified the Kyoto Protocol as his first act after being sworn in as Australia's prime minister. And Barack Obama, in his first press conference after winning re-election in 2012, shared: "I am a firm believer that climate change is real, that it is impacted by human behaviour and carbon emissions. And as a consequence, I think we've got an obligation to future generations to do something about it."

Of course, while this insight can be used for helping the world reach agreement for the benefit of all, unethical negotiators will also use exactly the same insight to create puppet regimes to further their own agenda.

Needs of groups, entities, coalitions, bodies, clusters, troops, gangs, factions...

While it is easier for us to remember concepts where there are only a few distinct nuances, you may well realise that we again (as with power, status, dependence and so many other concepts) have identified a spectrum. At one end of the spectrum we are talking about the needs of an individual, and at the other end we are talking about the needs of humanity, or the planet. Every level in between will have a distinct set of needs. For instance:

* the needs of a team within a company;

* the needs of a division within a company;

* the needs of the company;

* the needs of different sub-group of people who share race, religion, culture, location, nationality, dietary requirements, political convictions, etc;

* the needs of all people on the planet;

* the needs of all current and future generations of people; and

* the needs of the planet.

This list is for illustrative purposes, and I acknowledge that the order of some items could change based on our assumptions.

Often the needs of the group will be those that are shared among its individual members. Sometimes only a majority will agree (e.g. in the case of a functioning democratic nation). In other cases the needs of the group may only satisfy a couple of members (e.g. in the case of many dictatorships, or companies where members work for a salary while disagreeing with the company values, or sects or gangs where members may not believe there is an option to leave).

External | internal

Groups (entities, coalitions…) will typically have separate sets of external and internal needs. For example, terrorists may perceive external needs to justify killing a hostage (e.g. to further a political agenda), or internal needs for killing a hostage (e.g. to improve team cohesion). If we as external observers only recognise one set of needs (typically the external), then we may fail to anticipate how the group (entity, coalition…) will act — e.g. terrorists executing a seemingly politically unimportant hostage.

INTRINSIC | EXTRINSIC

There are things we want to do because they satisfy a deeper need. We call this *intrinsic* motivation. Sometimes we do things we don't want to do because we get some form of reward (or avoid some form of punishment) by taking the said action. We call this *extrinsic* motivation, and this captures the first two approaches to influence (rewards and punishment). Both play a role in motivating people to take action. However, extrinsic rewards typically do not create lasting commitment, although there are some exceptions.

This distinction between intrinsic and extrinsic is important for several reasons. Let us briefly revisit the failed negotiation in the section on Personal | organisational needs. We can now see that the personal needs driving the lead negotiator down the wrong path were actually extrinsic. The negotiator may very well have wanted to do what was in the best interest of the company, but was extrinsically incentivised to do otherwise.

The key takeaway here is to pay careful attention to ensure that incentives are set up to motivate behaviours that will result in the *agreed* and *desired* outcome. Organisations consistently fail to achieve their desired outcomes specifically because incentives for team members, or even for external parties, are not aligned with desired outcomes. Of course, crafting incentives that motivate the desired behaviour, and only the desired behaviour, can be a difficult task. But simply ignoring the incentive structures that are in place altogether is dangerous. I would suggest *difficult* is better than *dangerous*.

MOST IMPORTANT NEED RIGHT NOW

I was having coffee with the lead union negotiator for a well-publicised negotiation in the aviation industry. This was a great meeting with both parties very engaged in the conversation. Suddenly the union negotiator's eyes glanced towards a TV located in the café. I turned around and saw breaking news on the airline he had been negotiating with.

No matter what we had been discussing, hearing what was in this news broadcast became his most important need for about three minutes. So I stopped talking mid-sentence and sat quiet. When the segment was over I suspected his most important need would be to make sense of the news, and to think through how it would affect his current negotiations. So those were the questions I asked him. Once he had spent a few minutes organising his thoughts, we continued with the original conversation.

In any negotiation, the large list of needs that we identify for the other party during our preparation sessions may become completely trumped by other needs at various points in the negotiation. This may be a temporary need that only exists in that short span of time, or another more permanent need that for some reason or another becomes the main focus at this point in the negotiation. This emphasises the importance of a situational approach to negotiation — we need to continuously stay aware and attentive to the context, and adapt accordingly.

DISCLOSED | UNDISCLOSED

While some negotiation styles (e.g. integration and maximisation) can greatly benefit from free information sharing, the reality of negotiations is that parties will typically not disclose everything.

Let's create an example: a banking employee has been accepted into the police force, and the intake is nine months from now. If the employee were to disclose this to his or her employer, it would provide the employer with options for creating value — the handover process could be planned, the employee's current tasks could be documented, and the search for a new candidate may start. If playing the integration game, some of this value could reasonably be passed back to the employee.

However, the employee may elect not to notify his or her employer just yet, perhaps out of fear that the employer will choose to play the division game now that a shared future is no longer expected.

- The employer might find a replacement too quickly and choose to terminate the current employee's contract before the nine months have passed.

- Government changes may affect the offer with the police force, and the size of the intake may get reduced in seven months' time, resulting in the banking employee losing his job offer. If a replacement has been found at the bank there may not be an option for the employee to cancel his or her resignation.

- The employee may psychologically prefer to have the choice to stay, even though he or she believes him/herself unlikely to use that option.

One of the main insights here is that there will be more factors relevant to our negotiations than we are aware of. This is yet another reason not to label people as irrational or difficult. If what they do doesn't make sense to us, then it's because we don't see the world the way they do — possibly because they don't want us to.

Note that there may be either positive or negative intent behind not disclosing needs. This is one reason why we may wish to avoid the term "hidden agenda", as it carries negative connotations of malicious intent. And at this stage the reader will fully appreciate the pollution we inject into the process if we incorrectly assume malicious intent.

It is certainly possible that the agenda is hidden because the other party is trying to take advantage of us. It also just as possible that the agenda is hidden (or rather, the needs undisclosed) because the other party either can't, is not allowed to, or simply doesn't know how to disclose those needs to us.

This happened to a vendor that was selling services to a start-up company. A deal was agreed with the intention to deliver services in two weeks. But suddenly the start-up company ceased communications with the vendor. The vendor wasn't sure whether this was a tactic, if the deal was off, or what else could be going on?

About ten weeks later the start-up company broke the silence and shared that after the deal had been agreed, a private equity company had taken a majority stake in the start-up company. The valuation of this deal was heavily dependent on the present financial year profit figures, which would be finalised in coming months. This had thus introduced a new temporary need for the start-up company: to hold off on expenses. So there was no malicious intent towards the vendor; the start-up still wanted the deal, but simply didn't know how to inform the vendor given the secrecy around the private equity investment, and the awkwardness (cognitive dissonance) of reneging on an agreement. Sometimes when people struggle to cope with a situation they chose to withdraw while hoping things will work themselves out.

So where does that leave us if we feel that the other party hasn't disclosed everything? Do we assume good or bad intent? As we discussed earlier, this is context dependent. In most cases, assuming good intent is safe and helps prevent pollution of the process. In other cases we may decide to assume neither, and instead collect more information.

AWARE OF | UNAWARE OF

Of course, we also need to understand that one plausible reason for us not disclosing some needs is that we aren't aware of those needs to begin with. This is just as true for us as it is for the other party. The more skilled we become as negotiators, the more easily we will recognise needs. At some point we start to see patterns and will begin to start predicting what needs might play a role.

Now, rather than assuming we are right, we are better advised to verify our guesses with the other party. This is still a valuable process because the other party will often, either consciously or unconsciously, give us indications of whether or not our hypothesis is right.

For example, "Would you say that you prefer to talk in concrete terms rather than in abstract terms?" could for instance provoke either of the following.

- Confirmation: "Yes, you're right! I never thought about that."

- Denial: "No, I prefer talking in abstract terms."

Whether or not our guess is correct, we still end up with the right answer, *and* we raise the other party's awareness as well. Of course, the other party may get their answer wrong. For instance, if we asked: "Would you say that you have a sensitive ego?" then my prediction is that most people would say "no". However, the way they answer this question can still give us indications of what the accurate answer is. For instance, if the answer is, "No, absolutely not! And I'm insulted that you would even imply that!" then I would be inclined to make a mental note to in fact tread very carefully around this person's ego.

NON-NEEDS AND NON-ISSUES

Negotiators who specialise in the competitive division game would be familiar with introducing fake issues into the negotiation. This may for instance involve:

- the door-in-the-face tactic, where we ask for something that we don't want, and when we don't get it we say, "Oh, but can I at least get this other thing?" — in this instance what we really care about is the other thing; or

- introducing constraints that don't exist to make it appear harder for the other party to get what they want, e.g.: "Oh, well, if you want the BMW Z4 in blue, then we can't give a discount — they are very popular and hard to come by."The seller may tell this story even if he has exactly this car, in blue, and it's been sitting on the shop floor for twelve months.

Such tactics are intentional. As we keep reiterating, the division game unfortunately rewards lies, deceit, and manipulation. It serves us well to consider the list of demands or issues, and consider the possibility that some of them have been invented merely as bargaining chips.

In addition to intentional tactics used by the other party, we also need to recognise the possibility of so called non-issues. This is when we believe we have to negotiate to get something even though it is ours to begin with. As a result of our ignorance, we may end up trading something of value in order to get this non-issue.

A customer might open a negotiation with, "I will only buy this item if you throw in a six-month warranty," not realising that the product already comes with a twelve-month warranty. An unethical salesperson would jump on the opportunity to use this non-issue for a trade: "Oh, six months' warranty? I may be able to do that for you, but only if you purchase the item today, spend at least $500 in the store, and pay in cash."

SUB-OPTIMISATION

I derived this negotiation concept from the field of software development, so let us begin with an analogy from that profession. There are several criteria that a piece of software should ideally tick.

- If the code is kept flexible and generic, then that will make bug fixing, changes to the software, and integration with other systems and operating systems easier.

- If the code is written in a manner that mimics real-world

interactions, then many bugs become easier to find, and many bugs also become completely preventable.

- The software can be optimised to run faster, or require fewer systems resources, e.g. less memory. This allows the software to run on devices with lower specifications (e.g. a tablet or smartphone), or allows the programmer to add more features (e.g. more realistic effects in a computer game).

- The software can also be optimised from a user experience point of view, e.g. by making controls intuitive and self-explanatory.

- If the code is well documented, then that makes it much easier to add to, as well as to change or replace the developers who are working on the software

There are of course *many* more criteria. For our purposes, I simply wish to share that there are many needs to be satisfied in order for successful software development to take place (i.e. a successful outcome).

Sub-optimisation occurs when the programmer continues to focus on one aspect long after that aspect is good enough. Not only does this reduce the time available to work on the other aspects, it may also make it much harder to make the other aspects good enough. For instance, if the programmer chooses to optimise execution speed to the extreme, he or she will in the process have to make trade-offs on the flexibility of the code. At some point even the user experience may have to suffer, because the software logic is now arranged to fit the computer's hardware rather than the user's brain.

Sub-optimisation is extremely common in negotiation. In particular, the division of money usually gets far more attention than is appropriate. In a salary negotiation between an employer and a new recruit, the employer may take pride in winning the price negotiation. In the process, he or she is likely to neglect the other ten, twenty or a hundred needs that the company actually wants satisfied through this appointment. And if the hiring manager uses too much power in trying to force a low salary, then it may become much harder for the company's other needs to get satisfied going forwards.

10

CONSIDER ALL RELEVANT PARTIES AND STAKEHOLDERS

———

I go to the hairdresser. We negotiate which haircut I should have. We both agree, the services are rendered, money changes hands, and the deal is done. Right? Wrong!

Afterwards I go home and find that my girlfriend doesn't like my haircut. So my girlfriend calls my hairdresser (they are friends) and negotiates what my haircut should look like. Next time my girlfriend comes with me to the hairdresser and negotiates with the hairdresser on my behalf. I had failed to consider the needs of all stakeholders, and now one stakeholder (namely the decision maker) decided to interfere with my negotiation.

Many books and training courses treat stakeholder analysis as an advanced topic, or not at all. I would be inclined to suggest that having a firm understanding of all the parties directly and indirectly involved, affected or related to the negotiation is fundamental to setting up the right negotiation to begin with.

Several cultures have figured this out and incorporate behaviours such as including empty chairs at every meeting. These unfilled seats serve to remind those present of the stakeholders who are not present at the table. Who is a stakeholder? In its simplest terms a stakeholder is someone who can either affect the outcomes of the negotiation, or will be affected by the outcomes of the negotiation. Many stakeholders will hold both roles at the same time.

We next expand our understanding of stakeholders. However, if we launch straight into the comprehensive version I'm afraid that I'll demoralise you; we rarely, if ever, have time to do all the work that proper stakeholder analysis requires of us. So let's start with a more basic version that will get you through most negotiations.

THE BASIC VERSION

Here we acknowledge that we have stakeholders, and the other party has stakeholders. So, how do my stakeholders affect my negotiation? Well, at least in two ways.

- They may give me the brief to begin with, i.e. the parameters of the negotiation and the desired outcomes.

- They may also need to approve any final agreement that I reach with the other party.

This applies to the other party as well. Now, the average negotiator might simply accept the brief from his or her stakeholders, negotiate, and then check with the stakeholders for approval. But skilled negotiators realise that these interactions are in fact also negotiations. Thus we have already added four negotiations in addition to the "main" one (negotiation #1).

Let me explain. Remember that the way we set our desired outcomes or goals affect what game we can play. And what game we play will affect the likelihood of us creating value and achieving outcomes that we are happy with. So, we may need to negotiate the brief (negotiation #2) to ensure that it allows us to set up the most appropriate negotiation process for the outcomes that we wish to achieve.

In response to the negotiation with the other party, we may come up with ideas for options that could work for all parties. In some instances we may first discuss with the other party, and then negotiate with our own stakeholders (negotiation #3) for approval. Remember that if we treat the other party as a partner who can help us in the pursuit of creating value, it is possible that the other party helps us find outcomes that our stakeholders could never envisage.

In other situations we may actually want to ensure that our stakeholders will approve an option *before* we mention it to the other party. This would be true for example in a hostage negotiation where we make an offer to the perpetrator. If we make the perpetrator excited about the option, but then have to renege because our stakeholders say no, then we risk loosing credibility with the perpetrator. In such crisis negotiations trust and rapport is even more critical than in everyday and commercial negotiations, so we may want to be extra careful that we can deliver what we promise.

And now we consider the other party, who will also negotiate their brief, and negotiate for final approval (negotiations #4 and #5). It may very well be in our interest to help the other party with these negotiations. If negotiating with our stakeholders can help open up the scope of the negotiation, and that can lead to better outcomes, then we can expect the same benefit from the other party's negotiation with his or her stakeholders.

Let's now focus on negotiation #5. What if the other party does not expect his or her stakeholders to approve the deal? Will he or she then agree with us to begin with? Probably not. Thus, if we want to get the other party to agree, we had better ensure that:

- the agreement will satisfy the other party's needs;

- the agreement will satisfy the other party's stakeholders' needs;

- that the agreement is such that it will make the other party look good to his or her stakeholders; and

- the other party is equipped with the confidence and arguments to convince his or her stakeholders to accept the deal.

I hope these insights, together with many more in this book, will persuade you even more of the limitations of the division game. If we win the negotiation game, the other party loses. How will that negotiator feel about selling that loss to his or her stakeholders? Could embarrassment, a loss of pride or resentment cause the negotiator to deadlock the negotiation rather than face his or her stakeholders only having achieved the worst possible deal? At least a deadlock can be blamed on us being unreasonable. The lesson here is that it is rarely helpful to make the other party look incompetent to his or her stakeholders. Just as it is rarely helpful to destroy a relationship.

So we have now identified five separate negotiations that are present as soon as we consider stakeholders. In some cases a couple of these negotiations will be trivial. In other cases one or more of these peripheral negotiations will be the key to unlocking value.

But we aren't done yet. There is also a chance, opportunity or risk (depending on the context) that our stakeholders will communicate directly or indirectly with the other party's stakeholders (negotiation #6). In that case we (as negotiators) may want to influence our stakeholders to act a certain way, come across a certain way, or communicate a certain way (negotiation #7) in interactions with the other party.

A concrete example would be a negotiator representing a community of landowners in their negotiations with a large mining company that is interested in buying their land. If playing the division game, there is a benefit to the landowners to negotiate as a group, and a benefit for the mining company to negotiate with landowners individually. Thus we may need to negotiate with our group of landowners to ensure that no one breaks off from the group to have individual negotiations with the mining company.

Another example might be two countries that are both flexing their military muscles by having a military presence in an area (e.g. the Persian Gulf or the South China Sea). While the intention of the respective governments may simply be to signal strength, a serious negotiation will be needed with some of the stakeholders (in this case the military personnel in the area) about how they need to behave. A simple misinterpreted action, e.g. one country's military ship in the wrong region, or a single soldier killing an innocent civilian, could be sufficient to trigger an escalated conflict.

These would be two examples of negotiation #7, the one where we ensure that our stakeholders behave in a manner that is conducive to us achieving our desired negotiated outcome. Of course, the other party may have to have this negotiation with his or her stakeholders too (negotiation #8).

Add to this that the other party's negotiator may seek to bypass us and influence our stakeholders directly (negotiation #9). And we can of course do the same (negotiation #10). So that is at least ten possible negotiations among two negotiators and two groups of stakeholders, and this was the basic version of stakeholder mapping. How keen are you to launch into the comprehensive version?

THE COMPREHENSIVE VERSION

So you want to do a proper stakeholder analysis? Good! Let's begin by asking ourselves the following questions:

- who is our negotiator?
- who is our decision maker, or who are our decision makers?
- who are our internal stakeholders?
- who are our external stakeholders?

- Who can advise us on the negotiation, e.g. negotiation expertise, cross-cultural expertise, industry expertise, legal issues, knowledge about people involved and their histories?

- Who could be a potential ally for us in the negotiation?

- Who has relationships with key people in the other party's organisation?

- Who is a potential leak of information to the other party, e.g. a disgruntled past employee?

- If the other party escalates the negotiation, who would become involved on our side?

- Who do we expect is giving the other party advice on us, e.g. how to negotiate with our culture?

And here are questions we might ask regarding the other party.

- Who is the negotiator?

- Who is the decision maker, or who are the decision makers?

- Who are the internal stakeholders?

- Who are the external stakeholders?

- Who can the negotiation be escalated to if necessary?

- Who can connect us to the decision maker?

- Who can indirectly influence the decision maker on our behalf?

- Who is next in line to replace the decision maker if the current one is out of the picture?

- Who can provide us with information on the other party?

- Who can coerce the decision maker?

- Who influences the flow of information and opinion?

- Who is trusted by everyone to keep secrets?

- Who is the person that everyone likes?

- Who controls the budget?

- Who will implement the deal (or be in a position to raise any other constraints, barriers or concerns before the outcome is achieved)?

And as we consider external parties we might ask these questions.

- Who could replace us in the deal if the other party wants to negotiate with someone else instead?

- Who could replace the other party in the deal if we want to negotiate with someone else instead?

- Who are the benefactors, i.e. all the parties that would derive benefit if there were a deal between us and the other party? (Note that this changes based on what the deal is!)

- Who are the victims, i.e. everyone that would be adversely affected by a deal and would therefore oppose it? (Again, this changes based on what the deal is!)

- On that point, who are the benefactors and victims of the status quo? Who is unhappy/happy if there is no deal?

- Who is the referee who could force an outcome?

- Who is better positioned to negotiate on our behalf?

- Who could add value if included in a deal? E.g. in terms of resources, reputation, credibility or relationships?

- Who can facilitate a deal?

- Who or what organisations need to approve the deal?

- Who or what organisations can stop the deal?

- Who can influence those who can stop the deal?

- What external parties will be part of implementing the deal?

- Who is the poison, who if included would worsen or ruin the deal?

- Who controls the flow of information, e.g. in the media?

- Who might be watching the negotiation and may use the outcome as a precedent, or preparation for their future negotiations with us or with others?

Now, given all of these parties, let's ask these questions.

- Who has needs that they want satisfied? Everyone! Absolutely everyone! So the ideal option, solution or agreement that we come up with should do a good job of catering to everyone's needs!

- How will the stakeholder map change if we change the issues? What if we are discussing a complex issue with various sub-issues? That may result in unique versions of the stakeholder map for each sub-issue!

- Who negotiates with whom?

- Who likes whom?

- Who dislikes whom?

- Who agrees with whom? On which of the issues? What about future issues? Is support based on issues or relationships?

- Who depends on whom? Who has power over whom?

- Who controls resources?

- Who has a history with whom?

- Who has stakeholders? Who are they?

- Which parties form coalitions, e.g. for political reasons or because they share deeper beliefs or values?

- Who is best positioned to influence whom?

- How could each stakeholder be influenced to in turn help us influence the other party (or parties)?

- What does each stakeholder need to know? What do they want to know? What type of message is most suitable to influence each stakeholder? E.g. facts for the other party and simplified public relations for the public?

- Who does each individual piece of communication appear to be directed to? Who is it actually intended to influence?

- What external reality and system is each stakeholder facing currently? Does this make each stakeholder temporarily stronger, weaker, tougher, more desperate, more agreeable or more flexible? How are bonds between stakeholders affected?

- What external reality and system do the stakeholders (or coalition) together face? E.g. an imminent alien invasion would probably incentivise people to stop arguing about differences and think of ways of cooperating instead.

- Is a stakeholder one individual or several people? How unified are they in their views, opinions, positions, needs, values, beliefs? Are they in complete agreement or fifty-one per cent vs. forty-nine?

- Is this stakeholder map static? No! It changes constantly. If stakeholders change so do relationships. Therefore our strategy may need to change.

Another negotiator once told me: "Clients don't need questions, they need answers." I would respectfully agree with the merit in his argument, and then reframe and suggest that this depends on the questions. Clients will be able to answer most of these questions, but they typically don't because no one is asking them.

NEGOTIATING THROUGH A THIRD PARTY

We have mentioned that sometimes there will be a third person or party who/that is better positioned to influence the other party than we are. Using a third party may also provide a natural way of stalling or slowing down the negotiation if this is desired, e.g. in a hostage negotiation. Depending on the negotiation, this may very well be a decision that makes all the difference to the outcomes.

There are, however, a few considerations to keep in mind. Firstly, the third party will become a stakeholder, and as such will have needs of his or her own. Some of these needs may not be perfectly aligned with the outcomes that we desire. This is a similar challenge to the one we discussed when pointing out the difference between personal and organisational needs.

In fact, the third party may bring in much more than his or her own set of needs. The third-party negotiator may have a prior relationship with the other party that is either positive or negative, or perceived to be positive or negative. And the third party may bring a completely different risk profile, temperament and personality into the negotiation.

For instance, in law enforcement crisis negotiations, third parties are occasionally allowed to speak to the perpetrator. They may be a psychologist, and the task may be to assess the subject's personality. However, sometimes the psychologist will fall back into his or her default mode of operation, and may start to treat the subject. It is therefore of grave importance to brief the third party on the role we want him or her to assume.

Also, as with any stakeholder analysis, we need to carefully consider what hidden agendas parties may have. This goes for the third-party negotiator too, even though we would like to hope that he or she is on our side.

An example could be that of a union negotiator who is supposed to represent us, but may have a personal need to maintain a reputation for being a tough negotiator who always puts up a fight and never backs down.

In such a scenario, the third-party negotiator may pollute the process and hinder a negotiation where parties might otherwise have been ready to agree.

The other aspect to keep in mind is that negotiating through a third party introduces yet another layer of communication. So we essentially double the number of opportunities for misunderstandings and diverging perceptions. Consider also the reverse of this — that the use of an interpreter essentially makes the interpreter an intermediary negotiator. While the intention is for the interpreter to merely translate from one language to the other, there are a large number of reasons why meaning will be lost or distorted in the process.

- As previously discussed, languages don't match perfectly and translating from one to the other without changing the meaning is virtually impossible.

- The interpreter may not mimic all the body language, tonality etc of the negotiators when translating the message, and specific elements of body language, tonality may mean very different things in different languages and need to be changed to convey the intended message.

Of course, there are also advantages to using a third party or an interpreter.

- Using an intermediary negotiator can be an effective excuse to not have decision makers at the table. This allows for various tactics used in the division game.

- Using an interpreter, even if the negotiator is familiar with the other language, slows down the process and increases thinking time.

- If the third-party negotiator brings a strong relationship, then this may significantly improve the level of rapport and trust in the negotiation.

- The third-party negotiator may be more skilled in the process of negotiation than we are.

- The third party negotiator may bring expertise regarding the content, the culture or the system.

Every process option we have available to us in negotiation has pros and cons, and will be the most appropriate one in at least one situation. Your job as a negotiator will be to consider the advantages/disadvantages, and pick the most appropriate process option for the current situation.

For instance, a common approach to resolving disputes is using an impartial third party, i.e. a mediator. Having a mediator carry messages between the two parties allows that person to remove all the pollution in the interaction and facilitate a rational problem-solving process. However, because parties don't interact directly with each other, they have little opportunity to build rapport and trust, or adjust their approach in real time based on how the other party reacts. Add to this that, everything else being equal, we run the risk of dehumanising others and treating them worse if they are absent than if they are in front of us. Again, the decisions we make need to be situational.

11

CREATE VALUABLE AND COMPELLING OPTIONS

——— ——

We will continue to refer to "the other party", but encourage the reader to stay aware that options may exist between any number of parties on the stakeholder map. We have now hopefully identified all the parties, and a long list of needs for each party. The next step is to find options that parties can and want to agree on. In this section we unpack this concept a bit further.

OPTIONS TOOLBOX

The approach of identifying needs and satisfying them with options works in the majority of negotiations. Still, if we analyse a large number of successful negotiations, then we will also see a number of other techniques popping up fairly often. I call these the options toolbox. Many of these are quite specific, but can make a big difference in moving certain types of tricky negotiations towards agreement.

Preventative options

Sometimes needs are truly conflicting. Most of the time when we identify perceived conflicting needs we have the option to drill deeper to try to uncover other needs that are shared or unique. But when the deepest needs, e.g. values and beliefs, are in conflict then we may not find deeper needs and therefore we'll have to try something else.

Let's take an example. In one episode of *The Daily Show*, host Jon Stewart had a candid disagreement with then Republican presidential candidate, Mike Huckabee. Stewart and Huckabee had taken opposite sides on the topic of abortion. Some way into the discussion Stewart suggested that the parties might never agree on who is right on the topic of abortion, but perhaps both parties could agree that they would both like to see less abortion.

If the parties would instead focus their efforts on how to reduce the need for abortion, then that would reduce the need to have the difficult conversation of whether abortion is right or wrong. Ultimately, if the need for abortion were eliminated, the agreement on whether abortion was right or wrong would become redundant.

While I developed this tool to deal with truly conflicting needs, we can often use it as a shortcut to avoid other difficult discussions. In one scenario two companies were struggling to figure out what price would be fair if one party were to acquire the other. The discussion became so difficult that at one point my colleague applied the preventative option. He said: "How can we both get what we want without having to agree on a price?" The clever use of the question "How?" bypasses the question "Can we do it?" and makes the parties work on the assumption that they can find a solution. The parties realised that they could still do everything they wanted if the relationship changed from ownership to a service-level agreement. Now the conversation changed from the difficult task of agreeing on the value of the company for an acquisition, to only having to agree on the value of the services the company would provide. The perceived conflicting issue was thus eliminated.

In summary, whenever we find an issue that we can't resolve by any other means, consider instead how we could make agreement on that topic redundant.

Contingent options

Sometimes parties struggle to agree on how they believe the future will pan out. This disagreement might be well camouflaged and may need some detective work to identify, e.g. by using the ladder of inference.

Say that two parties disagree on the price of a company that is for sale. The parties have fully analysed and satisfied their respective and collective needs, and the only remaining issue is to agree on a price. Let's also say that the parties have shared their respective thinking processes and data that lead them to reach different conclusions about price. Let's also say the parties agree on everything apart from one assumption: the future performance of the company. We try to deal with this difference, but find that both parties are confident that their individual expectations are right.

How do we resolve this? Neither of us knows what will happen in the future, but still we are convinced that our guess is more accurate than the other party's. One option is to simply acknowledge that we don't know, and let each party bet on being right.

A contingent option is one where each party gets what they want provided that their forecast of the future is right. In this example, the parties may agree to have the actual company performance determine the price, and have the price paid in instalments over the next five years. If the company performs (and is therefore valuable) the price will end up being higher. If the company underperforms then the price will be lower. This has the benefit of putting parties in the same boat, with the same incentives, i.e. to make the company as profitable as possible for the next five years. This would discourage undesirable practices such as massaging the financials of the company in order to artificially increase the company's valuation at the time of sale.

Of course, some effects of contingent options may be undesirable. For instance, the seller might have preferred to have all their money at the time of sale, and the buyer might have preferred to not have the seller around to interfere with the running of the business for the next five years. These variations can often be accommodated.

If we look around we will find that contingent options typically explain how insurance and financial instruments such as futures, derivatives, and interest rate swaps work. With these instruments the negotiation is a zero-sum game, and one party will be a winner and one will be a loser. However, remember that at the time of agreement both parties are entirely confident that they are correct, and therefore confident that they have struck the best deal for themselves at the expense of the other party. Essentially this is a bet where both parties are convinced that they will win.

We may bundle together all assumptions for each party and make the agreement contingent on the final performance of the company. This is not viable in all cases, perhaps because the buyer will not continue operating the entire company in its current form. In such cases, we can still make the agreement contingent on the individual factors that will impact on future performance, e.g. future inflation rates, market growth rates, or anticipated political decisions that may affect the profitability of the industry.

Contingent options also work for differences in estimates of likelihoods, probabilities, preferences with regard to time, preferences with regards to liquidity and sensitivity or assessment of risk.

- If two entrepreneurs have widely different expectations of what the profit will be in the first year (say $100,000 and $1 million, respectively) of operation, they may agree that one party will get the first $100,000, and the other party may get the next $900,000.

- If a baseball team considers hiring a star player with a history of health problems, and the player is confident that he is healthy, then both parties should be happy with a generous remuneration package that is reduced for every game the player misses due to health reasons.

- If an employee is confident that he or she will generate twice the profit of other employees, then both the employee and employer should be happy to agree on uncapped variable compensation.

Impact check

We have discussed how conflicting values and beliefs can be inherently difficult to deal with. With preventative options we removed the need to have the conversation. But what if we must have the conversation? Sometimes we may be able to still change the topic.

Let's take the difficult issue of using US federal funding to pay for abortions for rape victims. If the negotiation is held at the ideological level (focusing on what the federal government should pay for, or whether or not abortion is acceptable) then parties may never agree. Why? Because we are negotiating about our values, and about right vs. wrong. And none of us will accept that our values are wrong.

If we instead change the topic to "How much will it cost?" and we arrive at a cost of $0.002 per taxpayer per year, then this cost might be laughably small compared to the cost of even having the conversation. It may feel a lot easier for one party to concede $0.002 per taxpayer than to concede on an ideological issue. Specifically, it makes it easier for us to rationalise that the issue is trivial, and therefore we won't feel cognitive dissonance from acting contrary to our values.

In this particular example we could of course go further and also calculate the added cost to taxpayers of *not* approving abortions for rape victims. Maybe there would be increased counselling costs, allowances for parents, and so on. By offsetting all these saved costs, perhaps the $0.002 cost per taxpayer actually becomes a *gain* of $1 per taxpayer? Again, I am deliberately sitting on the fence on the content of this issue. Rather I'm merely illustrating that changing the topic away from values, beliefs and ideology towards material needs can equip negotiators with an excuse to reach agreement.

Path of least risk

This is a tool that I developed after watching many debates about climate change. In this case the two camps (climate activists fearing the effects of climate change, and climate sceptics denying various aspects of climate change) have several different needs. This is not an exhaustive debate on climate change, but rather an excuse to demonstrate another tool.

- Both camps fear something. Climate sceptics fear unnecessary regulation and a negative impact on the economy. Climate activists fear the negative impact on themselves, future generations, and the planet.

- Both camps believe something. Some climate sceptics don't believe the climate is changing, and some don't believe it is caused by human activity. Climate activists believe in both the effect and that human activity is causing it. (Alternatively climate activists may not believe in climate change, but rather use it as a proxy for getting people to work for a healthier environment.)

As with the example of abortion, part of this discussion is values based, and focussed on which camp is right. In the abortion example we used preventative options, so let's try that here too. An example of a preventative option could be to change the source of energy used to one that doesn't produce emissions with negative side effects on our environment. This option may not be available to us at the moment.

How about contingent options, where we let the future happen and then we find out who is right and who is wrong? If climate activists are right than this is a dangerous gamble!

And because the stakes are high for climate activists the impact check won't work to persuade them. However, the impact check may be feasible to persuade climate sceptics if it turns out that saving the environment by curbing greenhouse gases can be made cheap (or even profitable).

A completely different option is for us to acknowledge that we can't agree on who is right and who is wrong. But we can acknowledge that there is some uncertainty and that either party could be wrong. It may then be in the interest of both parties to manage the risk of both sides being wrong.

- Implement as many carbon-emission-reducing options as possible, with the exception of those that will hurt the economy or require significant intervention.

- Continue monitoring the correlation between emissions and climate change. The data should confirm or deny whether the adjustment in emissions had an effect. If it turns out climate sceptics were right, then we didn't waste money and effort unnecessarily. If it turns out the climate activists were right, then we have made progress towards more sustainable behaviour and hopefully steered ourselves away from disaster.

A while after I wrote this section, Hurricane Sandy hit New York. On 2 November 2012 New York Mayor Michael Bloomberg wrote: "Our climate is changing. And while the increase in extreme weather we have experienced in New York City and around the world may or may not be the result of it, the risk that it might be — given this week's devastation — should compel all elected leaders to take immediate action."

Here we used climate change as an illustrative example how this tool can work. For the actual climate debate there may be several mutually beneficial outcomes available. It may be the case that converting society to green energy would bring with it a bigger positive effect to the economy than the savings from avoiding carbon taxes, thereby satisfying the major needs for both camps. There may also be the option of reframing the debate from climate change to sustainability by arguing that all fossil fuels are finite and solar power is effectively infinite. And if we accurately account for all the costs with each approach, we may find that the monetary cost of intervention now is miniscule compared with the financial and health impacts on all future generations from pollution, let alone climate change. We could also reframe the topic to align with additional needs of the climate sceptics. The options are endless.

Many of us already use the path of least risk. Whether or not we are experts in physics, many of us would probably prefer that the CERN particle accelerator does not carry out a particular experiment if a sufficient number of experts raise the risk of the earth potentially imploding as a result. We don't know which experts are right, but we may wish to avoid the path that carries the greatest risk.

Similarly, some people interviewed about why they believe in a religion cite the risk of not believing. Specifically, they may be unsure of whether their chosen religion is right, but of their two choices (believe or not believe), believing carries the lowest risk.

Path of least risk thus has links with how we think about insurance. When we take out hurricane insurance we don't take sides when parties argue about whether a hurricane will strike this year or not. We simply acknowledge that *if* a hurricane strikes, then the cost is prohibitive, and we therefore accept the risk of paying for insurance we may never use. Similarly those of us who get vaccinations wish to avoid the risk of getting a particular disease.

Values cherry-picking

We would probably like to believe that our values are consistent. But this is not always the case (as illustrated by our "What would you do if you could be invisible for a day?" example). We hold multiple values, and many of them are actually incompatible. In the section on perception we discovered that we could adopt multiple frames of reference to evaluate the right thing to do. This relates well to how we view our values; we often self-servingly cherry-pick and rationalise our values based on the outcome we want.

So while our values are inflexible, we have multiple values that aren't necessarily compatible with each other. This gives negotiators an opportunity for influence. What if we could influence which values the other party is using to make a decision? This is not a hypothetical question, because we can! For instance, let us assume that there is a person who considers himself a climate sceptic, and also feels strongly about national security.

Now, let's pause for a second. If we happen to be a climate activist, what do we want? Do we want agreement on the issue that climate change is a problem? Yes, but this need is merely instrumental to us getting something else. We hope that agreement on climate change being a problem will lead people to take action to reduce greenhouse gas emissions, which we hope will provide for a healthy environment.

So if we are stuck in the climate change debate, could we get our needs satisfied another way? What might be the outcome if we instead engaged the other party in a debate on national security? Perhaps we could reach agreement to reduce our dependency on foreign sources of energy. Perhaps these sources are primarily carbon based, and perhaps we have limited carbon-based energy sources domestically. So limiting our dependency on foreign energy may require us to increase our focus on alternative energy sources locally.

Is it conceivable that selecting a *different* negotiation that triggers *different* values could end up give us everything we initially wanted in the climate change debate? Yes.

Chunking

Sometimes the problem or issue that we are confronted with is simply too large to deal with. Take gun control as an example. Most people will have a view as to whether we should have restrictive gun control laws or not. Taking positions on the issue will simply lead to the divisional game of negotiation, and the longer we discuss this issue the more polarised our positions will become. And we now know that positions cause two big problems: they limit how we think about our needs, and they limit how we think about satisfying those needs.

We have discussed that we can instead play the integration game, identify the shared and unique needs we have, and find options for satisfying those needs. And we also know that this process may get stuck if we discover that deeply held values and beliefs are conflicting. And we discussed that we may then try preventative options to make resolving the differences a moot point.

But for the gun-control issue it may be difficult to find a preventative option. "Can we at least agree that it would be better if there were fewer guns?" may be met with "No!" Likewise "Can we at least agree that it would be better if there was less need for guns?" could also be met with "No!" by someone who likes to use guns for recreation or hunting.

A challenge here is that the topic is too complex — we are discussing gun control for everyone and every purpose in one go. And whether we want to or not, the issue may be interpreted as being directly tied to one's values (e.g. in the case of the US, where the right to bear arms is enshrined in the constitution: arguably a position in itself). If we instead subdivide the issue into smaller components, we may find that several sub-issues are easy to agree on (i.e. they become shared or different), and in the process we reduce the scale of the remaining disagreements (i.e. perceived conflicting issues). For instance (and here we focus on increasing agreement on what to do, not yet how to do it):

- Can we agree that neither of us wants to be killed by a gun?

- Can we agree that we do not want innocent people, children or police officers harmed by guns?

- Can we agree that we don't want children under the age of ___ to have access to guns?

- Can we agree that we don't want criminals to have access to guns?

- Can we agree that we don't mentally unfit people to have access to guns?

- Can we agree that we do not want guns in schools, bars, sporting events, libraries or hospitals?

- Can we agree that we don't want guns approved for one person to use ending up in the hands of another person?

- Can we agree that guns used purely for legal recreational purposes such as hunting, shooting range target practice and competitions are OK?

- Can we agree that guns for the use of defending oneself, one's loved ones and one's property are OK in the event that police are not yet present and use of the guns are in accordance with the law?

- Can we agree that it is reasonable that some weapons are too powerful for private use (atomic weapons, aircraft carriers, hand grenades, assault rifles...)?

In some cases this process can lead to complete agreement, and in other cases we simply reduce the size of the remaining issues that we still disagree on. In either case we are better off than when we started. The process we are following is similar to how we make an angel statue out of a block of marble. Even if we don't know how to shape the angel we can at least start by removing the parts that are *obviously not part of the angel*.

Chunking can be done in three directions: up, down and sideways. So far we have described chunking down, i.e. breaking into smaller pieces. Sometimes it is useful to chunk up (i.e. group several issues) or chunking sideways (e.g. using analogies or separate examples that we are not emotionally attached to).

Another insight is that chunking offers an explanation for why parties often try to trump each other in relation to perception needs — and chunking also offers a solution. We tend to assume that e.g. status and power are indivisible units of measurement, and that we have to have more status or power than the other party. But once we realise that there are multiple components of status, then each party can be best at their respective components. While negotiator A derives status from having a PhD, and negotiator B derives status from thirty years' experience, negotiator C may derive status from having been exposed to more approaches to negotiation. Note that by chunking down we replaced a conflicting need (status), with unique needs (status from research skills, from experience, and from breadth of knowledge).

Follow the money

A common negotiation scenario in business is where one more powerful party (e.g. a giant retailer), asks the other party (e.g. its supplier) to improve (i.e. reduce) prices compared to the previous year "…if it wants the benefit of doing business with the more powerful company". The follow-the-money tool offers a few alternative choices.

- Track forwards. As the supplier, one of the first things we can do is change the negotiation from "We need to give them a discount!" to "How can we both make more money?" If there are more end-consumers, if they buy more products each, if they select higher margin products, or if they pay more for each product, then we will all make more money. If the costs associated with getting the product to the retailer and to the consumers are reduced, then we can all make more money. So, how about we focus on that?

- Investigate internally. If we have to accept the price reduction, then what can we do internally to achieve that reduction in price? Can the retailer assist us in that? Can another third party help us cut costs?

- Track backwards. Can we motivate our own suppliers to take on some of the cost reduction? Can we together improve efficiencies? Can we perhaps consolidate our suppliers and get economies of scale? Can we improve inbound logistics?

Follow-the-money can work regardless of which side of the table we are on. One client in the mining sector had taken with a position of demanding a discount on rental of gas extraction rigs. As negotiators we don't always get the time or opportunity to help our clients better understand their own needs, and in this instance we had to run with this position. By tracking backwards, we looked at the supplier's business and understood that they incurred considerable cost and wasted capacity the more frequently they moved the rigs between clients. Thus quadrupling the duration of the contract (which was no issue for the client) allowed the supplier to significantly reduce the price charged to our client.

While our client started with a position, we avoided a process where the other party would have to give up value to our party. Rather we still managed the process to allow both parties to find value creation opportunities.

Add resources

What do we mean when we say that options create value? One way of answering that question is to say that the value comes from the complementary needs and resources that parties bring to the negotiation, and any synergies that may result. I may have unique needs that I can't satisfy on my own, but which *you* can satisfy because you have the resources. Both of us may have shared needs that we can only satisfy (or can satisfy better) by combining our resources.

So one insight is that it is often possible to increase the available value by adding the right person or party to the deal. This party may bring resources, or satisfy other needs such as credibility, access to clients, relationships, reputation, and power. When we think about it, we may realise that this is what most companies are; collections of individuals and resources that together create more value than the sum of their parts.

This tool simply raises the awareness that we can often increase value one step at a time by including for example another person who either brings value to the rest of us (perhaps through their reputation and network of potential customers), or unlocks value for all of us (perhaps by complementing our skills so that we can all together deliver a new product or service).

Importantly, the added person may also bring a new need into the equation, and this may actually help us satisfy our needs better. Let me share an example. I once approached an IT professional for some help. He wanted money in return, which I was not in a position to give at the time. So what could we do? I offered him a place in my negotiation course, but he was not very interested in negotiation. By including his employer, however, we added both a resource (a training budget for the IT professional), and a need (the company wanted to see him improve his negotiation skills). Suddenly we ended up with a perfect match of needs and resources.

- I could provide negotiation training; the company wanted it.

- The IT professional could provide IT services; I needed them.

- The company could provide some funds; the IT professional needed them.

So the option we came up with was for the company to send the IT professional to my course. Once I got paid I could then pay the IT professional for his IT services. And the company was happy since the IT professional now had improved negotiation skills.

Not a win/win, but rather a win/win/win!

Share resources

I developed this tool while helping an entrepreneur deal with her growing business. Demand was picking up to the point where she needed a reliable assistant to help her out. The challenge was that she really only needed the assistant to do one hour of work per day, but scattered over many small tasks over the course of each day. No assistant would like to tie up his or her entire day to only get paid for one hour. And the entrepreneur could at this point only afford to pay for that one hour of work. How could she get the reliability and responsiveness she needed from the assistant, while only paying for the work the assistant actually did?

Working together we identified a number of other entrepreneurs in the same position as her. Collectively they had enough work to warrant a full-time role, but they each only had to pay for what they used.

Many businesses are built on the concept of the assistant. Whether we look at providers of call centres, accounting or legal services, we observe that value is created by specialisation, better capacity utilisation, and less duplication of effort.

Eliminate worst case scenarios

In most deals, there will be some elements of uncertainty: some things we simply won't know about until they happen. Thus when we assess how valuable an option is to us, we consider several different scenarios, and how likely they are, and then we arrive at some form of average or expected value.

Often negotiators will focus on making the most desirable scenario more desirable. This is good, because it increases the expected value. But we can also increase the expected value by improving the *least* desirable scenario. This may also involve reducing the likelihood of that scenario, or even eliminating it. Specifically, parties can increase expected value by agreeing on what they will *not* do.

For example, if I am acquiring your company I may price in the risk of you leaving, of your employees leaving with you, and of you taking the customers with you as well. Or perhaps I price in the cost incurred if you stay in the business but resist the restructuring that I have in mind. By guaranteeing that none of these undesirable scenarios will take place, I will be able to justify a higher price for your company, because the expected value of your company just increased.

Eliminating worst-case scenarios is the main focus of the crisis negotiation game, but it is of course still a useful insight for the other games.

Remove negative value

When we design options from scratch, we build those options so that they satisfy needs. Sometimes we don't have this luxury and we are simply presented with an option that we can modify and then attach a value to.

Often in such cases we observe an exclusive focus on price, which translates to the division game. An improvement is to realise that the price is for something in return, and we can work to adjust the value of that something. If we want a higher price for a company we are selling, for instance, then we may look at how to increase the profitability of that company.

One aspect that is often missed is to specifically seek out and eliminate the negative value. For instance, some companies may have sub-units, contracts or projects that have a net negative effect on the company. Removing these then actually increases the value of the company.

Similarly, many positive professional and romantic relationships are clouded by negative value from various kinds of pollution. Strengthening such relationships might actually translate to merely removing the negative value — i.e. the pollution.

Quick options

After reading this book you will hopefully want to apply maximisation at every chance you get. You want to increase the scope, and create an extraordinary amount of value for all parties — way more value than the other party expected. But you may find yourself sitting opposite a negotiator who just wants to negotiate a five per cent change on last year's contract, and that's it. There are many possible reasons for this.

- He or she only has the mandate to negotiate that deal.

- He or she is only incentivised on achieving that deal.

- He or she only has time to negotiate that deal now.

- He or she is not sure a more creative negotiation process will reach an outcome, and prefers to at least have an outcome.

All of these reasons are barriers that will make it harder to bring the other party with us on the maximisation journey. One way forward is to realise that the other party has a need to have *a* deal. We could help satisfy that need by first finding a good enough deal, and then try to open up the scope to improve that first deal. The rule is simple: we try anything but will only change the deal if it is at least incrementally better for both parties.

Now the parties have nothing to lose. There is no pressure to reach another outcome. It doesn't matter if the negotiations don't lead anywhere. If worse comes to worst the other negotiator will go back to his or her stakeholders with the good enough deal. We have thus created a gain frame. This more relaxed and open attitude may be just what we want if we want to bring someone with us on a journey to find more value.

Of course, negotiators need to be aware of the risk that the other party won't agree to further negotiations, so we can't blindly agree to anything in that initial agreement. The initial agreement thus still has to be good enough for us as well.

GENERAL INSIGHTS ON OPTIONS

Both/and vs. either/or

The following is a small change in our language that can have a tremendous effect on our negotiation performance. Negotiators over and over again present ideas and options with:

- "Either we can do this, or we can do that."

- "Which do you chose, this one or that one?"

- "In the end, either we do what you want, or what I want."

- "My way or the highway."

Skilled negotiators don't accept the implicit forced choice, and rather use inclusive language wherever possible:

- "How about we do both this and that?"

- "What if both you and I could get what we want?"

The either/or construct has a tendency to lead us towards division. The both/and construct is more likely to lead us towards integration and maximisation.

Present options or develop options together with the other party

We may start the options generation process independently of the other party, and then present our fully developed options to the other party as offers. Or we may collaborate with the other party to develop the options together.

There are benefits and risks with both approaches. Thinking about options before involving the other party is good as it means that we are preparing before the meeting. This may give us much more time for options generation than we would have in a meeting. We can involve more people on our team and therefore have more brainpower and more perspectives (although all partisan to our side of course) by involving other departments that need to give input.

The obvious drawback is that we don't involve the other party, and therefore run the risk of not adequately understanding or satisfying the other party's needs. We also run the risk of becoming married to our options, and not flexible enough to alter them once we meet with the other party. If we negotiate in a consensus-driven culture, then it will be very difficult for us to be flexible once we've agreed on an option. We run the risk of having a whole range of the decision traps we mentioned earlier (reactive devaluation, partisan perceptions, confirmation bias) work against us. We will struggle to build the other party's commitment (more on that in the commitment section) but we will in the process run the risk of becoming too committed to an outcome (effort justification, commitment bias). All of this increases the risk is that we end up in the division game between our preferred options and those of the other party.

If we instead discuss options together with the other party, then it is more likely that we will arrive at options that will work for both parties. Because neither party typically has a complete understanding of its own needs, we keep discovering our own needs in the options generation phase. If we collaborate during options generation then these needs are more likely to surface and we can take the opportunity to modify the option to satisfy the need we previously missed.

Drawbacks of including the other party straight away include the difficulty of having internal team discussion to evaluate which options suit us and why. We may want that discussion to be open to every stakeholder affected in our organisation, but we may not want the other party to listen in to this debate.

In keeping with the insight from the previous section, our recommendation here is not an either/or choice, but rather a both/and option.

- Think about options before meeting with the other party, but keep them as options.

- Then meet with the other party and develop options together. We don't necessarily have to present any of the options we prepared before the meeting. In fact, as we will see later, we may prefer if the other party raises those options. Ideally we merely wish to give the process small nudges in the right direction as necessary.

Limit choice

In the section on options generation we encouraged brainstorming a large number of options. This is not because more is better, but rather because the longer we spend creatively looking for solutions from different perspectives, the more likely we are to identify high-quality options. (And of course more low-quality options too, which we will later reject.) In the end we will typically pick just one option, and we are interested in the highest-quality option.

A common mistake is to not perform the options generation well enough. So for most negotiations, simply instructing parties to think of more options is a step in the right direction.

But this is a Band-Aid fix and introduces another risk: too much choice. This can be debilitating. If there are too many choices, then parties are likely to:

- perceive that there is a higher probability that they will not choose the best option (the fear of having made the wrong choice reduces our satisfaction with the option we eventually choose);

- feel more responsible for the outcome (if there are only two options on the table, then we can credibly tell ourselves, "I'm not entirely happy, but then again I only had two to chose from," but if there are ten, twenty or one hundred options, and if we don't leave with a good enough option then it is likely to be our fault); and/or

- concoct unrealistic expectations of what is possible (if there are one hundred available options, then we run the risk of dreaming up a fictitious, superior 101st option that cherry-picks the most desirable traits of the other options, and in comparison all hundred options seem not good enough).

So in conclusion, we want to stick with the options generation process long enough for us to identify the best possible option. But we also want to make sure that we don't present ourselves, or the other party, with too much choice. Ironically this means that even though we may be in a position to offer the other party total flexibility, and this would allow them to maximise value, they are likely to feel more comfortable with the process and more satisfied with the outcome if we artificially limit choice.

Of course, while we as ethical negotiators use this insight to help the other party make the choice that best satisfies everyone's needs, unethical negotiators use the same insight to artificially limit choice to options that favour them.

Lessons from motivation

We can also look at the motivation we have to move in a certain direction. In the competitive division game, we are typically motivated to move in opposite directions. In the integration game we rather find a common goal that we can work towards together. In each of these cases, the goal is simply an option.

So it may help us to unpack the process of motivation and apply the insights to get parties to work towards a common and desirable goal. What does the process of motivation look like? Here is one.

- Present state. We figure out where we are now, and where we are going if we don't change, and think about the pain we will feel if we continue along this path.

- Desired state. We set a new goal that motivates us — that will satisfy our needs in the future — and anticipate what achieving that goal will feel like.

- Path. We identify the path that we will follow to reach the goal. If the path is unknown and we can't see the link from the present to the future we may get discouraged.

- Obstacles. We identify the obstacles along the way and figure out how to work around them. The trick here is to be specific about the obstacles (problems), which will make it easier to find a way around them (solutions).

◆ Leverage. We attach sufficient pain to the status quo, and sufficient pleasure to the desired goal, that it becomes clear for us that we must change.

◆ Interrupt. We interrupt the patterns of behaviour that may take us away from our desired goal, and install new patterns that will take us towards our desired goal.

The first steps to this uses concepts that we already know.

◆ Present state. The current path we are on (on autopilot) is a pattern, and the reason we are looking to motivate ourselves to change is because the pattern leaves several of our needs unmet.

◆ Desired state. The goal is an option (the what) that is derived from the needs we wish to satisfy (the why).

What we haven't yet discussed are the subsequent steps, which address additional reasons why parties in a negotiation do not accept options. So what are the reasons parties don't like particular options and pursue others?

◆ Desired state. One reason is of course that the other party doesn't think that the option will satisfy his or her needs.

◆ Path. If we peek at the motivation framework above we can also gather that negotiators may turn down options if they can't see how the options can practically be realised.

◆ Obstacles. Likewise, if the other party can immediately identify obstacles, or reasons the option would fail, then he or she may also reject the option.

◆ Leverage. It is also possible that the other party intends to follow through with the option, but at some point the status quo or other alternatives become more desirable, easier, or more tempting for another reason.

♦ Interrupt. Finally, negotiators may agree to the proposed option, but their behaviour on autopilot may still be wired to stop them from realising the option.

These are things that may stop the other party from accepting an option, or from doing their part in pursuing or realising the option. It is, as we've mentioned so many times already, just as likely that these insights will explain why we reject or fail to pursue or realise an agreed option.

Paint a picture of the final outcome

We have discussed that one of our needs is to move away from pain and towards pleasure. If we want to motivate the other party (or ourselves) to pursue a particular outcome, then one option is to create a very attractive image of the final outcome.

By describing the picture of the future we not only get the opportunity to emphasise all the positive (pleasurable) aspects. We also allow the other party to, in the present, anticipate what it will feel like to achieve that outcome.

These techniques are used with great success by crisis negotiators dealing with hostage takers or suicidal subjects. The crisis negotiator will help the subject think through actions, reactions and consequences, and create a picture of the desired outcome that satisfies the key needs of the subject.

And the same technique can also be used for motivational purposes to create commitment to a certain action. For a person trying to quit smoking the desirable vision of the future may include putting the money saved on cigarettes towards a beach cottage to be enjoyed until old age with a life-long partner. And the undesirable picture may involve being sick with cancer in a hospital ward surrounded by crying children and grandchildren who will feel resentment towards the person who selfishly killed him- or herself through smoking.

Trigger emotions

We sometimes fail to recognise that a future event will trigger emotions. Thus if we imagine a future event we might just reason rationally about it. As a result we may incorrectly predict our behaviour because we fail to consider the emotions that will drive our decision in the future.

For instance, if asked how you would feel in a fairly clear-cut scenario such as winning a million dollars, chances are that you would be pretty accurate in anticipating the type of emotions. And you could actually feel those emotions in the present.

However, if asked what you would do on finding $100 on the ground next to a sleeping homeless person, your prediction of what you will do may be less accurate. This is because it may be less obvious now which emotions will influence your decision then. Compassion? Guilt? Greed?

Negotiators can use these insights to influence how people reason about future options. We may for instance help the other party identify specific emotions that will make the option more or less desirable. If your partner is offered a job in Paris and you are happy for him/her to go, you may seek to trigger all the positive emotions: "That sounds amazing! Can you imagine us walking down the streets of Paris on a mild summers day, with the mouthwatering scent of gourmet food in the air. And the sense of freedom having all of Europe at our doorstep, only a short road trip away through beautiful scenery."

Or, if you want him or her to stay: "I don't know. I mean, you are very close to your family and friends here. How will you manage being that far away? I reckon it could be very lonely on holidays and birthdays. And how might your mother feel about you not being around now that she needs you? And just the stress of getting rid of all of our stuff and starting from scratch again. Feels kind of exhausting just thinking about it, doesn't it? And we haven't even spoken about the winter, the cold and the snow. Brrr!"

This example is only for illustrative purposes. Please don't manipulate your partner! But it does illustrate how even when content remains unchanged, by changing our focus we can change how people perceive and feel about an option. Ultimately, we influence their decision. This is a powerful example of the fifth approach to influence: manipulation of perception and feelings. Please use it ethically.

Constraints

What are all the factors that limit the range of options, and the value of each option? Negotiators will often be faced with constraints that we have to work within. However, in order to create value it serves us well to thoroughly understand which of these constraints are real, and which are artificial.

Artificial constraints may include rules, laws, tradition, policy, precedent, mandate and so on. The creation of OzHarvest illustrated how many such constraints in the system can be renegotiated and eliminated.

Some constraints will be real, or real for the time being. The lack of a particular resource might limit the number of products that can be manufactured. Then again, maybe the product can be redesigned to use different resources. Maybe the system can be changed so that there is less need for this product and more need for another product without these resource constraints. And maybe fluctuations in the economic environment will make this resource affordable in the future. Remember, creativity is our best tool for creating value.

In some instances we mention constraints because we truly believe that we have to work around them. Skilled negotiators know to investigate these constraints further. If a shop-floor salesperson says he or she cannot authorise a higher discount, then we may wish to find a person who does have the required authority.

In other instances we raise the constraints because we sincerely want help in eliminating them. A perpetrator in a hostage situation may say that he can't surrender because his gang members will later punish him for appearing weak. Here a creative option could involve agreeing with the perpetrator to allow him to pretend to visibly offer resistance (within reasonable limits) while he is taken into custody.

Yet another reason we raise constraints is that we don't like a proposed option and we simply make up a constraint — we lie. For instance, if I offer you the opportunity to help me paint my house on the weekend, and you feel obliged but really don't want to, then it is possible that you will come up with a false constraint, e.g. you may suddenly remember that you have prior commitments. This approach is very common in cultures that put high value on saving face. Here an effective "No" may actually be constructed as "Yes, as long as this other impossible thing happens."

As negotiators we want to test the validity of constraints. We also want to avoid having the other party lose face by being caught lying. For instance, let's assume that we are trying to arrange a meeting with a potential business partner and she replies with: "At this time, I am sorry that my work commitments prevent me from offering to spend some time with you."

If we suspect that this is a polite way to say "No", we may wish to test our theory by offering to eliminate the constraint: "Not a problem; I fully understand. Would you be OK with me contacting you in a few months to see if you might have time then?"

If the other party acknowledges our solution, and even appreciates it, then that is an indication that the constraint is real. The appreciation stems from us helping them solve a problem. However, if the other party ignores our solution and immediately gives us another constraint (e.g. "Actually, given my role I'm probably not the right person for you to speak with"), then that is pretty good indicator that the other party is inventing the constraints.

Let the other party think

We want to avoid interrupting the other party when he or she talks. Similarly we want to avoid interrupting if the other party is thinking about options. Rarely do we need to evaluate his or her options in this very moment. Rather we appreciate that having the other party think about options (as opposed to objections, problems or constraints) is desirable, and sometimes an achievement in itself. If uninterrupted, the other party's process of looking for options can often yield golden nuggets that we never would have thought of ourselves. In short, if the other party is looking for options and solutions — let them! And if the other party goes off track, merely raise or emphasise the needs that we want satisfied. They are already solving problems, so we may just need to clarify "the right" problem to be solved, i.e. the one that satisfies our collective needs.

Risk vs. reward

What is the risk, and what is the reward of taking an action? This is a question we should ideally ask ourselves in hundreds of places throughout the negotiation, and before every decision. When it comes to options, we may want to evaluate the risk and reward of:

- discussing a certain option;
- discussing a certain option now;
- proposing an option;
- saying yes to an option; and
- saying no to an option.

For instance, by discussing an option too early, there is a risk that the other party will not fully understand why it is in his or her best interest. Specifically, the other party may not have a clear understanding of what needs he or she would like to satisfy. If the option is rejected now it may be more difficult to get it back on the table later, partially due to the cognitive dissonance that would be triggered by changing one's previously stated opinion.

A risk of proposing an option at any point may be that the other party will be subject to the reactive devaluation bias, where he or she values the option less simply because we proposed it. Another risk is that the option may be viewed as an offer, and trigger the other party's autopilot behaviour of playing the division game and making a counter-offer. A perceived offer could also trigger expectations that this offer is secured, and therefore trigger the endowment effect, making it more difficult to change or withdraw.

A risk of saying yes to an option may increase the risk that we get over committed to the outcome (e.g. commitment bias). This would make us more susceptible to tactics such as *withdraw offer*, or *feign walking away*, where the other party essentially starts playing the division game and increases their power at the same time.

And if we say no to an option we may risk that the other party leaves the negotiation and starts pursuing their BATNA.

These are just examples of risks, and we may come up with a hundred more. The important insight is to remember to ask ourselves: "What is the potential risk or reward of my next action?" And don't forget to consider possible reactions to and consequences of each action.

Still no?

So we have performed a thorough needs analysis for both parties. The other party confirmed that we understood all of their needs. We created an option together that satisfied all needs of all parties. And *still* the other party rejects the option.

Rather than arguing, let's put our problem-solving hats on and try to figure out why we didn't reach agreement.

- Is there an unmet need that the other party or his/her stakeholders are not aware of?

- Is there a need or an agenda that the other party hasn't disclosed?

- Does the other party actually not want agreement?

- Has anything changed since we did the needs analysis?

- Have we in the way we negotiated accidentally caused a process or relationship need to be unsatisfied for the other party?

- What else...?

If a trialled option doesn't work

OK, so we came up with several options, agreed on one, we tried it, and it failed. What do we do? Do we pick the next best option on the list? Perhaps.

We could also recognise that we probably learned something from trialling that first option. And perhaps the added experience and insight will help us create a new, even more desirable and practical option. Similarly, the system may have changed (e.g. the stakeholders, their needs, value in the system, etc) since we generated the last set of options. So we may therefore decide to re-run the entire needs discovery and options generation phases.

Consciously consider level of abstraction

In the section on perception we discussed how we might be discussing, debating or negotiating the same thing but communicating at different levels of abstraction. We wish to reiterate this point in relation to options generation, because the option will invariably be at *some* level of abstraction. The levels of detail that have not yet been discussed will in all likelihood need to be discussed at some point in the future.

For instance, in a job interview where you are seeking employment with my company, we may come up with an option whereby you work X days per year, for Y dollars. That is an option! But which days will you work? How are holidays calculated? What other benefits do you get? What are my performance expectations of you? Which desk will you sit at? Will someone else use it when you don't work?

All of these things are part of the option; they just happen to be at a finer level of detail than we have yet discussed. It is important we realise that if details are omitted, we are likely to *generalise* and fill the blanks with our own assumptions, and this can later lead to diverging expectations, surprises, and loss of trust. In particular, it may lead to the need for more negotiation.

Value creation vs. fear of value destruction

I have been involved in several coalition-building exercises, many of which occurred before I realised that I was a negotiator. Usually the aim was to create great amounts of value that could only be realised if the parties joined the coalition.

Often those parties who were reluctant to join demonstrated the same pattern. This pattern was very much related to the status quo bias and loss frame. Despite the projects having tremendous value-creation potential, parties would not want to join if they perceived a risk that they could lose *any* value compared to the status quo. In simple terms, if they had $100 today, and the project could create $500 for them, then they would still be reluctant to join if they perceived that the outcome *could* be that they were only left with $75.

When this happens, the other party is sharing a need to have their fear of potential loss addressed before they are ready to look for value creation. If we don't realise this, then we may waste our efforts in continuing to try to maximise the value creation potential.

12

REACH AGREEMENT

―――― ― ――――

ASSUME AGREEMENT

What? Assume agreement? But what if we don't actually agree? What if we leave the negotiation believing that we agree and then it turns out that the other party never actually agreed to the outcome? Isn't it dangerous to assume agreement if we actually have disagreement? Yes — before we seal the deal negotiators certainly wish to ensure that all parties have the same understanding of what was agreed. So your concerns with this heading are well founded!

But I selected this heading to emphasise that we are very prone to make the opposite mistake of assuming there's disagreement when there is none. And as soon as we perceive disagreement, we run rather destructive patterns on autopilot. Typically we will incorrectly assume that our position is the right one (partisan perceptions) and we will become preoccupied with supporting our position (confirmation bias) in order to win. In the process we stop listening, we get stuck in first position, and we pollute the process with assumptions, judgements, accusations and anything else that can help make us feel like winners and make them feel like losers. This process will lead to disagreement.

Rather than assuming there is disagreement, negotiators assume that there is misunderstanding. That is, if we aren't agreeing at the moment, it is not because we have incompatible opinions, but rather because we don't yet understand how our opinions actually *are* compatible. What's more, we don't fall victim to the temptation of blaming the other party for not understanding us. Rather we assume we don't understand each other, and allow all parties to clarify their views and check their understanding. We suggest that this process can always lead to agreement.

AGREEMENT THROUGHOUT

Successful negotiations are less likely to follow this pattern: disagreement-disagreement-disagreement-disagreement-disagreement-AGREEMENT!

Successful negotiations are more likely to follow this pattern: agreement-agreement-agreement-disagreement-agreement-AGREEMENT! It is of particular importance to begin with agreement as this sets the tone of the whole interaction.

When we find ourselves in disagreement we are talking about differences. And the longer we talk about differences the more we will find. The more disagreement we find, the less convinced we are that agreement is possible. Also remember the guiding principle that in negotiation we are more likely to find something if we look for it. If we look for disagreement, we'll find it…easily!

However, if we start to focus on agreement then both of us will feel that we are making progress. We will enjoy the interaction more, which builds rapport, trust, and our perception of the relationship. We will also start feeling more confident that we will be successful in finding agreement in the end. This anticipation of success can be a critical motivator to help us when we eventually hit a sticking point in the negotiation.

If we have generated a large amount of agreement, then any

disagreement is more likely to feel like a smaller bump (contrast principle) than an impenetrable wall. If we ever reach an impasse we have the option of revisiting all aspects of the agreement: "It seems that we struggle to reach agreement on this aspect. However, given that we have agreed on everything else, I'm sure we can find a way to resolve this final piece too."

Agreement also sets a positive precedent. If either party feels like reneging on what we've already agreed on, that party is likely to experience cognitive dissonance from having acted inconsistently with what it said it would do.

Agreement is not tacked on at the end of the negotiation! Rather we seek to build in as much agreement as possible throughout the process. Remember that we like people who are like us. Part of being like us involves sharing our views, and we infer this by there being ample agreement. This agreement builds rapport, which builds relationships. A process full of agreement is more likely to result in parties perceiving a positive relationship, which we now know bring tremendous benefit to the negotiation process.

OK, so we have discussed that agreement is important, but how do we reach it? There are a number of ways!

Agreement is always available

Even in the extreme scenario where we feel that we disagree one hundred per cent with the other party's viewpoint, we can still find opportunities to agree.

- We agree that their view is one way to look at the situation.

- We agree that, given the context, situation and history of the other party, we can see how the other party arrived at that conclusion.

- We can agree that we understand (or don't understand, or can never truly understand) the other person.

- We can agree that we see some merit in the other party's logic (even if we disagree with the assumptions that feed into that logic, and the conclusions that are the result).

+ We can agree that this negotiation may be more challenging than others.

+ We can agree that there are indeed unresolved differences.

+ We can agree that we want agreement.

+ We can agree that we would both ideally prefer to have negotiated with someone else.

This is not simply a play on words. Next time you are in an argument (with a friend: start in a safe environment!) see if you can agree with every single statement he or she makes. Then monitor what happens to the emotions in the argument, and how long the argument lasts. It turns out that it is very difficult to keep a fight going with someone who doesn't want to fight with you.

US president Barack Obama demonstrated this technique at the Health Care Summit in 2010. John McCain raised a contentious issue about Florida cutting a sweetheart deal in relation to Medicare. McCain's body language, voice, volume, tonality and gestures all suggested that he was looking for an argument. Obama responded with, "I think you make a legitimate point," to which McCain had no response. After saying, "Well… um…maybe we…", it appeared to dawn on McCain that the two of them were in fact in agreement, and he rapidly ended with: "…thank you, thank you very much."

> If you are not convinced, i.e. if you disagree, then please take this opportunity to craft a response that is in agreement with what I just said.

You will recall that I applied exactly the same strategy for four full days with John, the "difficult" participant who negotiated by punching people in the face.

Find shared needs, opinions, values, beliefs…shared anything!

I found myself in a client meeting with a new co-negotiator who was simply not on the same page as me. After I opened the negotiation, he immediately interjected and said "I disagree" in front of all who were present. What does one do when this happens? Interrupting him and correcting him would certainly not look good. Taking a time out would also serve to bring more attention to the disagreement. What I chose to do instead was to listen, and in the process I managed to pick up the specific area of disagreement: he wanted to have the "how" conversation, and I had introduced the "what/why" conversation.

This might appear as a conflict in needs, and it is! Thankfully we can often reframe perceived conflicting needs to be shared or different. So I addressed the other parties present. "With your permission I'd like to clarify what this conversation was about. Both my co-negotiator and I really dislike wasting time (shared need). However, what we view as wasting time is different (unique needs). He dislikes staying idle, so he'd prefer we start work straight away. I dislike spending time on redundant work, so I'd prefer that we ensure we agree on the right option for us before we start work. So what we are agreeing on is that we both really care about making the best use of everyone's time. Would that be in your interest as well?"

No matter what the other party says, if we know what to look for we can still find reasons to agree. In every negotiation there will be shared needs; we only have to find them! In addition to shared needs, we may find shared opinions, taste, values, beliefs, behaviours or anything else. These are all candidates for building common ground.

Agree on the process and the relationship

We discussed agreeing on the frames of the negotiation as a means of improving the negotiation process going forwards. The added benefit is that you start the negotiation off with a significant number of points of agreement. There is no limit to the number of process and relationship elements we can agree on, and this therefore becomes an infinite source of agreement that we can draw upon. Examples include:

- "Can we agree that we prefer a constructive process without personal attacks?"

- "Would you agree that making good use of our time is of interest to both of us?"

- "Do you agree that no matter what happens in the process, we want to protect our relationship and our individual reputations?"

Separate areas of agreement and disagreement

All the content in the negotiation will be either in agreement or disagreement. If it is partial agreement then we can often break it down into smaller pieces (i.e. chunk down), some of which we are in complete agreement with, and some of which we are in complete disagreement with.

On autopilot some of us have a tendency to launch straight into resolving the problems and the differences. Our focus is on disagreement. We don't pay attention to what we already agree on, because that is already solved. What we miss though is the opportunity to demonstrate and emphasise how much we already agree on! Skilled negotiations would instead label all the content as either agreement or disagreement. Through this process even the biggest obstacles or disagreements will tend to dwarf compared to the huge body of agreement (contrast principle). This makes resolving the differences seem much easier.

For example, pick any fight between two people in a ten-year relationship. The issue may seem like the end of the world — but what happens when you actually compare it with all the good things that both of the parties have *agreed* on for ten years?

Start with agreement

Once we identify areas of agreement and disagreement, we are well advised to begin by going on to examine the areas of agreement. Leaving the (perceived) disagreement until later often results in many of the (perceived) disagreements never having to be resolved, or even brought up, in order for parties to agree an outcome that satisfies their needs.

For instance, if two parties have different religions, their value systems will have portions that are always going to be in conflict, regardless of whether these are discussed or not. Bringing them up is rarely constructive or beneficial — it is unlikely to help parties reach a mutually beneficial outcome. Beginning the negotiation with these is likely to position parties on opposite sides of a conflict.

If we instead introduce the negotiation by agreeing on shared needs, the process, on desired outcomes, acknowledging that both parties are human beings with needs that they want met, we are more likely to end up in a cooperative process. This process has a higher likelihood of leading to both parties getting their needs satisfied. And often the negotiation can end there, without parties ever having to explore all the ways in which they disagree or are different.

Pick our disagreements

Some things will need to be resolved for the negotiation to reach the point of agreement, understanding and commitment. However, many, many things that we discuss and disagree on in the process are not important for the outcome. So as outcome-focused negotiators we may consciously make the decision to not share our disagreement if we don't think it will help the process.

When a business partner of mine in a client organisation left his job, his replacement started the new job by unilaterally, via email, cancelling all work with external partners. The decision flowed from a new, unilateral strategy to stop relying on external consultants and instead rely on in-house expertise. In a subsequent phone conversation with this replacement I probably found twenty reasons to strongly disagree with what was said. And still my every word spoken was neutral or in agreement, and at the end of the conversation we agreed to seek new ways for our organisations to work together.

At the time I anticipated that some of the differences I could have raised would need to be discussed at some point, but launching into discussing differences with a new person, on the phone, and with a limited time would have made the rest of the negotiation difficult. One of the reasons was the lack of a strong existing relationship. So instead I started by building the relationship, sought to understand the other party's needs, started agreeing on what the process for interaction would be going forwards, and set up a face-to-face meeting to introduce myself in person.

Eventually our organisations reverted to the original agreement. And, to my delight, this happened without me ever having to resolve or even raise my disagreements with what had transpired. Instead we focused on agreement, and as a result we found…wait for it…agreement!

Non-verbal agreement

In my seminars I quickly demonstrate this insight by having a participant share something with me that is important to them. With the body language and tonality of someone bored senseless I respond, "Yes… absolutely…you are completely right…couldn't agree more…tell me more…please do tell me more."

It usually doesn't take long before the participant doesn't want to continue this roleplay. "How come?" I ask. "I was agreeing with everything you said, and verbally encouraged you to continue!"

"Yes, but you just didn't seem to mean it!"

Exactly: agreement is not just about what we say. Every channel of communication needs to be congruent for the other party to truly feel that we agree with him or her. That means our voice variation, our non-verbal behaviour, our actions, and everything else has to indicate agreement. Conscious agreement without unconscious rapport does not feel like agreement.

AGREEMENT VS. UNDERSTANDING

In the section on level of abstraction we mentioned that when discussing things at the general level it is easy to reach agreement but difficult to reach understanding. This is because general language omits all the details, and is therefore likely to mean different things to each of us. We may agree that freedom is a good thing, but we may have completely different views on what freedom should look like. As we add in more specific details we start to understand how different our views are. Thus our level of understanding increases, but so too does the likelihood of disagreement.

Thus, one way to quickly move from disagreement to agreement is to increase the level of abstraction and move away from detail. You and I may be working in a team tasked with creating a new strategy for the company. If we find ourselves severely stuck in disagreement on a detail, we always have the option of moving up in generality until we reach agreement: "Can we at least agree that we want to pursue a differentiation strategy rather than a cost leadership strategy?", or "Are we at least in agreement that the current strategy needs updating and we need something different?"

LEVELS OF DISAGREEMENT

If we assume that disagreement merely signals unmet needs, then we don't have to be afraid of the other party saying "no". Disagreement just tells us that we have to do a better job of discovering and satisfying needs. But does every "no" carry the same weight? NO! We are programmed to think in terms of binary decisions, black and white, yes and no, right and wrong, and us vs. them. It keeps things simple. It is also one of the counterproductive assumptions that limits our negotiation ability.

One key to negotiation is realising that we most of the time deal with a spectrum between two extremes. Specifically, we have a spectrum between complete disagreement and complete agreement. Thus "no" covers half that spectrum, from complete disagreement to almost agreement.

The strength of the "no" will be related to the amount of deliberation, intensity of emotions, and the unity of the decision makers. If it takes a long time for the other party to make a decision, it might suggest that it was difficult to decide between "yes" and "no". Likewise a split decision among decision makers may suggest that the "no" is close to a "yes", and might be influenced to a "yes" through stakeholder management. A highly emotional decision may signal a range of factors, e.g. fears, perceived uncertainties, risks, complexities or cognitive dissonance. And an instant decision may signal either strong preparation, or an unsubstantiated, inflexible position driven by beliefs or ego needs.

As with body language, we can't attach an absolute meaning to individual behaviours. However, we can raise awareness that there are different levels of disagreement, and we may find that the current "no" is in the grey zone right next to "yes".

DOCUMENTING THE AGREEMENT

We reached agreement! Now we shake hands and...done? The short answer is that it depends!

The saying "a verbal agreement is not worth the paper it is written on" is certainly a good guideline for negotiation, particularly for transactional relationships. We often want a written agreement to protect us from:

- either party changing his or her mind;

- either party forgetting what was agreed;

- either party's decision maker being replaced in the future with someone who has different intentions;

- confusion about responsibilities and liabilities in the event an issue needs to be resolved in a court of law; and

- either party misunderstanding what they agreed to.

So now we have a contract. Are we done? Not necessarily. As the parties start implementing the agreement, they will invariably realise that some things were discussed at too high a level of abstraction, and the parties may also have different perceptions of what was agreed. This now has to be negotiated. It is also likely that the negotiators reaching the agreement did not anticipate all the parameters and details that needed to be agreed upon in order to implement the agreement. This also needs to be negotiated. And circumstances invariably change for either one or both parties, and they will seek to renegotiate aspects of the contract.

OK, so the negotiations will continue after the contract is signed, but at least we have a contract. Does that protect us? Again, the answer is it depends. The contract has a lot of words, but do we look for agreement regarding the letter of the contract, or the spirit of the contract?

For example, if you and I create a joint venture then I want you to be committed to working with me to do everything you can to make the business successful, while not doing anything that would make me disappointed in you. There is no way that I can craft a contract that stipulates every single action that I want you to take, and what actions I do not want you to take. I am putting some faith into us being in accord over *the spirit of the agreement* — an accord that cannot necessarily be enforced.

And on that topic, can contracts be enforced? Some of them can. Some international contracts may not be enforceable due to the differences in legal systems in the different countries. And other contracts we simply can't afford to enforce.

Many negotiations and contracts will not have complete protection against the other party not keeping his or her end of the bargain. This insight should now increase the importance that we place on building trust and a strong relationship throughout the process. It should also increase the effort we invest in trying to ensure that we play integration or maximisation to ensure that all parties derive maximum benefit from continuing working together. All of these mechanisms provide a safety net that reduces the need for having to revisit the contract. In contrast, if we play competitive division, then we are unlikely to have this type of safety net and instead may have to put our faith in our lawyers, the legal system, and a complex contract that covers every conceivable transgression.

Who documents?

There are many benefits of controlling the contract. One is that the way we phrase clauses will affect how they will be interpreted in the future. Also, some items may have been discussed at too abstract a level in the negotiations, and a call has to be made when writing the contract regarding what the concrete details should be. Unless the parties meet to clarify these items, the contract will reflect the perception of the party that writes it.

The above paragraph reflects the recommendations you might read in a lot of negotiation texts. My view would be that anything we do that surprises the other party is also something that risks damaging trust. Therefore I would typically want to discuss all the details with the other party before we (together) put them in writing. This of course assumes that we are playing integration or maximisation. In competitive division I would agree that we prefer to be the party that writes the contract. Whether or not we elect to use the above tactics, we at least prevent the other party from using them.

To make things more complicated (and thereby emphasise the need for our situational model to negotiation), we may in some instances want the other party to document parts of the agreement — subject to our final approval. Specifically, the task of writing the agreement is an investment in effort, and we know that can trigger the commitment bias or effort justification, both of which can increase the likelihood that the other party will honour the agreement.

PREPARE FOR POTENTIAL FUTURE DISAGREEMENTS AND DISPUTES

Just as it is easier to agree on the process of negotiation before we launch into it, it is easier to agree on how to deal with a disagreement before we find ourselves in the middle of one. This is true for commercial deals, for treaties between nations and it is true for marriages. We want to agree how to deal with the difficult times now when parties don't expect them to come. In the present, when the future disagreement is merely hypothetical, parties can dispassionately have that conversation in third position. Once a divorce is on the table parties are likely to be stuck in first, with all the pollution that brings to the process.

Contingent agreements

We can probably all relate to having felt stuck with a contract we wanted to get out of. Perhaps we wanted to leave our apartment because our new neighbours were having parties until three am during the week. Perhaps we married someone we shouldn't have. Or perhaps we signed up a supplier that didn't deliver.

As negotiators we should be able to predict quite a few reasons for wanting to exit a contract in the future. Often we want to exit because the value or the other party's performance is not living up to our expectations. Because we are dealing with expectations of the future at the time of signing the contract, we may wish to make such contracts conditional on performance, value or success, just like our contingent options.

For example, let's say that I want to move my day spa business from the suburbs to a shopping mall. My rent will be higher, but the mall operator assures me that this will be balanced by the additional benefits a mall can provide, in particular the benefit of high traffic of potential customers. Rather than me relying solely on the salesperson's word, I may wish to make our contract *contingent* on these assurances being true — so the duration of the contract is contingent on a minimum monthly traffic of X customers passing the store.

When we think about it, perhaps we would ideally want this type of contingent contract in all areas of our lives; of course we often do in the form of money-back guarantees. In our negotiations it will be our responsibility to make sure that we have this guarantee by making our final agreements contingent on what was promised, implied or assured.

AGREEMENT VS. COMMITMENT

"What is a successful outcome of a negotiation?" I ask my participants. One of the first responses is usually, "To reach agreement" (closely after, "To win!"). But is that true? Should we be happy if we reach agreement? Well, we are probably interested in having the agreed outcome delivered in a manner consistent with the agreement. Agreement itself is merely a step on the way.

Sometimes the final outcome won't be achieved for decades after the agreement. Imagine a proposed new coalmine with a lifespan of thirty years, and that we are in charge of negotiating contracts with different operators. Yes we may agree now, but it will take thirty years until everything we agreed has been delivered. So agreement is not a goal in itself.

Do we always want agreement? Well, no. Maybe we don't even want to negotiate. Maybe there is no ZOPA. Maybe we at some point realise that the current deal is not going to be better than our alternatives elsewhere. If we focus too much on reaching agreement, we may find ourselves accepting a bad deal.

And what if the other party actually does not want agreement with us? Has that ever happened — that we spend time negotiating with someone who says they want to agree, but stalls the process so that agreement is never reached? This may happen for several reasons, and one to look out for is when the other party prefers the status quo.

For instance, let's say that you complain about the noise that is caused by some very expensive air-conditioning units that were just installed in the building next to your home. If your neighbours are to abrogate the noise they will probably incur a cost, so their preferred option is to leave things the way they are. One division game strategy would be for them to agree with you, say that they are looking into things, and then stall until you get tired and give up.

This is an important lesson: we do not want to find ourselves in a situation where we believe we have reached agreement and expect compliance, but in fact the other party has no interest in following through on their part of the deal.

Imagine that I offer you four weeks of contract work for me. The fair price of the project work is probably $40,000. But because I know that you have no other work at the moment I know that you are desperate enough to accept anything that pays your rent. So I offer you $2000 for the work. Will you accept? Quite possibly. Do you feel fairly treated? Unlikely. Do you feel taken advantage of? Probably. Do you resent that I coerced you? Yes. Do I have your commitment to deliver the best work you can do? I wouldn't count on it. Do I have your commitment that you will stay for the entire project if someone else offers you a better deal? Probably not. Will you help build my reputation when you interact with others? Unlikely. May I have even gone so far as to motivate you to get back at me somehow in the future? There is certainly a risk.

Sometimes we may reach agreement without commitment. This insight has huge repercussions for how we negotiate. If I negotiate merely to get agreement then I can use any of the tools from the competitive division game, including coercion, unethical psychological tactics, threats based on my alternatives or your dependency on me, manipulation, lies and verbal ploys. We can often force someone into a reluctant agreement, but that does not generate commitment. A final agreement without commitment is rarely useful to us. In fact it can become very expensive

This should be another reason for making the extra effort to changing the game to integration or maximisation. Yes, the tools in the division chapter will help you win the division game, but what do you win? Commitment? Most definitely not!

NEGOTIATE FOR COMMITMENT

So what do we want commitment to? In short, ideally we want commitment to anything that we want agreement to.

Build commitment throughout

As with agreement, commitment is *not* tacked on at the end. As a general rule, the earlier we start building commitment, the more likely we are to have it strongly in place by the end of the negotiation. However, the process of achieving commitment is not the same as for reaching agreement.

Let the other party choose

Stronger commitment, ownership and responsibility are created when people perceive that they choose their own path, as opposed to being directed. We have a need to be in control of our lives, so letting the other party believe they have choice allows him or her to feel in control without triggering reactive devaluation. If we ask questions and they give the answers, then they feel like the choice is theirs. Once a decision is made they will rationalise that this behaviour is consistent with who they believe they are or what they want. Because there are no visible extrinsic rewards, they don't have the option of rationalising that they are doing something they don't want to do. Partisan perceptions and confirmation bias will help them selectively manipulate information to rationalise that they have made "the right" decision. Because a choice has been made, post-decision relief kicks in and they will incorrectly attribute that relief to having made the right decision.

Ownership of the idea

Similarly, it turns out that we get more committed to ideas that are "ours". For instance, let's say that I'm your manager and I have directed you to carry out a project in a certain way. If you start experiencing difficulties then you always have the option of blaming me for:

- not having thought things through; and

- not having given you adequate instructions, resources, and so on.

In fact, as you learn about the situation and get the 20/20 clarity of hindsight, you may even blame me for not realising things that were impossible to know at the time.

However, if we instead discussed the project together, and you came up with the idea, then you now have a lot more at stake. Chances are that when you face difficulties you will be more focused on finding ways to solve the challenges, because giving up will mean that you had a bad idea. And by now we know how important it is for us to believe that we come up with good ideas.

Public announcement

Building on this, if I can get you to publicly announce your plan then you will dramatically increase your commitment to the task. Just think about how easy it would be to quit a weight-loss program if no one would know about it. Now imagine how difficult it would be to quit if you had announced your weight loss plans to all your friends, family, and all the viewers of the reality TV weight-loss show that you decided to join. Suddenly the potential damage to your ego has skyrocketed, and it may actually be less painful to just complete the weight-loss program. Thus, in our negotiations we would prefer if the other party (and our team too if we want to increase our commitment) announce publicly what we have agreed to achieve.

Public announcements also work by capitalising on our need for consistency. If we say that we are going to do something but we don't do it, then we will experience cognitive dissonance. To relieve the dissonance we will either change what we say, or change what we do, so that the two become consistent. The public announcement makes it very hard for us to change what we say, so it is often easier to just change our behaviour to be consistent.

This also means that if we want to change someone's view, then we benefit from doing so before the other party publicly announces their position. Learning from commitment bias, we wish to influence before the other party takes action. In fact, drawing on partisan perceptions, we wish to influence the other party even before they make their mind up what they want to do!

Sometimes we miss this opportunity, and instead have to influence the other party after they have made a public commitment and taken a stance against our preferred outcome. In that case we need to facilitate the other party graciously retracting that public commitment. Sometimes this can be achieved by controlling the flow of information. In other instances we may help the other party provide a rationale or justification for why the first public commitment wasn't really a commitment.

Start taking action towards the outcome

Taking action also triggers cognitive dissonance. We will subconsciously want our action to be consistent with our beliefs. So if we take an action that is contrary to our beliefs then we may rationalise this to mean that we must have wanted to take this action. And in the process of taking action we also increase the chance of triggering commitment bias and effort justification, all of which increase commitment.

Eliminate the status quo (and other alternatives)

If I have a backup plan, e.g. to do nothing, then I may choose only to work with you as long as you can offer me something better. This thinking is very clear in the negotiation models that are centred on the BATNA; i.e. you and I only negotiate to see if we can create a better deal than our respective BATNAs. The concern here is that even if we collaborate and agree, then at any point in the future, one of our BATNAs may become more attractive, and we may henceforth leave the deal, and our negotiation partner.

The status quo may simultaneously be the most attractive option *and* our BATNA. The status quo bias and the omission bias both suggest that we will overvalue the status quo because we are afraid of making a change that we could regret in the future. So if we want to negotiate with someone who struggles to commit to a new option because they perceive their status quo is attractive, then we may want to eliminate the status quo.

One example could be conflict between two cities along a river in a developing country. The upstream city may have profitable industries that pollute the river, to the detriment of the downstream city. In this negotiation anything the upstream city does to remedy the issue will incur a cost, but doing nothing incurs no cost.

Here the downstream city may struggle to get the negotiation concluded as long as the status quo is an option. One way to eliminate the status quo may be to lobby for pollution controls that make the upstream city's pollution costly or illegal. Another option may be to make it unattractive for foreign companies to have their operations in the upstream city through revealing media coverage in the home countries of those companies.

Gain commitment when the option is most desirable

At this point the reader will have a good grasp of how we can change perceptions to make options (deals, offers, proposals…) seem more or less appealing. For instance, we may use the contrast principle and compare the option to something less desirable. We may associate the option with the status quo and thereby create a loss frame around missing out on the option. We can emphasise scarcity by emphasising that the opportunity may be lost if we don't act now. And so on.

Because we have so many tools to influence the attractiveness of options, we can probably acknowledge that the perceived attractiveness of options will vary throughout the negotiation process. So when do we want the other party to publicly commit to the option or to a course of action? That's right, when that option or action is most attractive.

For instance, salespeople typically try to convey scarcity to artificially increase the appeal of the product we are looking at: "I'm afraid that the car you are looking at is in such demand that it will take at least six months to deliver." At this point the customer wants the car even more simply because he or she can't have it. This is when the salesperson seeks to gain commitment: "I tell you what, if you are serious about buying this car (gaining commitment), then I might be able to pull a few personal favours to get one delivered sooner."

Progressive entanglement

Sometimes a person is not prepared to make the leap from option A (e.g. the status quo) to option B (what we want them to consider). In that case we may have more success by breaking down that journey into a number of trivial steps.

As an example, I grew up in Europe and eventually moved to Australia. Making the decision to move halfway across the globe alone at a fairly young age was too big a decision for me to handle. But I picked up a brochure about studying abroad — why not? I then sent an application to a university in Australia — a small investment of time and what's the worst that could happen? After I got an offer I though I'd explore funding options — still not committed to going, and not investing too much time. A long story short, I eventually found myself in a position to simply say "yes" or "no" to moving, because all the logistics had already been taken care of. And because of the investment of time and effort, commitment bias and effort-justification kicked in and made it more attractive to choose the option of following through.

Progressive entanglement can be a very powerful tool to lead someone (including ourselves, as just described) to move from one option to another. An ethical implementation requires that each step is made to feel positive, so that the person voluntarily makes it. The smaller the steps, the more likely that our approach will be invisible to the other party, and the lower the risk that they will resist.

As individuals we are under the illusion that we act according to who we are, what we believe and what we want. But in reality the opposite tends to happen — that we first observe our behaviour and then infer who we are, what we believe and what we want. After we have led the other party through many small steps to our desired outcome, he or she is likely to think: "Hey, I took every step voluntarily to get here, so this must be what I want."

I also know a negotiator who has perfected a competitive and arguably less ethical version of progressive entanglement. It is similar in that the jump from option A to option B is broken down into several trivial steps. The difference is that in each step the other party does *not* want to move, but does so because of *guilt* and *pressure to conform* or *appease* the negotiator. He has been very successful in using this approach to manipulate people into doing things they absolutely do not want to do. Once he even manipulated a vegetarian to give in and end up at a meat-only restaurant for dinner!

So I wish to reiterate that the ethical application of this technique is to ensure that the other party always *wants* to move towards the option we prefer. We simply make the journey easier and more psychologically comfortable for him or her.

Commitment and coalition building

When we negotiate with multiple parties and want their commitment, we may draw upon lessons from group dynamics in social psychology. For instance, research suggests that people resist being the first person to disagree with a group that is in consensus. This was elegantly illustrated by Solomon Asch's experiments on group conformity. I recommend that you read up on this study, or at least view the entertaining video clips on the web.

For now, let's just worry about the implications for our coalition-building strategies.

- We don't want to be the first person to confront and disagree with a group that is already in consensus.

- The need to conform drops dramatically if there has been even one other dissenter, even if that dissenter doesn't share our view.

- The greater the number of people that are part of the consensus, the harder it becomes to disagree with them.

- The number of people in the group who are yet to be asked to give their view also affects our need to conform. For example if everyone is in consensus and we are the last person to give our view, there is no chance of finding an ally if we were to disagree with the group. But if only ten people are in consensus, and there are another ninety to be asked, then we may feel it likely that other people will also disagree.

So imagine now that we are the US government after 9/11 and we want to build a "coalition of the willing". Who should we ask first? Should we start with those most difficult to persuade? No, because they are likely to share their deeply held belief, which is to disagree with this particular cause.

Should we make it clear that we will ask all countries for their view? No, because then countries make up their mind at the same time, with no indication of what other countries will do. And in this case, there was probably good reason to expect that most countries would prefer to *not* start another war.

So, if we instead apply the lessons of group conformity, we should talk to parties one-by-one, and in the order from most agreeable to least agreeable. Thus we ensure consensus throughout the entire process. Every party we ask would feel the discomfort of being the first to disagree with a group in consensus. Also, as we approach more and more disagreeable parties, the group of consensus will be bigger and bigger — thereby putting more pressure to agree on the parties least willing to agree. And because we haven't said that we'll consult everyone, we can always make the case that the country we speak with now is the last one we will ask, thus eliminating the expectation that the country currently being asked will find an ally in dissent.

In some situations we can create this group dynamic even if no one has yet joined us in building a consensus. For instance, sharing that we are talking to other parties and expecting them to agree can still be as powerful as if we say that we have talked to other parties and they *do* agree.

Taken to the extreme, we can even present each party with a hypothetical final scenario: "If I got everyone else to agree, would you also say yes?" This approach can sometimes *still* invoke the group conformity effect. And what happens if we present all parties with the same question and they say yes. That's right, we just created consensus with the snap of our fingers. I am still astonished by how often this last technique works.

Don't over-sell

Whenever we try to convince the other party that a particular option is desirable for them, we also need to recognise the point where they change from "unconvinced" to "convinced". Often, this will be a good time to stop "selling" our view. Continuing "selling" past this point essentially creates the set-up we warned against in the section on good and bad arguments, where every additional argument risks undermining the one the other party has already accepted.

We can also look at this as a risk/reward calculation. If the other party is already "sold", then we have little potential for making him or her "more sold", but everything we subsequently say or do could be something that will give the other party a reason to change his or her mind.

Build commitment into options

We said that commitment is not tacked onto the end of a negotiation and that we can affect the level of commitment simply by the way we create and present the options. Let's start with the less effective strategies and move to the more effective ones.

First up, we can always coerce, threaten or otherwise force the other party to do something. As we saw in the second approach to influence, this does not build commitment. In fact, we are instead likely to produce negative by-products we are now familiar with.

How about I just tell you my suggestion? This will be less likely to cause resentment so that's a step in the right direction. However, there is nothing that creates ownership of the idea so you are likely to blame me if it is not perfect or if something goes wrong.

How about I ask you *and* I give you an extrinsic reward for complying? Again, as we shared in the first approach to influence, this approach does not build commitment. It is also expensive, and may undermine the intrinsic motivation that was already there.

So how about I just ask you with no bribe or reward? If you say yes we get more commitment. Unfortunately this is also the easiest approach to decline.

It is better if I can give you multiple options to choose from. Often we don't question why these are the only options available. We simply fall for the illusion of choice and can now tell ourselves that *we* decided in the end, and therefore we will feel more committed.

If I involve you in the process of crafting the options we would build even more commitment. This allows you to feel heard, which is almost always a need. While you may have shared the needs you were aware of, now that we develop the option you will most likely realise that you have additional needs. This allows us to tailor the option to better suit you. You also invest time, thus increasing the commitment bias and effort justification. You will also feel that the process is fair, and therefore be more accepting if we can't get you the outcome you desire in the end. Finally, simply by being involved, the illusion of optimism suggests that you will perceive a higher likelihood of success.

Ultimately, a negotiator wishes to just plant the seed of an idea in your mind, and only give you minimal nudges in the right direction to allow you to develop the idea for yourself. (This is why *Inception* is such an excellent negotiation movie!) And, because you came up with the idea we completely circumvent reactive devaluation on your part. The more voluntary action you take to develop the option, the stronger need (cognitive dissonance) you'll feel to have a belief that is consistent with those actions, thus you will persuade yourself that you like the option.

There is actually one approach that generates even more commitment. We don't have much control over that one, but it is nevertheless important for us to be aware of it. It is very possible that the other party will come up with an idea without any intervention from us, and this idea may be far better than anything we thought of! This idea will come pre-packaged with maximum commitment from the other party, and all we have to do is to capture the opportunity and agree. We want to be open to persuasion!

ANTICIPATE AND PLAN FOR THE UNEXPECTED

When will parties be most committed to each other? Well, it depends. (You probably knew I was going to say that.) It is quite possible that if parties build a strong relationship going forward then commitment can keep growing with time.

However, as negotiators we need to acknowledge that the future doesn't always turn out as agreed or planned, and this can cause the level of commitment to drop. In particular, we want to plan for any changes that could negatively affect commitment in the future. Here are some examples.

- The system can change due to external shocks outside our control.

- The organisations can change e.g. priorities, needs or goals.

- The individuals can change e.g. their priorities, needs, or they may even leave the organisation.

- The relationship and interdependence between the organisations or individuals.

- Perceptions and emotions related to any of the previous points.

We also need to acknowledge that while we are building commitment throughout the process, we still may not reach agreement in the end. This is not necessarily a bad thing — we may simply have realised through the negotiation that both parties' needs will be better satisfied separately elsewhere.

However, if one party is considerably more committed to the process and outcomes at the time negotiations cease, that party is likely to feel greater resentment towards the other party. If we subscribe to the practice of always leaving relationships in a better state than we found them, then we are well advised to manage the balance of commitment during the process so that it doesn't become too asymmetrical.

Even if we do go ahead and strike a deal, overly asymmetrical commitment may also lead to differences in expectations — which we also know is undesirable.

Enforce commitment

Enforce commitment? But didn't we spend this entire chapter discussing the benefits of making the other party *want* to be committed rather than being *forced* to being committed? Yes we did. I still maintain that we build stronger commitment in that way, if that option is available. That's why we started there.

Sometimes we are negotiating with someone who really does not want to commit to a particular outcome. Perhaps this is an athlete who is tempted to dramatically improve his or her likelihood of achievement in sports by taking steroids. Perhaps this is a manager in the financial sector who can gain huge rewards for himself by taking leveraged bets with other people's money.

In such cases, if we fail to build the desired level of commitment, we may need to enforce it. And as we saw in the above section, even if we build commitment today, anticipated or unanticipated future events may reduce or eliminate commitment.

So the recommendation is that we in some negotiations may need to plan for how to enforce commitment if necessary, or for how to move forwards if commitment can't be enforced. For critical negotiations we cannot afford to figure this out when the time comes. For instance if we create a joint venture with a partner in a country with less developed legal and political systems, what mechanisms are in place to ensure that our interests will be protected? We may find that there is no practical legal option available to us, as a small foreign company, should our partner choose to disappear with our money.

Managing commitment, trust, alternatives and potential negative behaviours is very tricky — bringing these issues up can hurt the negotiation, but so will ignoring them. Specifically, while we caution you against taking actions that unintentionally create a low-trust environment, some of the insights in the section on managing negotiations with low levels of trust will also be relevant for enforcing commitment.

NEGOTIATE FOR SATISFACTION

We have indicated that in negotiation we build more commitment by having people *want* do to something rather than feeling that they *have to* do something. This is true for building commitment that lasts.

However, in specific instances we can influence parties to build complete commitment by coercing them to feel that they have no choice. For instance, if one of our close relatives or children was taken hostage by kidnappers, then we may feel committed to agree and comply with anything that will ensure their safe release. Thus it is possible to get someone's commitment to an outcome that is not good for them. This is not sustainable so can't be our only criteria for success.

So far we have shared that agreement is important, but negotiating for agreement alone can lead to undesirable outcomes. Similarly, commitment is important, but negotiating for commitment alone can also lead to undesirable outcomes. Perhaps we wish to add a third criterion, and that is to negotiate for satisfaction — the satisfaction of all parties. And perhaps, we want agreement, commitment, *and* satisfaction. Rather than assuming that either criterion is better than the other, may I suggest that we simply aim to check all three boxes whenever we can.

So how do we build satisfaction? Part of this relies on the third approach of influence, where we seek to ensure that each party gets his or her needs satisfied. However, how do we feel when we get everything we want too easily? That's right, we often feel unsatisfied because we realise that this is probably not *the best available deal*. Thus, successful negotiation ensures we get what we want (content) in a manner (process) that makes us also appreciate the outcome when we get it. This means drawing on the insights from the fifth approach to influence as well, in order to maximise satisfaction.

Note that this can be done in an ethical or unethical manner. We, as always, advocate the ethical approach.

CONCLUSION

——— ——

INTRODUCTORY CASE REVISITED

Let's revisit Tom and Ivan, introduced in "A case in point" at the beginning of this book. Please take a few minutes to read it again.

So how does it read this time? I hope very differently! Let's walk through it together and see if the concepts you've been reading about can explain what is taking place. First of all, where is the focus in terms of content, process and relationship? That's right, entirely on the content. Ivan didn't even try the most basic rapport building and instead launched straight into content.

No attention was given to negotiating the process or the frames around the negotiation. Ivan didn't ask permission to begin the negotiation. Neither party sought to clarify the common outcomes, the desired behaviour, or any of the other negotiation frames.

Who was on autopilot? Both of them! Both parties lost their temper, got defensive, and argued. Neither party stayed process aware.

What game did they play? Both parties took positions on the laptop. Tom wanted it three weeks ago, and Ivan would only agree to provide it once it is fixed. Division, division, division.

But is that the entire truth? Did anyone experience a crisis at any point? And what were their needs? It is quite easy to spot them now, right?

Tom was primarily concerned with getting his laptop fixed immediately so that he could deliver his work and look good to his stakeholders. He also wanted to be treated with the respect that his position in the hierarchy warranted. Tom probably also wants his employees to follow procedure and not simply storm into meetings. Once he became visibly upset and raised his voice, we knew immediately that he had a need to vent his frustrations, feel heard, feel understood, and then discuss a solution to the problems. Tom was completely uninterested in placing blame, he just wanted the outcome achieved. In fact, the failure to get such a simple task completed may cause frustration in itself for a powerful man with so much responsibility. On top of that he was most definitely feeling the pressure of time, and anticipating all the work that he couldn't do now and therefore would have to do on the weekend. He already felt that future resentment in the present. Tom also had no interest in hearing or understanding the technical details of the problem.

This takes longer to read than it took to diagnose. Within seconds a skilled negotiator would have identified these needs in the situation. With sufficient practice, needs stand out like bright neon signs compared to the rest of the conversation.

How many of these needs were satisfied? Tom didn't have a functioning laptop. And a lowly IT-support employee was arguing with him and seemingly showing no respect for his status. And this was probably made worse by having an audience, i.e. me. Was Tom allowed to vent? Did he feel heard? Understood? Did he get to speak uninterrupted? Did he at any point hear Ivan talk about solutions? No, Ivan only raised problems and obstacles. How did having to hear about all the technical details affect Tom's perception of time pressure? It made it significantly worse.

If Ivan were a skilled negotiator he would have been able to immediately identify Tom's needs, and adjust the approach to satisfy those needs. All the tools in this book would have been helpful, so let's just pick a few to illustrate how the situation might have been more constructively handled.

- First of all, check permission to interrupt the meeting.

- Start by acknowledging the pressures that Tom was facing.

- Stay in second position; show empathy, listen and learn about Tom's needs, and demonstrate an understanding of those needs.

- Don't offer resistance by arguing.

- Don't interrupt while Tom is talking.

- Focus on agreement.

- Paraphrase understanding: "Just let me verify that I get the key point, you want a laptop — any laptop — that can provide the functions you need, and you want it now so that you can deliver all the work that has piled up? Would that be an accurate understanding?"

- Label emotions: "I can understand that you are upset: this should never have happened in the first place!"

- Start proposing options for satisfying content needs: "One option that would work is to get you a brand new laptop. It will probably cost _____ dollars. Given the circumstances, how do you feel about that option?"

Now, Tom was not the only person who had needs. Ivan needed:

- to not get blamed for any wrongdoing because he had done everything he could within his set of responsibilities;

- to not be spoken down to — his job is also important; and

- to educate Tom so that there was an appreciation that while things have failed, it was due to external circumstances and not because of Ivan.

While Tom never blamed Ivan, this was not enough to satisfy Ivan's needs — he was still anticipating it and therefore interrupted and argued every single point from a perspective of "You can't blame me." All Tom had to do was to explicitly assure Ivan that no blame would be placed on anyone — his only concern was to put all of this behind him and be allowed to get back to work.

Also, rather than being frustrated that Ivan kept focusing on problems rather than solutions, Tom could have investigated and neutralised those obstacles. "Ivan, it looks to me that the limitations you face in terms of authority are making it difficult for us to solve my present problem. Let me assure you that every hour I don't work costs us more than any solution will cost us. So, *if* resources were not an issue, how could we get me in front of a working laptop within two hours?"

This is not too different from what actually happened in the end. Tom made use of the impact check technique from the options toolbox.

IVAN: *[explaining the obstacles] ...and I have spoken with Microsoft support and they said there is no way to get the three monitors working with the docking station that you have —*

TOM: *How much would it cost to get a docking station that allows me to work the way I want to work?*

IVAN: *Eighty to 150 dollars.*

TOM: *Done! Buy it! Now! Hurry!*

Well, that's what Tom could've said. But as you can probably guess the conversation first went down another path (or detour).

TOM: *WHAT? 150 dollars?! WE HAVE WASTED THREE WEEKS OF MY TIME FOR 150 MEASLY DOLLARS?!*

As expected, there was again a need to vent and feel heard before moving on to the solution.

Now that you are equipped with a mountain of negotiation insights, and are probably in third position while reading this, it may seem absurd that neither party figured this out earlier. But when parties are stuck in autopilot, stuck in first position, ignore the relationship, experience a crisis, or have limited awareness of the process, negotiations simply go off track.

CLOSING COMMENTS

I hope you now experience the feeling of being filled absolutely to the brim with new insights. I hope that you even feel some trepidation regarding how huge a task it will be to master everything. That is good! Negotiations are very complex, and one of the biggest dangers is underestimating that complexity. Rest assured that my expectation is not that you will master, or even remember everything from reading this book once. Rather I hope the book will serve as your companion for years to come.

I also know that some of you will instead have the feeling that everything in this book was just common sense. That is also a great reaction — because it *is* common sense...though, I argue, hidden in plain sight.

It also makes you a victim of the curse of knowledge, which states that once we understand something we can't fathom how someone else can't understand it. Let's just say that it was no accident that we asked you early on in the book to take a few minutes to write or draw the way you negotiated before reading this book. Please revisit your notes. If history is any guide, then I would predict that you will draw a very different picture today.

Going forward I encourage you to:

- pick two skills to practise in every interaction you can for the next month. This will educate your autopilot. Then repeat this process and pick two more skills every month going forward; and

- evaluate progress. What worked? What didn't? What do you reckon is the reason for that? What can you try differently next time?

If you feel that this approach is too slow, please remember that it is only the skills that we apply in negotiations that make a difference to the outcome. And for us to apply them in the heat of the moment while keeping track of everything that goes on in the interaction (that we are now aware of!) we need to install these behaviours into our autopilot. Unfortunately the process for doing that is "practice, practice, practice".

To help reassure you that this is a powerful approach, please read the following few paragraphs that a former participant sent me after attending one of my negotiation courses:

> *I made a conscious effort to do only two things from the course to the best of my ability at that time: 1. To listen, and 2. To find where their memories of the past lay and move them slowly to a positive future. Here's where it got me.*

> *We just agreed a new six-figure deal with the same individuals who vowed never to work with us again.*

> *We agreed a new six-figure deal with the same individuals WE vowed never to work with again.*

Our planet will be better off if we live in a sustainable manner. And our interactions, relationships and outcomes will be better off if we negotiate in a sustainable manner.

ENDNOTES

1   p17 Inspired by Allan Parker

2   p93 "Conscious Competency — The Mark of a Competent Instructor", *The Personnel Journal, Baltimore, July 1974, Volume 53, pp538–539*

3   p172 Inspired by Allan Parker

4   p266 Strenz, Thomas, *"The Cyclic Crisis Negotiations Time Line", Law and Order, March 2005*

5   p285 This breakdown is inspired by Allan Parker's material | symbolic | deep categorisation of needs.

INDEX

www.ingramcontent.com/pod-product-compliance
Lightning Source LLC
Chambersburg PA
CBHW050625280326
41932CB00015B/2524